TABLE OF CONTENTS

preface

INTENDED AUDIENCE

Exploring the Art and Technology of Web Design offers the reader that rare opportunity to gain an overall understanding not only of the art of Web design but also of the vast array of software available. Unlike other books about Web design that go into great detail regarding one specific program, this book offers a general overview of some of the major programs used and how they can interact with one another. The reader is introduced to essential features of basic Web design programs—HTML, Macromedia Dreamweaver, and Macromedia Flash—as well as how these programs interact with the Web design features of Adobe Photoshop and Adobe Illustrator.

The book takes the holistic approach designers need to succeed in a client-driven work environment, delivering a thorough understanding of all of the elements that go into great Web design. This approach to understanding both technology and conceptual design principles will lead to the creation of striking Web sites.

Exploring the Art and Technology of Web Design is intended for both educational and professional settings. It is appropriate for high school to college digital media departments and upper division fine art schools. It is geared to the student just beginning a foyer into Web design and the graphic designer well-versed in print design who wants to delve into Web design.

EMERGING TRENDS

The World Wide Web is absolutely fascinating. It is revolutionary, in part because it is accessible to everybody, but even more so because it is revolutionizing our culture. The WWW provides common accessibility to information, images, music, grassroots politics, and cross-cultural story sharing. The trend toward more sophisticated and interactive Web sites will continue as long as there are WWW users. Each generation will demand more of its designers and Webmasters, yet basic design components will remain constant.

BACKGROUND OF THIS TEXT

I wrote this book because I needed it. Teaching in the fine arts department of a university, I was required to cover the major basic programs in Web design in one semester, a rather daunting task. There wasn't a book out there that could assist me and I ended up purchasing books on each piece of software, plus several more for design concepts.

This book is a result of my research, teaching a Web design class for several years, and experimenting with my students to discover the best methods to teach the subject matter. After talking to other educators, I discovered that there was a broad need for a book like this.

This book assumes a print-based understanding of both Adobe Photoshop and Adobe Illustrator but little to no understanding of Web design and authoring software.

TEXTBOOK ORGANIZATION

Exploring the Art and Technology of Web Design contains 16 chapters and is organized into two basic theoretical approaches to creating Web sites: HTML and scripting. Included are techniques for creating powerful images in each approach and what it takes to get from A to WWW. Using Photoshop and Illustrator as tools for creating images is discussed throughout the book in relation to the software and technology currently being examined. The important art elements of color, line, text, movement, and visual organization are also discussed throughout the text specific to each technology. Each of the three main sections include how to organize a Web site, develop powerful images, create the technology to be understood by a browser, and get your Web site onto the Web. The glossary and back of book CD help to support the exercises and understanding of the text.

The discussion of HTML in the text is divided into two sections: writing code in HTML in Chapters 1 and 2 and using Dreamweaver to write code in Chapters 3 though 7.

Chapters 1 and 2 delve into HTML, Web-safe colors, the power of images, and understanding the technology that delivers images over the WWW.

Chapter 3 presents an overview of Macromedia Dreamweaver and pixel technology. Site design and developing Web-ready images in Adobe Photoshop and Illustrator are explored, as well as linking and targeting.

Chapter 4 looks at Web site Navigation in depth to discover the unique design considerations as well as the technology involved in getting the user from one location to another within a site. Concurrent with this is learning to develop navigation images in image software and prepare the images for use in Dreamweaver.

PREFACE

Chapter 5 continues the exploration into site navigation and takes a look at creating images and technology that respond to mouse rollovers. Additional Dreamweaver organizational tools are examined, including frames and framesets.

Chapter 6 further examines navigation, using additional elements that respond to human gesture. This chapter also explores the important ingredients of type, metaphor, icons, and styles.

Chapter 7 puts everything together and discusses how to connect to the WWW and upload files. This chapter also takes a brief look at many of the additional features of Dreamweaver.

The third section of the text, composed of Chapters 8-16, is devoted to scripting software, focusing on the scripting environment of Macromedia Flash.

Chapter 8 introduces Macromedia Flash and vector technology. Symbols and frame-by-frame animation are explored.

Chapter 9 examines Animation through the Flash technology of motion tweens. The interaction between Illustrator and Flash is also explored.

Chapter 10 teaches readers how to work with masks, understand the interaction between Photoshop and Flash, and use the Break Apart and Trace Bitmap tools.

Chapter 11 explores the Flash scripting language ActionScript. Reducing the technology to basic, understandable ingredients, this chapter also reviews navigation aesthetics.

Chapter 12 examines the usefulness of movie clips, as well as how to use type in Flash.

Chapter 13 looks at importing and managing audio and video clips in Flash.

Chapters 14 and 15 explore two very different ways to organize a Web site through Flash. The chapters examine when to use which organizational tool as well as additional tools to augment a Web site.

Chapter 16 ties together all of the earlier chapters, teaching the reader how to optimize and publish a Flash Web site. Quality versus quantity is discussed, as well as hosting, connecting, and uploading to the Web.

HOW TO USE THIS TEXT

The following features can be found throughout the book:

▶ Objectives

Learning objectives start off each chapter. They describe the competencies readers should achieve upon understanding the chapter material.

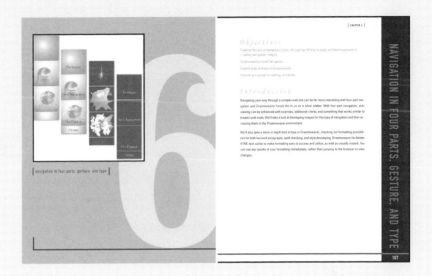

▶ Sidebars and Notes

Sidebars and notes appear throughout the text, offering additional valuable information.

▶ Color Inserts

The color inserts provide helpful tools as well as examples of chapter discussions and existing Web sites that can inspire.

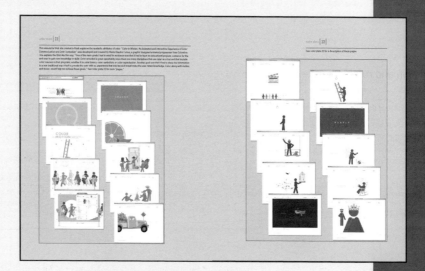

▶ Review Questions and On Your Own

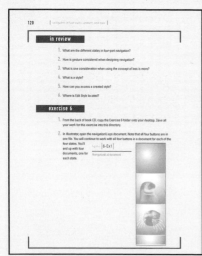

Review questions are located at the end of each chapter and allow the reader to assess understanding of the chapter. Each On Your Own section contains exercises that reinforce chapter material through practical application.

FEATURES

The following list provides some of the salient features of the text:

* Straightforward presentation of the differences between authoring software and image software equips users with the knowledge to explore the more advanced features of each program.

* Complex topics such as site design are reduced to a basic structural approach in order to promote comprehension and retention of key concepts and techniques.

* Step-by-step exercises show how to link technical procedures with such key design concepts as navigation, color, and aesthetics to create a compelling user experience.

* Chapter discussions offer an in-depth look at the power of images, their function in a Web environment, and the appropriate software to deliver them.

* Comparisons give users the knowledge and skills to confidently decide which software program is best suited to any specific Web design project.

* Theories and concepts behind the validity of using the World Wide Web to introduce new subject matter and powerful images are presented for careful consideration by the reader.

E.RESOURCE

This guide on CD was developed to assist instructors in planning and implementing their instructional programs. It includes sample syllabi for using this book in either an 11- or 15-week semester. It also provides chapter review questions and answers, exercises, Microsoft PowerPoint slides highlighting the main topics, and additional instructor resources. Finally, additional images are provided as an extra resource.

ISBN: 1401881564

ACKNOWLEDGMENTS

* Special thanks to my daughter, Dionne Anderson, for her constant support and love.

* Special thanks to Lisa Bloomfield, Dr. Betty Ann Brown, and Sue Maberry for their confidence in me as faculty on their respective staffs.

* Special thanks to all of my students through the years including Jody Doyle, Lori Lindland, Orly Osman, Francisco Ruiz, Yuko Sawamoto, Ricardo Trujillo, Eric Wong, and oh-so-many more whose work has inspired me and kept me enthusiastic about education.

* Special thanks to Susan Boyle, Elizabeth Canelake, Kathleen Forrest, Anne Gauldin, Cheri Gaulke, Suvan Geer, Susan Gray, Mary House, Starr Goode, Christine Papalexis, Mary Peterson, and Rose Marcario for great collaborations we shared.

* Special thanks to Melissa Cogswell for her careful technical assistance.

* Thanks to my students and friends who helped fill this text with stunning images.

* Finally, my warmest thanks and gratitude go to James Gish, acquisitions editor, whose enthusiasm and belief in this book from the very beginning encouraged and guided me, and to Jaimie Wetzel, my development editor, without whose support, guidance, and constant encouragement I could not have written this book.

Thomson Delmar Learning and the author would also like to thank the following reviewers for their valuable suggestions and expertise:

Steve Campbell
Graphic Design and Web Design Department
Lewis and Clark Community College
Godfrey, Illinois

Gary Crossey
Visual Communications Department
American InterContinental University-Buckhead
Atlanta, Georgia

Stephanie Cunningham
School of Arts and Letters
Florida Atlantic University
Fort Lauderdale, Florida

Rebecca Gallagher
Chair, Digital Media Communications Department
Katharine Gibbs School
New York, New York

Kimberly Harder
Visual Communications Department
International Academy of Design and Technology
Troy, Michigan

Bruce Huff
Visual Communications Department
Dakota County Technical College
Rosemount, Minnesota

Ruth Ann Anderson
2005

QUESTIONS AND FEEDBACK

Thomson Delmar Learning and the author welcome your questions and feedback. If you have suggestions that you think others would benefit from, please let us know and we will try to include them in the next edition.

To send us your questions and/or feedback, you can contact the publisher at:

Thomson Delmar Learning
Executive Woods
5 Maxwell Drive
Clifton Park, NY 12065
Attn: Graphic Communications Team
800-998-7498

Or contact the author at:

http://moonlightdsn.com
moonlght@pacbell.net
CSUN-Northridge: http://www.csun.edu/~hfart010/People.html
OCC: http://www.orangecoastcollege.edu/academics/divisions/visual_arts/digital_media_arts_and
_design/Faculty.htm

about the author

Since graduating with her MFA from California State University at Long Beach, Ruth Ann Anderson has built a successful graphic and Web design business. She began teaching in the Fine Arts department at California State University at Northridge and in the Digital Media Arts department at Orange Coast Community College in Costa Mesa, California, where she continues to teach today. Ruth Ann's art and written work have been featured in several art books highlighting noted women artists. She has received numerous awards and grants and has participated in several public art projects. Her artistic concerns extend to social and cultural issues and her work frequently reflects this. She currently serves on the Board of Directors of the Woman's Building, an art and cultural center in Los Angeles active from 1973–1991. She maintains a Web site featuring her student's work that is truly inspiring.

Photo by Les Nakashima

introduction

The World Wide Web has been around since 1989. It was the brilliant, revolutionary concept invented by Tim Berners-Lee about 20 years after the beginning of the Internet. Berners-Lee was working at CERN at the time, a particle physics laboratory. He developed the WWW as a way to easily share global information. He wrote the first browser editor in 1990 as a way to view the information. The WWW has since become the quintessential metaphor for how we currently experience our world. We can process multiple channels of information, choose autonomous paths of interaction, work in a non-linear environment . . . and we can do so regardless of ethnicity, economic status, religion or country. The Internet is truly the great equalizer and bridge for humanity.

So what makes the WWW so revolutionary? It not only made the Internet accessible to everybody, it is also revolutionizing our culture. Witness the profound accessibility to information, images, and music.

Think back on the recent grassroots political campaigns and fundraising, and reflect on the success and political clout of newly organized political organizations and their influences in the 2004 presidential race. Moveon.org was begun by two Silicon Valley entrepreneurs as an online petition to move beyond the Clinton impeachment "mess." After 9/11, moveon.org was enhanced by Eli Pariser's Move On Peace Campaign. When Michael Moore's book, *Dude, Where's My Country*, was held up at the publishers due to controversial content, Librarians went to work. A massive e-mail campaign soon convinced HarperCollins to change its mind.

Finally, look at the way our language has changed: Buzzwords original to the Internet are now prevalent in all of mass media—*home page*, *download*, *search engine*, *upload*, *cookies*, *navigation*, and *blogging*, just to name a few.

It is the intent of this book that you will begin to understand the basic ingredients to Web design, gain sufficient technological knowledge to produce compelling Web sites and confidently participate in this new culture as a dynamic creator.

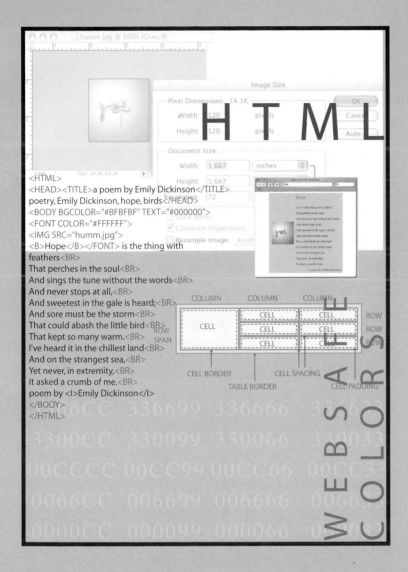

HTML

SECTION

| onstage: html |

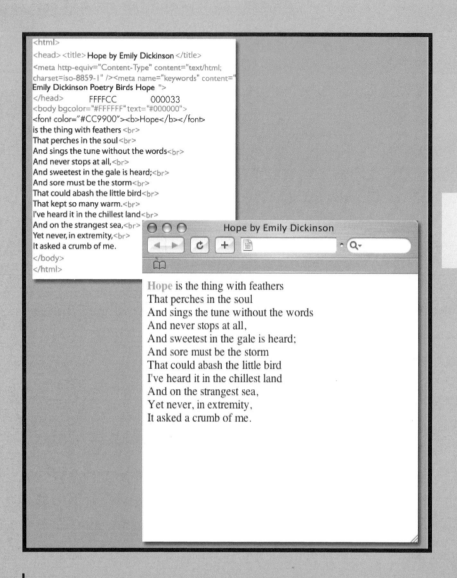

CHAPTER 1

Objectives

Learn about a few Web Design concepts.

Examine the Internet and the World Wide Web.

Discover protocols.

Explore color on the World Wide Web.

Understand the basic concepts of HTML.

Introduce tags.

Introduction

Web design. Is there such a thing? It's a legitimate question. Web design has become a powerful buzzword in a relatively short period of time. It has implied riches, mystery, and the future. Yet when I surf the Web, I see anything and everything from intelligent content that is poorly designed (or lacks design completely) to poor (or no) content that is beautifully designed. Anyone can publish a Web site. A site can be anything from a child's stick drawing of a bird to a scientific thesis on the migratory habits of the Golden-crown Kinglet. And when it comes to design, the child's site might actually be more interesting than the scientific thesis. See Color Plate 1 for an example of a well-designed Web site.

figure | 1-1

A nicely designed student Web site. Ricardo Trujillo's portfolio site, http://www.csun.edu/~raa/1399/SPR02.swf

DESIGNING FOR THE WORLD WIDE WEB

Let's assume there is such a thing as Web design. As an incredibly vast subject, with so many books and software programs available to assist with the task, it is difficult to know where to begin. Any Webmaster or Web designer that you talk to will have his or her own favorite way of doing things and, most likely, each one will tell you something different. So let's start at the very beginning.

Perhaps the most important thing to do to start is to educate your eye. Surf, surf, and surf some more. Spend at least an hour a day surfing the Web during these initial weeks of learning. Learn what works and what doesn't work. How long does it take a download to bore you to tears? Are you interested in a site beyond ten seconds? Will you bother to scroll to view an entire image that doesn't fit in your browser's window, or will you be satisfied to view only that part of the image that shows? Do those flashing images and rotating globes drive you nuts? Do you want to throw your monitor through the wall when you can't figure out how to get back to the beginning of a Web site? What engages you? What imagery entices you? Does interactivity pique your curiosity? Does the navigation urge you toward further exploration? The more you surf, the more informed your eye will become. Your answers to the above questions will become more discriminating and refined.

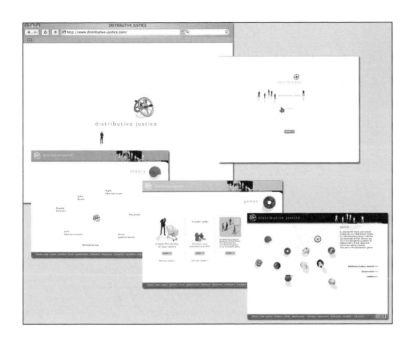

figure | 1-2 |

A captivating Web site.
http://www.distributive-justice.com

Today's Web users are sophisticated, intelligent, and tech-savvy. Do not expect them to be patient while your 50 K image downloads. They have been exploring this media for over a decade. So before you begin building a site, educate yourself. Learn what works and what doesn't. Be diligent in this process. See Color Plate 2 for two student Web sites that are nicely designed.

| NOTE |

Surfing the Web

The word *surf*, when applied to the Web, has become a cross-platform, cross-cultural, cross-status term that everyone understands. It is a simple metaphor borrowed from the hip culture of water babies who ride the ocean's surf on a board. Likewise, we can surf the oceans of knowledge and information on the World Wide Web riding the air waves.

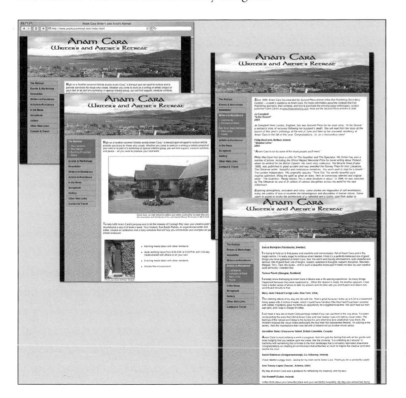

figure | 1-3 |

A well designed Web site.
http://www.anamcararetreat.com

THE INTERNET

To understand Web design, let's begin by poking around what's behind the World Wide Web—the Internet. The Internet is simply a network of computers used to move data around. Using a common protocol or set of rules that allows digital communication across a variety of computer platforms, it includes e-mail, FTP (File Transfer Protocol), listservs, newsgroups, bulletin boards, chat rooms, and the World Wide Web (WWW). In other words, the WWW is a subset of the Internet and cannot exist without it. Conversely, the Internet can and does exist without the WWW.

PROTOCOLS

Let's take a look at the *protocols*, or set of rules, that communicate digital transactions.

HTTP and HTML

First and foremost is HTTP. HTTP is an acronym for Hypertext Transfer Protocol. Web pages travel the Internet via Hypertext Transfer Protocol. HTTP is a set of rules that link documents, or pages, together. These pages are then displayed on computer monitors through browser software.

The browser interprets page content with another set of rules. This is the programming language Hypertext Markup Language, more commonly known as HTML. HTML provides you with the necessary rules to format text, add graphics, sound, and video; determine colors and division of space; and talk to search engines.

URL

Still, HTTP and HTML would be useless without a universal addressing system—a system that every computer can understand. An *IP address* is a number that identifies a specific computer connected to the Internet. And every Web document on the Internet has its own unique address or URL, Uniform Resource Locator.

URLs are like an address on a street. There are specific parts to the address. Take, for example, http://www.domainname.com/pathname/filename.html. The first four letters of this URL define the protocol for transfer: HTTP. The next set of letters is the address of the *server* (the host of the Web site, the company you pay to store your Web site): www.domainname.com. Rather than using the name of your Web host, you can register you own *domain name*. Your Host will then create a virtual domain on their server so that your Web site *looks* like it has its own domain name. The domain name can be claimed and copyrighted. There are several companies on the Internet who will research a domain name for you and charge you a fee to register the name as yours.

Domain names include a common set of extensions that can be internationally recognized. Although these extensions are not as strictly governed as they used to be, they can include:

- .com— a commercial site

- .edu— an educational site such as colleges and universities

- .gov— a government site, such as a state site or the White House

- .org— a nonprofit organization, such as a museum or a charity

- .mi— a military site

- .net— a network site, such as a service provider

Additionally, many countries have their own two-letter code, such as .au for Australia or .fr for France.

The next set of letters in the URL will define the *directory path*: /pathname. The final set of letters will name the *file*: /filename. The directory paths and file names speak to the organization of the site itself and are specific to HTML programming.

An URL can actually tell you a lot about a site. For example, the URL http://members.aol.com/screen name/filename tells you that this is a site sponsored by America Online (AOL) and the creator was limited to using AOL's development parameters and publishing restrictions. The URL http://www.csun. edu tells you that this site is an independent educational site with its own domain name. Having your own domain name increases the presence of a professional appearance.

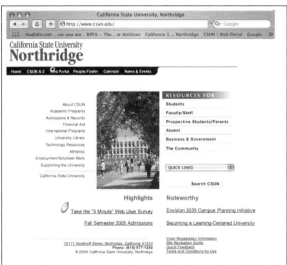

figure | 1-4 |

Browser window showing
http://www.csun.edu

THE WORLD WIDE WEB

The WWW has emerged as the quintessential metaphor for how we currently experience the world. We can simultaneously process multiple channels of information, choose autonomous paths of interaction and pursue a whole new career all, without even getting out of our pajamas. We can choose how we receive world news. We've become a nonlinear culture concentrating on the details of life rather than the big picture. That which emerges from this grassroots rebellion becomes the marketing tools of tomorrow's dominant corporation.

| NOTE |

The World Wide Web

The WWW remains the source of subversion, diversion and honest experience and it offers that experience regardless of race, economic status, religion, or country of origin. It is the great equalizer of humanity.

The WWW is that rare environment where advertising can truly be avoided. True, much of the information available on the Web is commercial, and we all hate those pop up ads. However, we can choose to avoid these influences consciously. Whereas in the rest of our lives we are surrounded by advertising—it is our environment, whether we pay attention to it or not. In fact, advertising influences us most if we are not paying attention to it since it is intended to speak to our emotional selves rather than our conscious selves. The WWW speaks to our conscious selves, giving us choices, autonomy, and the ability to create our own experience.

figure | 1-5 |

Desktop of a Mac

In 1984, Macintosh introduced the concept of the computer as a metaphor using the monitor as a desktop with icons of an office profile—folders, files, and even a trash can.

When HTML came along for the Web, another set of icons began to evolve with its own new interpretations of language—*pages*, *maps*, *navigation*, and *home*, to name a few. By 1995, HTML included tables. With this simple technology designers began a whole new level of subversion, manipulating the technology and forcing the browser to do things for which it was never really intended. An indigenous design language quickly began to take shape, one that didn't refer to any other mass media. Now, in this third generation of Web design, the technology is highly sophisticated, with a number of intelligently developed software programs that allow the designer unlimited creative potential. Yet most software programs are still based on the concept of forcing the Browser to interpret coding in a way that it was never originally designed to do. This behavior increases the importance of understanding the basics of HTML, particularly when you need to figure out a workaround to achieve a certain goal.

COLOR

The use of color in Web design is exceptionally important. We will return to this topic over and over, but for now, let's start with the basics. Too many colors and/or lots of bright colors will indicate to your viewer that you are a new designer lured by the magic of the Web. A more sophisticated approach is to choose a simple color palette and stick to it throughout the Web site. Choose only two or three basic colors with one or two accent colors. The basic colors could be analogous or monotone, with the accents as complements. See Color Plate 3 for a Web site with a great color scheme.

Let's take a brief refresher look at the color wheel on Color Plate 4, CMYK color wheel. This is a handy tool when developing colors. Just to help with future discussions, here are a few important definitions in relation to color:

figure | 1-6 |

A great Web site.
http://www.itvs.org/beyondthefire

- Hue—the tone/color name
- Monochromatic—uses tints and shades of one hue
- Analogous—colors that are adjacent to each other on the color wheel
- Complements—colors that are opposite each other on the color wheel

Take some time again to explore the WWW. Notice that it doesn't take long for your eyes to get tired. The more colors that your eyes have to adjust to, the sooner they will tire. For this reason, some of the most sophisticated sites use off-whites, soft grays, and one or two contrasting bright colors. Take another look at Color Plate 3 for a great color scheme.

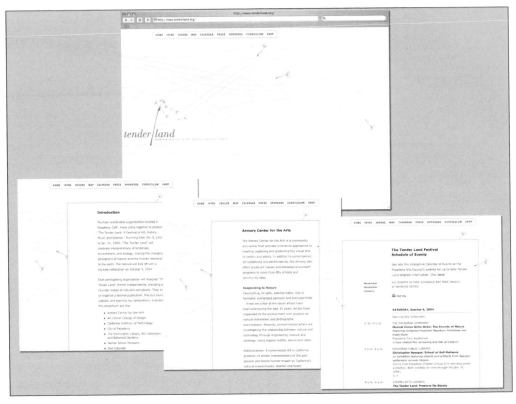

figure |1-7|

Web site in gray tones with one accent color:
http://www.tenderland.org

| NOTE |

A chaotic site reduces the look of professionalism.

The design of your site communicates not only your aesthetics but also the level of professionalism you have brought to it. A cluttered and chaotic site is difficult for the user to maneuver. Remember: Too many colors add to a sense of chaos.

Web-Safe Colors

Web-safe, or cross-platform, colors are a whole new way of thinking of color. There are only 216 cross-platform colors. It's important that you stick with this limited color palette. If you don't, your viewer's computer will do one of two things with your color. It will either dither the color or it will shift it. To *dither* means that the browser's palette will mix colors that are available in order to approximate the color. To *shift* means that the browser will shift the color to its nearest palette equivalent. In either case, you have lost control of the color.

There are two primary sources of producing color. One is a process called CMYK. CMYK is an acronym for cyan, magenta, yellow, and black. It is a color mode that uses light that reflects off of the surface of a printed page. Cyan acts as a red light filter, while magenta is a green light filter. Yellow filters out blue light. Because less ink leads to lighter colors, this is called a *subtractive color model.* This color model is referred to as four-color process and is the most common model for printing color on a page. Process inks are measured in percentages. Combinations of these colors and their percentages produce an almost unlimited range of color.

The other primary color model—and the one that we need to use for the Web—is RGB. RGB is an acronym for red, green, and blue. The RGB color mode is created from white light that passes into your eye through cones in the retina and mutates into nerve impulses. Red, green, and blue are the primary colors of light. Computer and television screens fool your eye by speaking directly to your cones. Full intensities of all three light colors produce white, therefore producing an *additive color model*. RGB is for screen viewing only, whether it be the Web, computers, television, film, or video. Make sure that all of the images that you produce for the WWW are RGB.

The 216 cross-platform Web-safe colors are RGB light-source colors.

Web-safe colors are developed through conversion values in hexadecimal. It helps to understand the concept behind this, although you can easily refer to a Web-safe color chart when you are actually developing your site. There are six shades to each color, which results in the Web 6 x 6 x 6 color cube. The six shades in decimal values are 0, 51, 102, 153, 204, and 255. These translate to 00, 33, 66, 99, CC, and FF in hexadecimal. In percentages, they translate to 0%, 20%, 40%, 60%, 80%, and 100%.

Thus Web-safe colors are specific combinations of these six values. The first two values in a Web color refer to red, the next two to green, and the last two to blue. FFFFFF is white and 000000 is black. A Web-safe color is FFFF33; 100% red, 100% green, and 20% blue. That translates to yellow. See Color Plate 5 for a Web-safe color chart.

Let's look at this hexadecimal table compared to percentage of light just to get the basic idea.

| **NOTE** |

Print vs. Monitor Viewing
Printed CMYK colors will not necessarily match a monitor's RGB display. The RGB color range is larger than that of CMYK and the callibration of a monitor may not match the printers CMYK palette.

| **NOTE** |

216 vs. 256
There are 256 Web-safe colors but only 216 that are cross-platform safe.

Decimal	Hexadecimal	Percentage of light
0	00	0%
51	33	20%
102	66	40%
153	99	60%
204	CC	80%
255	FF	100%

figure | 1-8 |

Hexadecimal interpretations of light compared to percentage interpretations of light

You can also take a look at Adobe Photoshop's Web-safe color cube to better understand this concept. In the Swatches Palette, choose the triangle at the upper right and scroll down to Web Safe Colors. Then double-click on the Fill color box in the Tool Box. This will bring up a color cube. Select different hues in the scroll bar to see the variations. Check out Color Plate 6 for some examples of this color cube.

In addition to the cross-platform colors, there are 16 predefined colors identified by names that browsers can recognize. They are white, silver, aqua, black, blue, gray, lime, fuchsia, red, maroon, yellow, green, navy, purple, olive, and teal.

HTML

Now let's take a closer look at the language for the Web: HTML. By understanding the basic concepts of this language, you will not only be able to write HTML code but you will also be better informed to understand and work with designer-friendly programs. Additionally, this knowledge can help you discover the source of a problem that may otherwise have been a mystery when working in other programs.

HTML is the required extension for a browser to recognize a home page. Your home page must therefore be uploaded as index.html or index.htm.

Page Tags

HTML uses the concept of *tags*. A tag consists of greater than and less than brackets < > with information inside of the brackets. A simple direction informs the bracket. Basic page tags are:

- <html> </html>
- <head> </head>
- <title> </title>
- <body> </body>

Notice that there are two tags in each case. The second tag includes a forward slash. This is the closing tag. If you forget to add a closing tag, then a page will probably display incorrectly in the browser. Frequently, when a student new to HTML opens a freshly designed page in a browser and the page doesn't display correctly, it is because there is a missing closing tag somewhere on the page.

A basic HTML page looks like this:

```
<html>
<head> <title> to be displayed in title line of the browser </title>
</head>
<body bgcolor="#FFFFFF" text="#000000">
   all information to be displayed in the browser
</body>
</html>
```

figure | **1-9** |

HTML page with basic codes

You must also be careful about spelling. If a tag is spelled wrong either in the opening tag or the closing tag, the browser will not recognize the code and will display the page incorrectly. You don't need to add any spaces between your text and the tags.

An HTML page always begins with the tag <html> and always ends with the closing tag </html>. This is mandatory for the browser to recognize the language enclosed within these tags and interpret it correctly.

After the <html> opening code, the next bit of information gets inserted in the <head> tag. This information is not displayed in the browser. First is the title information. This begins simply with the tag <title>. Whatever you put in here will display in the information window or "Title Bar" of the browser, as well as become the identifier for pages that are bookmarked. So it is important that you put something intelligent and informative here. Keep it short and simple. And don't forget the closing tag </title>. TITLE tags are required by HTML. The title element sits inside of the head code. So it looks like this:

<head>

<title>Art 301 Spring 2004</title>

</head>

This is the only required element inside of the <head> element.

Additionally, inside of the HEAD tags you can add keywords and a short description of the site's content. Keywords and descriptions are special words and instructions for browsers and search engines. Thus you want to include any information that will help your pages be found when a search engine is locating pages that match what a user is looking for. For example, if a user is searching the Web for information about women-owned businesses and your Web site is about a business owned by a woman, if you have included this information in the head, the site will show up in the search results.

Some search engines limit the number of keywords that they will review and are equally conservative about the length of the description. For this reason, keywords should be chosen wisely and be limited to about 10 to 15 words that will best describe your site's contents. Likewise, keep your description short and simple.

A META tag identifies keywords or content-type (description) for a browser. The <meta> tag is followed by the codes "keywords" or "content-type." So on the page it might look something like this:

figure | 1-10 |

HTML page showing the HEAD element with TITLE and META elements, including keywords and content-type description

```
<html>
<head> <title> Writers at Work </title>
<meta http-equiv="Content-Type" content="text/html;
charset=iso-8859-1" /><meta name="keywords" content="Terry
Wolverton Writing and Poetry Workshops Educational Programs
Retreats Los Angeles Fiction Nonfiction Screenwriting Consultations
Manuscript Review">
</head>
<body bgcolor="#FFFFFF" text="#000000">
  all information to be displayed in the browser
</body>
</html>
```

Additional data such as character encoding and author and copyright information also exists inside of a META tag. The META tag does not need a closing tag. However, don't forget to add the closing HEAD tag after the TITLE and META tags.

Next is the body of the page. This will include everything that is actually displayed by the browser. The tag used here is <body> </body>. First you need to add all of the information that tells the Browser how to display your page. This includes the color of the background, the font, font color, font size, and more. These pieces of information are inserted inside of the opening BODY tag.

When adding color to your HTML page, you need to begin the color with the pound sign and sur round it by quotes: "#FFFFFF." Without the pound sign and quotes, some browsers may not recognize the code.

Tags for body color and text are:

<body bgcolor="#FFFFFF"> (Page background color is white.)

<body text="#000000"> (Text color is black.)

At the end of the page is the closing tag </body>, followed by </html>.

Using all of these tags, a typical page would look like this:

```
<html>
<head> <title> Hope by Emily Dickinson </title>
<meta http-equiv="Content-Type" content="text/html;
charset=iso-8859-1" /><meta name="keywords" content="
Emily Dickinson Poetry Birds Hope ">
</head>
<body bgcolor="#FFFFFF" text="#000000">
Hope is the thing with feathers <br>
That perches in the soul <br>
And sings the tune without the words<br>
And never stops at all,<br>
And sweetest in the gale is heard;<br>
And sore must be the storm<br>
That could abash the little bird<br>
That kept so many warm.<br>
I've heard it in the chillest land<br>
And on the strangest sea,<br>
Yet never, in extremity,<br>
It asked a crumb of me.
</body>
</html>
```

figure **1-11**

A simple HTML page showing the chapter exercise

Text Tags

Within the BODY tags are additional codes, such as codes guiding or formatting the text. Some commonly used text codes are listed below.

- <p> is a paragraph tag.</p>
- <h1> is a header tag. Header styles number 1 through 6, with the text getting larger as the number gets smaller.</h1>
- <i> will italicize the text.</i>
- <b> will bold the text.</b>
- <blockquote> indents text together in a block. </blockquote>
-
 is a break tag and is one of the few tags that doesn't need a closing tag.
- <hr> is a horizontal rule and also doesn't need a closing tag.

Ninety percent of tags need a closing tag. It's similar to using parentheses when writing. You always need to add the closing rounded bracket. In HTML, you almost always need to add the closing tag. There are a few exceptions, such as the break tag: <br>.

Beginning to Write Code

You need to develop your HTML page in plain-text-only software. Writing your code in software that already has built in code (such as Microsoft Word) will create conflict. The code from the software will usually take precedence over the code that you write. So start with something like TextEdit or Notebook, using the plain-text option.

Again, the first page of your Web site must be saved as index.htm or index.html. This is a universal protocol for the default page on the server directory to be recognized by the browser.

Remember: Begin with the <html> tag. Develop your HEAD, TITLE and META information. Next, develop the BODY coding. Finally, close both the BODY and HTML tags at the end of the HTML page. (See Figure 1-11.) See Color Plate 7 for an HTML Reference Tool.

SUMMARY

In this first chapter, you've been introduced to a few basic Web design concepts, WWW protocols, and examined some of the features of the World Wide Web. You've learned about Web-safe colors and why it is important to use them as well as color design theories for the Web. You've begun to understand tags and how they function to enable someone else on a different computer to view your coding.

in review

1. What is a protocol?

2. What does HTML stand for?

3. What are Web-safe colors?

4. What punctuation marks are required when defining a color?

5. What tags are absolutely necessary to define a Web page?

6. How can you provide additional information for a search engine?

exercise 1

1. Begin by sketching a simple page using the following poem:

   "Hope"
   By Emily Dickinson
   Hope is the thing with feathers
   That perches in the soul
   And sings the tune without the words
   And never stops at all,
   And sweetest in the gale is heard;
   And sore must be the storm
   That could abash the little bird
   That kept so many warm.
   I've heard it in the chillest land
   And on the strangest sea,
   Yet never, in extremity,
   It asked a crumb of me.

2. Concentrate on developing color schemes for this first exercise. Look at Color Plates 4 and 5. Use Color Plate 4 to help you identify analogous and complementary colors. Use Color Plate 5 to identify the Web-safe color formula for your choices. You could choose two analogous colors for the type and one complementary color for the background. Consider your choices based on easy readability and appropriateness to the theme of the poem. Try out different ideas.

3. Next, open a plain-text-only software such as TextEdit or Notepad. From the menu bar, select Format>Make Plain Text. Deselect any Rich Text Formatting the software you use may offer.

figure **1-Ex1**

TextEdit Showing Make Plain Text Option

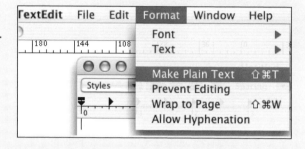

4. Add the HTML, HEAD, TITLE, and META elements. Your document should look something like this:

figure **1-Ex2**

HEAD elements in TextEdit

```
<html>
<head><title>Hope by Emily Dickinson </title>
<meta name="keywords" content="Emily Dickinson
Poetry Birds Hope ">
</head>
```

5. Next, type an opening BODY tag and include the color scheme you selected. (Remember to replace the color, header, and font size choices in the following examples with your own.)

   <body bgcolor="#FFFFCC">

6. Try a header tag for the word *Hope*. Change the color for this word using your color scheme.

   <h2><font color="#FF9900">Hope</h2>

7. Add a paragraph tag and choose a new color and font size for the body of the poem.

   <p><font size="5" color="#000000">Hope is the thing with feathers

   That perches in the soul

8. Continue typing the poem, adding the BREAK tag at the end of each line.

9. Add the </p>, </body>, and </html> tags.

10. Save the document as exer1.html and open a browser. From the Pulldown menu in the browser, choose File>Open. Scroll to your newly created page and open it. It should look something like this:

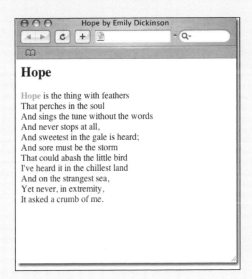

figure | 1-Ex3 |

How the browser interprets HTML

If code shows up in the browser window, something is wrong. More often than not, that something is a misspelled tag or a missing closing tag. Check your HTML page for spelling, closing tags, and brackets. This should prove worth your while.

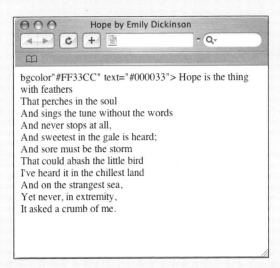

figure | 1-Ex4 |

Browser view showing code

11. Return to your plain-text-only software and the HTML page. Bold the word *Hope* in the first line. Change the color of this word, again referring to your color scheme. Don't forget to close these tags.

12. Save the changes to your page and return to your browser. Browse to your file and open it. Use the Refresh/Reload button in the browser to view your changes. Your page should look something like this:

figure │1-Ex5│

HTML page with <b> tag and color change added

```
<html>
<head> <title> Hope by Emily Dickinson </title>
<meta http-equiv="Content-Type" content="text/html;
charset=iso-8859-1" /><meta name="keywords" content="
Emily Dickinson Poetry Birds Hope ">
</head>
<body bgcolor="#FFFFCC" text="#000033">
<font color="#FF9900"><h2> Hope</h2></font>
<p>
<font color="#CC9900"><b> Hope</b></font>
is the thing with feathers <br>
That perches in the soul<br>
And sings the tune without the words<br>
And never stops at all,<br>
And sweetest in the gale is heard;<br>
And sore must be the storm<br>
That could abash the little bird<br>
That kept so many warm.<br>
I've heard it in the chillest land<br>
And on the strangest sea,<br>
Yet never, in extremity,<br>
It asked a crumb of me.
</p>
</body>
</html>
```

on your own

Develop a new color scheme. Explore Color Plates 4 and 5 and how colors are viewed in a browser, then examine different font color choices on different background colors. Take the time to truly get a handle on this. It will serve you well in the future. Additionally, play around with the heading choices and font sizes. Try out the ITALIC and BLOCKQUOTE tags. Experiment. You can refer to Color Plate 7 to try different coding possibilities.

notes

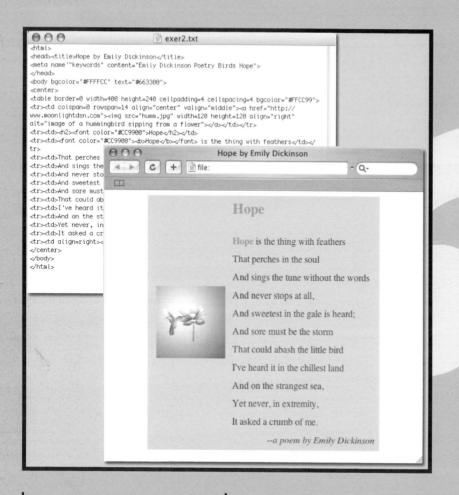

images, links, and html tables

CHAPTER 2

Objectives

Consider the power of images.

Understand how to format images in preparation for HTML use.

Explore vector versus pixel images.

Learn how HTML tags access images.

Introduce HTML TABLEs and necessary tags.

Examine the subversive use of HTML TABLEs.

Introduction

To be able to build a truly enticing Web site, one that will keep your user actually engaged, you first need to explore the power of images and how they speak to us. In this chapter, we'll learn how to access images in HTML and subvert the system to design with them. In doing so, we'll learn about more complex tags, as well as how to create TABLEs in HTML.

IMAGES, LINKS, AND HTML TABLES

IMAGES

An image can speak a thousand words. You've no doubt heard that phrase many times. However, no matter how many times you have heard it, it still remains true. An image not only speaks a thousand words, it primarily speaks to our emotional selves. Our brains process images differently than they process words. We believe in pictures as truth.

When we read words, our brains engage in an intellectual process that can be filtered through our experiences and what we already know. We accept or reject the information, file it, and move on. Words engage us on a cognitive level. With images, we tend to unconditionally accept the information, take it into the non-thinking parts of our brain first, and respond solely on an emotional level. Later, we may filter the image through our intellectual selves and process it in a rational way. Initially, however, it's our emotional selves that are engaged. When we deeply connect to a very powerful image, it can stay with us for a very long time. See Color Plates 8 and 9 for additional examples of images that strike an emotional chord.

figure | 2-1 |

Untitled by student Nick Rickenbach

Consider your earliest childhood memories of a book. Have you ever read a book to a young child, say two or three years old? A child absolutely delights in identifying the images, responding on an emotional level to the picture first. When my daughter was three, her favorite book was *Hand, Hand, Fingers, Thumb* by Dr. Seuss. She would request that book over and over because she could connect the images of the hand, fingers, and thumb with her own hand, fingers, and thumb. She processed the images emotionally, accepting them as truth. She could identify them within her personal experience and then understand them on a cognitive level.

Alternately, think about love. Recall the first time you fell in love. Are you thinking in terms of words or images? Can words evoke the feelings that you associate with this recollection? It is at our deepest stratum of being that we take in images, and they can stay with us for a very long time.

So to truly engage your viewer, consider the importance of your images. Your goal is to create the most powerful images you can. Engage the user's emotional self—their intellectual self will

figure |2-2|

Honk by Mary Peterson

follow. Be sure to consciously look at images as you continue your eye's education by surfing the Web. Whenever you pick up a magazine or see a billboard with an image that makes you stop and look again, take a second, thorough look. Dissect the image. Understand why it engaged you. Educate yourself. What images do you connect to?

Image Formats

Images can be used on the Web in several different formats or extensions. HTML uses JPEG, JPG, GIF, PNG, and SVG. These are all forms of compression that allow a browser to access an image. Keep in mind that here is always a trade-off between compression and resolution. The higher the resolution, the longer the download time for your user. This cannot be stressed enough. Your average user today is so sophisticated that they will not wait more than ten or even five seconds for one image to download, never mind if you have several images that each take five seconds or longer.

Both Adobe Photoshop and Adobe Illustrator will indicate in the Save for Web window what the download time will be for different modem speeds for each type of compression with the

figure |2-3|

Imagine by Student Yuko Sawamoto

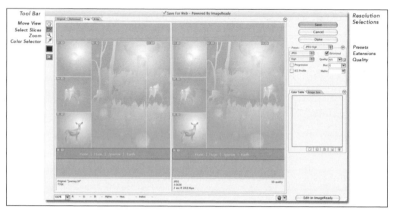

figure | 2-4 |

Annotated overview of Save for Web window

Cross-Platform Testing

You may want to test images, as well as fully designed Web sites, in various browsers. Different browsers on different types of computers will display images and interpret colors differently. Connection speeds will also affect a user's experience. Testing on various computers is referred to as *cross-platform testing* and is an important habit to develop. It really is not a good idea to assume that every user is going to see what you see. By cross-platform testing, you can get an idea of what needs to be changed to display best in most situations. If you do not have access to several different computers and connection speeds through friends or school, try your local library.

specific settings. Pay attention to this information. (See Chapter 3 for a detailed description and use of the Save for Web feature.)

JPG or JPEG (Joint Photographic Experts Group) references a form of compression that allows for the best quality. When you export a file from Photoshop or Illustrator for the Web as a JPG, a 1 MB PICT document can be reduced to 100 KB with little loss of quality. JPGs can be saved at low-, medium-, or high-quality settings. We'll look at JPGs more in the next chapter. This format is a choice that is best used for photographic or continuous tone images.

GIF (Graphics Interchange Format) is historically the most common format used for the Web. It is generally chosen for flat color graphics and has a tremendous compression rate. However, resolution of anything beyond flat color is definitely sacrificed when using GIF compression. GIF is a good choice for graphics such as icons, buttons, or directional arrows. GIFs can also be used with simple animation programs. In Photoshop, when you Save for Web as a GIF, you will have choices of low, medium, or high compression, using 32-, 64-, or 128-bit compression. GIFs (like PNGs, discussed below) offer the advantage of an alpha channel when a transparent background of the image is important.

PNG (Portable Network Graphics) offers the primary advantage of variable transparency. It is generally used instead of JPG when transparency is important. A photographic PNG will be larger than its equivalent JPG. You have a choice of PNG-24 or PNG-8 128-bit compression. As with JPGs, you can view your choices and compare your resolution quality and download time all within the Save for Web dialogue box.

SVG (Scalable Vector Graphics) is relatively new on the Web format scene. This is a vector file format used by XML (Extensible Markup Language). This format allows for interactivity and scalability and compresses to a small, efficient file size. Neither Macromedia Dreamweaver nor Macromedia Flash currently use SVGs, nor can all users access SVGs. However, SVG is a powerful compression tool that has no image resolution loss and therefore will no doubt become more usable as programmers include it when revising Web-authoring programs.

Experiment with these different settings. Try saving the same image as a JPG high, a GIF 64, and a PNG-8 124. Make a note of the download time, then view the image in your browser window (File>Open). Notice the differences in resolution and color quality. Consider these differences with the download times indicated in the Save for Web window. Make informed decisions.

Tags for Setting Images into HTML

Now let's take a look at how HTML tags set images into a page. The basic tag for an image is:

<img src="graphicname.ext">

This tag tells HTML to place the image on that spot on the page. There are inline images (graphics that are part of the flow of the HTML content), background tiling images, and horizontal rules. If an image is not a background tile, then it is an inline image. By default, graphics are displayed with their bottom edges lined up with the baseline of the surrounding text.

Background tiles are one image that is repeated over and over, filling the entire background of an HTML page. Coding <body background="image.gif"> tells a browser to fill the window with this image as many times as necessary. Background tiles are frequently misused, most often by those who are seduced by the cleverness of them. Background tiles need to be carefully thought out. It's best to not use them at all, but if you must, be cautious. Don't let them interfere with type, navigation, or the overall design. Some of the most amateur pages out there look that way because of the use of garish, obvious tiles that interfere with the text, making it difficult to read the content and impossible to understand the navigation. Background tiles are actually deprecated as of HTML version 4.

When adding an image to an HTML file, you need to not only name it, but also specify width and height attributes, border thickness, alignment, and the space around it. This information is specified in *pixels*.

Pixels? Okay. Let's pause here and talk about pixel versus vector. We'll look at this subject again and again. But for now, the simple explanation is that pixels are little squares and vectors consists of dots and lines—formulas really. The most important difference between pixel and vector images is that the latter can be sized without losing resolution quality. In other words, when you resize a pixel image it will become less clear, fuzzy, and funky—in other words, pixelly. When you resize a vector image, the quality of the picture will remain the same.

HTML can display only pixel images. Dreamweaver and Photoshop are pixel-based programs. Flash and Illustrator are both vector-based programs. Also, Illustrator supports Flash, offering greater drawing capabilities that translate to Flash beautifully. XML supports vector graphics through SVGs. See Figures 8-1 and 8-2 for scaled pixel and vector images.

Back to adding images in HTML. To begin with, you can obtain the width and height of an image through its Photoshop file. The information is under the menu bar of Image. Select Image>Image Size. When the dialog window opens, note the width and height of the image in pixels. Alternately, you can drag an image from the desktop into a browser window. On a Mac, from the menu bar of Window, you will be able to see the dimension. On a Pc, right click on the image and click on properties. In either case, write this number down. It has to be exact. Whatever pixels you specify in HTML will be how the browser displays the image. If your pixel numbers are, for example, ten pixels wider than the actual image, HTML will stretch the image to match the specification. This translates to a distorted image. So it is important to be accurate. Additionally, if you alter the image later and the size is affected, be sure to change the dimensions in the HTML document.

Also, in the Image Size dialogue window in Photoshop, make sure that your image is 72 pixels per inch (ppi). 72 ppi is the standard resolution for the Web.

Let's return to the coding for images:

<img src="graphicname.ext" width=pixels height=pixels>

This tag includes the width and height attributes of an image. Note that there are no spaces before or after equal signs, quotations marks, and numbers. The only spaces are between commands. Graphicname.ext refers to whatever name you assign the image plus whatever extension it has—for example, "bird.jpg".

figure | 2-5

Browser window showing an image with the wrong dimensions specified

Limit the names of images to eight letters or less. It's important to remember this naming convention, as once your Web site begins to grow, things can get pretty confusing.

The above example might look like this:

<img src="bird.jpg" width=120 height=120>

The image will probably still display if you forget to add the width and height dimensions, but the download time will be increased.

Other attributes and their coding are:

- <img src= "graphicname.ext" border=pixels>

  This attribute refers to the pixel thickness of a border or frame around an image. This number can be, and most often should be, 0.

- <img src= "graphicname.ext" align=left valign=top>

  These attributes refer to horizontal and vertical alignment in relationship to the adjacent text. By default, graphics are displayed with their bottom edges lined up with the baseline of the surrounding text. This is changed through the ALIGN and VALIGN code. ALIGN=left means that an image will sit to the left of the text. ALIGN=right means that an image will sit to the right of the text. ALIGN=center will assign an image to the center of the text. VALIGN uses *top*, *bottom*, and *center* to align the text to the top, bottom, or center of an image.

- <img src="graphicname.ext" hspace=pixels vspace=pixels>

These attributes determine the space around an image. It is a good idea to allow at least a few pixels (maybe five to ten) around the image to give it some breathing room.

You can use any or all of these attributes. They should all fall within the IMG SRC tag:

figure **2-6**

Annotated examples of ALIGN and VALIGN

<img src="bird.jpg" width=120 height=120 border=0 align=left hspace=10 vspace=10>

There are situations where images will not be displayed. This may be due to a user's inability to either see or access images or it may be that the user has such a slow connection that he or she has chosen to disable images. Given these possibilities, it is a good habit to add an ALT code. ALT code offers text as an alternative to an image and sits within the IMG SRC tag. It might look something like this:

figure **2-7**

ALT Tag in an IMG SRC tag

LINKS

Now let's talk about including links on a page. The basic anchor link tag that contains the image, text, etc. that you want to link is <a></a> .

So an example might be:

<a href="url"><img src="bird.jpg" width=120 height=120></a>

This code points to an URL using an image as the link. HREF refers to the attribute that provides the URL of the page to be linked to, whether it is an internal or external page, a different location on the same page, or a mail link. The URL can be absolute (includes the protocol and complete path name) or relative to the document currently displayed in the window. You need to provide an *absolute URL* if you are linking to a page outside of your Web site. You can provide a *relative URL* if you are linking within your Web site.

A link to a page outside of your own Web site is known as an *external link*. You must provide the browser with the protocol (http://) and specific URL, such as "http://www.name.com/pathname.html/subpathname." Wrap the URL in quotes. Follow the <a href=url> with the text or image that is the visual link and close the tag. In this example, the external link would look like this:

<a href="http://www.name.com/pathname.html/subpathname"><img src="bird.jpg" width=120 height=120></a>

By default, links will appear as blue underlined text or blue outline graphics in most browser windows.

mailto: is the protocol for linking to an e-mail address and causing the browser to pop up an e-mail window. The code looks like this:

<a href="mailto:name@server.com">linked text or image</a>

DIRECTORIES

You can organize your Web site by using directories, subdirectories, sub-subdirectories, and so forth. Each directory (or folder) can accommodate an entire page along with its images and any other organizational elements of your site. *Root Directory* refers to the top directory level. It is indicated with a slash at the beginning of the path name.

You may want to organize all of your images in a folder called "images." If so, you want to point the code to the path names of the images. If the graphic you are pointing to is in the same directory as the HTML file, you can simply specify the file name of the graphic in the IMG SRC attribute as shown in the previous code sample. Otherwise, point the code to the path name with a forward slash and the name of the folder.

To link to a page within your own site, you can use a relative URL, dropping the "http://" protocol. Your path name must include the directory in which you have placed your linked page. If the linked page is within the same directory as the linking page, then all you need is the pagename.html. If the linked page is in a lower directory, name this directory first, then the file name: directoryname/image.ext. For example:

<img src="images/bird.jpg" width=120 height=120>

In this example, images is the subdirectory that contains the file bird.jpg.

If the file is in yet another subdirectory, then name the subdirectory also: directoryname/subdirectoryname/image.ext. If the file is in a higher directory (such as when linking back to the home page), tell the browser to go up one level: <a href="../file> It is the ../ that indicates going up one level. Two instances of ../ translates into moving up two directory levels, and so forth.

TABLES

Now let's look at further ways to control how your HTML translates to viewing in a browser window. As I mentioned in Chapter 1, when TABLEs were introduced, a whole new level of subversion began to take place. Designers saw TABLEs as a way to control design rather than display data. Today, using columns and rows to develop empty space that controls the placement of images and/or text is just as common, if not more so, than using columns and rows to display data in an organized fashion. Tables can be used to organize the content of pages, format text, and add blank space. They can be used to divide a page into major sections. Left navigational items can be in one column while the rest of the page is in a larger column. TABLEs can also be used to hold together a multipart—or sliced—image. Prior to TABLEs, horizontal control of a layout was very limited.

TABLEs are made up of CELLs that are then arranged into rows and columns. CELLs are the containers for the content. CELLs can be spanned both horizontally and vertically to create even larger CELLs by combining adjacent cells.

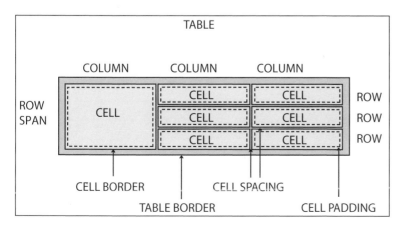

figure | 2-8 |

Annotated table and cells

Sketching

Get into the habit of sketching your ideas with pencil and paper first before you are lured to a computer's capabilities and magic. This will give you the opportunity to take your own ideas to a more sophisticated level. By sketching your design first, you can always go back and revise it to make it more—before starting in on the computer. This is your opportunity to deepen your ideas before being mesmerized by a computer monitor.

The sketching phase is a good time to plan the dimensions of a TABLE and its ROWs and columns. Blocking out the main areas of a TABLE helps you to plan ROW spans and column spans. Once you plan your column spans, start building the TABLE based on your sketch.

The basic information in a TABLE includes:

- the <table> tag
- the border, if any
- the width and height of the TABLE in pixels or percentages
- the CELL padding in pixels (the amount of space held between the contents of a CELL and the CELL border)
- the CELL spacing in pixels (the amount of space held between CELLs)
- the background color of the entire TABLE

Usually TABLEs look best without borders. This is part of the whole invisible design concept.

Here are the basic TABLE tags:

<table border=0> the pixel thickness of the border. 0=no border

<table width=number height=number> width and height are either in pixel dimensions or percentages

<table cell padding=number> amount of pixel space held between the contents of the CELL and the CELL border.

<table cell spacing=number> pixel space between CELLs

<table bgcolor="#number"> background color of the TABLE

Quotes are required around color callouts but are optional around other values.

Thus your opening tag could look something like:

<table border=0 width=520 height=200 cellpadding=6 cellspacing=4 bgcolor="#ffffff">

The next step is controlling the individual CELLs. This includes working with background color, CELL dimensions, alignment of CELL contents, and column and spanning.

A fundamental feature of TABLE is CELL spanning, or how a CELL can span several CELLs in the next row or column. Row spanning is when a CELL is stretched downward to span several rows. Column spanning is when a CELL is stretched to the right to span across subsequent columns. ROW and COLUMN spanning are controlled by the attributes rowspan and colspan, as shown here:

<td colspan=number>CELL</td>

<td rowspan=number>CELL</td>

You can specify the width of the columns, the height of the rows, the background color of CELLs, and the alignment of the elements within CELLs. All content goes inside the CELLs, which go by the tag <td> </td>. TD stands for Table Data. The ALIGN and VALIGN attributes control the alignment of elements within CELLs. Use these to position left, right, center, top, or bottom.

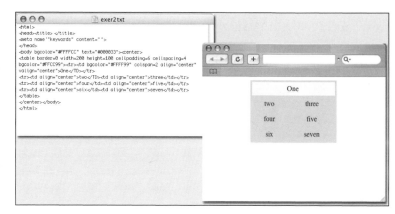

figure 2-9

TABLE with column spanning

TABLE ROWs are determined by the <tr> </tr> tag. CELLs are created with TABLE data <td> tags placed within each ROW. The number of columns is determined by the number of CELLs. Columns are implied by the sets of <td></td> tags.

You can have as many TABLE ROWs as needed, and background colors can be applied to <tr> or <td> tags as desired. Images, text, font information, links, height, width, and alignments all fall within the <td></td> tags. Thus a TABLE ROW could look something like:

<tr> <td width=100 height=100 bgcolor="#66CC99" align=center valign=top>My Name </td> <td width=100 height=100 bgcolor="#66CC99" align=left valign=top>My Favorite Food</td><td width=100 height=100 bgcolor="#66CC99" align=left valign=top>My Favorite Song</td ></tr>

Don't forget the closing tag for a TABLE. Putting it all together, a TABLE can look something like the following:

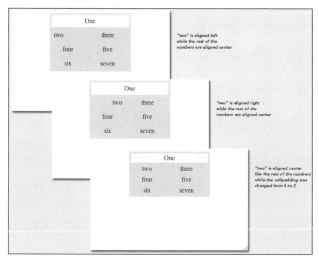

figure 2-10

Various align options applied to a CELL

figure | 2-11 |

TABLE in TextEdit

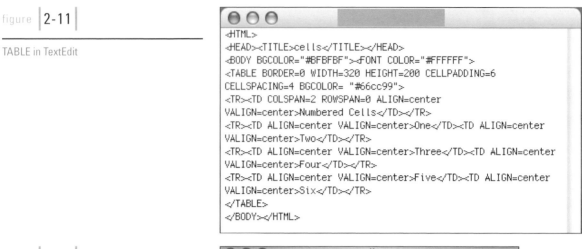

figure | 2-12 |

TABLE viewed in browser

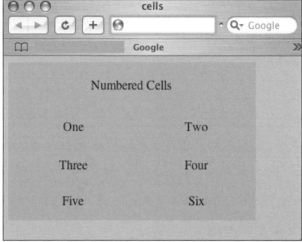

See Color Plate 10 for an example of a Web site that uses TABLEs in HTML. Also, remember that you can always refer back to Color Plate 7 if you have forgotten a code in HTML.

SUMMARY

Now we're getting somewhere with design. Using TABLEs, we can actually keep the relationship between an image and the text exactly the way we want it. In this chapter, you've learned about images, links, and TABLEs. We've discussed designing with TABLEs and have explored the relationship between images and text with and without the use of TABLEs. We've taken a look at the importance of color schemes, the power of images, image formatting, and the differences between vector and pixel graphics. In other words, we've looked briefly at many of the major design concerns for the Web as well as basic HTML coding. Even though we'll spend the rest of the book looking into Dreamweaver and Flash, this very basic knowledge will serve you well in understanding the theories and formulas behind the more complex programs that will code HTML for you. Additionally, when something isn't working quite right, you'll be able to take a look at the code to help uncover the solution. Being familiar with these basics not only helps you resolve problems and workarounds, it will also help you to be a better designer.

in review

1. Why are images so important?

2. What are some common image formats?

3. How do you create a link?

4. What is a TABLE?

5. When would you want to use a TABLE?

6. What does <rowspan> mean?

exercise 2

1. Copy the folder

   Exercise 2 from the Back of Book CD onto your hard drive.

2. Next, open Photoshop and then open the image humm.jpg from the Exercise 2 folder. Feel free to make changes to the image if you like.

3. From the menu bar, select Image>Image Size to view the pixel dimensions of the image.

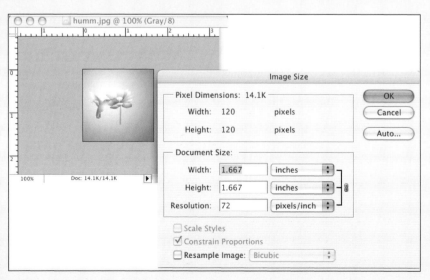

figure | 2-Ex1 |

Image Size window for humm.jpg

Write down the dimensions. Save for Web using the default settings for JPG High. Close Photoshop.

4. Using your HTML page from Chapter 1, add an image to see how that works. Open exer1 in your plain-text-only software and save as exer2 in your Exercise 2 folder.

5. Add the IMG SRC code for the humm.jpg image using the image from your Exercise 2 folder or one that you create. Add the code between the BODY tag and the FONT tag for the word *Hope*. It should look something like this:

<img src="humm.jpg" width=120 height=120 align=right>

figure | 2-Ex2

Complete HTML page with a placed image

```
<html>
<head><title>Hope by Emily Dickinson</title>
<meta name'"keywords" content="Emily Dickinson Poetry Birds
Hope">
</head>
<body bgcolor="#FFFFCC" text="#000033">
<img src="humm.jpg" width=120 height=120 align="right" >
<font color="#CC9900"><b>Hope</b></font> is the thing with
feathers<br>
That perches in the soul<br>
And sings the tune without the words<br>
And never stops at all,<br>
And sweetest in the gale is heard;<br>
And sore must be the storm<br>
That could abash the little bird<br>
I've heard it in the chillest land<br>
And on the strangest sea,<br>
Yet never, in extremity,<br>
It asked a crumb of me.
</body>
</html>
```

6. Now take a look at your code in a browser window. Open your browser and choose File>Open. Browse to the newly revised HTML file in the Exercise 2 folder and open it. It should look something like this:

figure | 2-Ex3

Exercise 2 displayed in a browser window

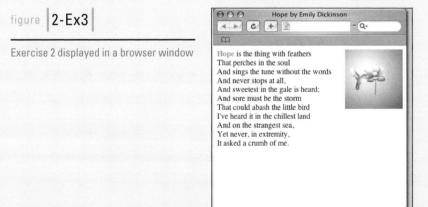

7. Return to the HTML page. Try out different ALIGN and VALIGN options and view them in the browser window.

Next add a link to the image by inserting the coding into the HTML IMG SRC tag. Use an URL that you know will work. Remember to add the protocol HTTP since this site is not contained within your directory. Your code should look something like this:

<a href="http://www.moonlightdsn.com"><img src="humm.jpg" width=120 height=120 align="right"></a>

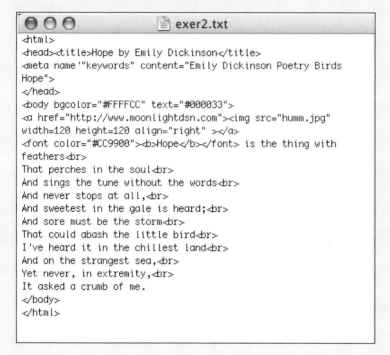

```
exer2.txt
<html>
<head><title>Hope by Emily Dickinson</title>
<meta name'"keywords" content="Emily Dickinson Poetry Birds
Hope">
</head>
<body bgcolor="#FFFFCC" text="#000033">
<a href="http://www.moonlightdsn.com"><img src="humm.jpg"
width=120 height=120 align="right" ></a>
<font color="#CC9900"><b>Hope</b></font> is the thing with
feathers<br>
That perches in the soul<br>
And sings the tune without the words<br>
And never stops at all,<br>
And sweetest in the gale is heard;<br>
And sore must be the storm<br>
That could abash the little bird<br>
I've heard it in the chillest land<br>
And on the strangest sea,<br>
Yet never, in extremity,<br>
It asked a crumb of me.
</body>
</html>
```

figure | 2-Ex4

HTML page with an image as a link

8. Return to the browser window and hit the Refresh button. Your page should now look the same as Figure 2-Ex3 but the image should link to the Web site that you included in the code. Try clicking on the link to make sure it works.

Any code showing up in your browser window? If so, something is wrong. Remember to go back and check the spelling of your tags. Also check to make sure that all of your brackets— < > —are correct and that you have all of the necessary closing tags.

figure **2-Ex5**

Exercise 2 and linked Web site
displayed in a browser window

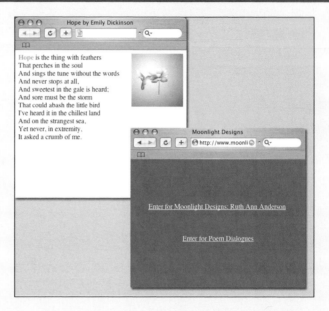

9. Next, add the ALT tag to the IMG SRC code. Type a description of the image in the ALT tag. Don't forget the quotes around the text.

10. Notice how little control you have over the relationship of the image to the poem. You can change that. Create a TABLE. To begin, take a look at how you can use TABLEs in your design. Start with a sketch of your page. Then find the grid and draw it over the sketch.

figure **2-Ex6**

Sketch of TABLE overlaid on poem and image

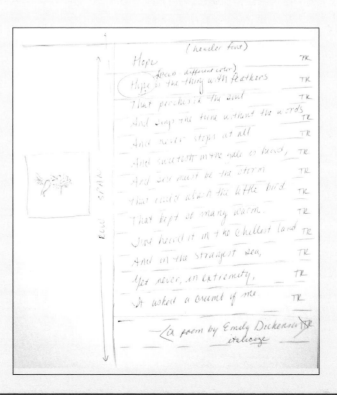

11. Now use TABLEs to control the way the poem looks with the image. Put the image in the first column and the text in the second column. In order to make that work, you'll need the first column to be a row span. Divide the second column into three rows: one row for the title, one for the poem, and one for the author name. Since the second column contains 14 rows, the first column should span three rows.

It should look something like this:

figure | 2-Ex7 |

Final HTML page

12. Save your document and return to the browser window. Open the file and refresh.

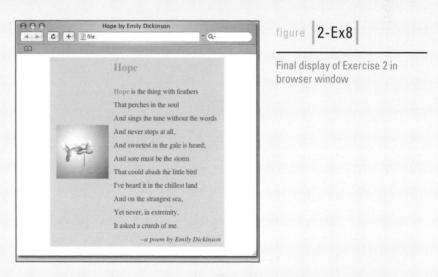

figure | 2-Ex8 |

Final display of Exercise 2 in browser window

If code is showing up, make whatever corrections you need to make. Experiment with the HEADER sizes, FONT colors, and ALIGN options until you are happy with the results. When everything looks perfect, save the page and show your friends.

on your own

In Photoshop, try creating your own images for the Emily Dickinson poem. There are additional images in the Exercise 2 folder that you can use also. For example, you could try creating an alpha channel (transparency) for the feather.tif image. Save for Web as a GIF with a transparent background. Then add the image into the table code. Instead of having humm.jpg occupy the entire row span, change it to a two-row span and add the feather image into the third row of the first column. You'll need to make sure that feather.gif is small enough to fit. Open the altered HTML file in a browser and refresh. Make adjustments as needed.

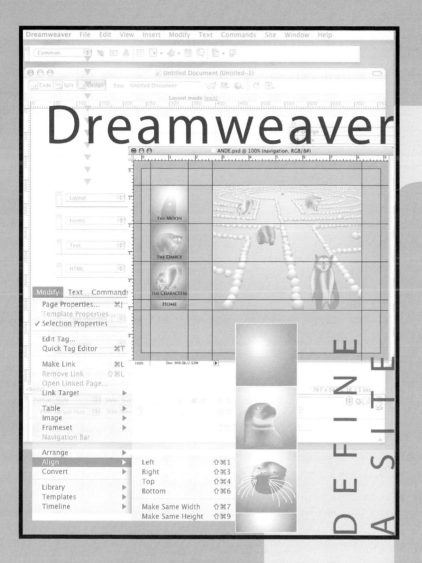

Dreamweaver

SECTION

| onstage: dreamweaver |

Sparrow

The ra...
I play
I hear
You a
Danci
Cocki
Wantin
Notici

Togeth
I am p
You a
I am c
the mo

The great sea has set me in moton.
Set me adrift
And I move as a weed in the river.

The arch of sky
And mightiness of storms
Encompasses me,
And I am left
Trembling with joy.

Eskimo Song

an introduction to site design, save for the web features, image maps, and dreamweaver

Objectives

Explore the organization and hierarchy of Web design.

Examine the Save for the Web feature in Adobe Photoshop and Illustrator.

Get acquainted with Macromedia Dreamweaver.

Understand Dreamweaver's toolbars, panels, and windows.

Discover how to create image maps in Dreamweaver.

Introduction

In Chapters 1 and 2, we took a brief look at HTML and the basics of Web authoring. Macromedia Dreamweaver is a WYSIWYG (What You See is What You Get) Web page editing software that can help you with HTML. It is truly comparable to weaving a dream. Dreamweaver can take care of the tags, create tables, edit frames, format type, and oh, so much more. Plus you can easily switch from code view to page view, allowing you to instantly see the result of your HTML (or vice versa to see your codes).

Dreamweaver can do wonders to assist you in creating a compelling Web site, but you still need to consider weaving together powerful images, engaging color schemes, compelling content, and clear navigation. In this chapter, we'll start at the beginning with the organization of content and the Save for the Web feature in Adobe Photoshop and Adobe Illustrator, as well as an overview of Dreamweaver.

SITE DESIGN AND STRUCTURE

The standard steps in the Web design process are:

- Conceptualization and research

- Content organization and creation

- Art direction—Sketch, sketch, sketch!

- Image preparation

- HTML production—Be very picky! Make sure there are NO typos and everything is precisely coded.

- Prototype building—Frequently called the "alpha release," the first prototype may be available only to the Web team. A "beta release" might be sent to a client for approval.

- Testing—Test in the major browsers and across platforms. Make certain that all of your coding and links work in each of them!

- Uploading and final testing

| NOTE |

Content and Organization
of a Web Site

Users' top frustrations in browsing the Web include not being able to find information, hitting dead ends, not being able to get back to where they started, and having to click through too many pages to get to the information they want. Clutter and chaos look amateurish.

A few helpful tips:

- Limit the length of your pages to one or two "screenfuls" since longer pages require lots of scrolling and scrolling is boring.

- Put your most important messages "above the fold," before any scrolling is necessary.

- Design for a screen size of 640 x 480 pixels if you want a global audience. 800 x 600 pixels is becoming more common but not everyone has a monitor capable of this display.

- Don't center everything on the page. It is too difficult to read and is a poor choice visually.

- Limit the number of colors that you use. Don't use rainbow dividers.

Organizing information can be a complex and highly subjective business. Entire careers, as well as college degrees, are based on the ability to effectively organize information. This is not a subject to be taken lightly. There are standard approaches to bringing logical order to information. In Web design, it is imperative to keep the user's perspective in mind.

Begin by identifying the contents of the site and giving it a basic structure. Organization can be:

- alphabetical

- chronological

- class (or type)

- "information clumping"
- hierarchical
- by order of importance

Next, create a diagram of the site. You can use boxes to represent pages with lines and/or arrows to represent the relationships (links) between the pages. Alternately, you can use index cards or sheets of paper to represent each page—write out everything needed for the page on an index card and place the cards in order on a table or bulletin board. Experiment with moving the cards around to look at different relationships between pages. When you have decided upon the best possible solution, you can either enter the design on a computer or take a digital image of it. At any rate, find a way to save the information. Also save the cards. They may come in handy later if you find that you need to restructure your site.

Most Web sites are organized hierarchically, starting with a top page that offers several choices and then successive layers of choices branching out below so that a "tree" is formed. Make sure that important information doesn't get buried too deeply. Also, make sure that the "branches" of the hierarchy tree are generally balanced.

In the last chapter, we talked about directories. This is a good time to determine subdirectories. To simplify things, consider having the organization of your files match the structure of your site. A single root directory can contain all the files for the site. The root directory can then be divided into subdirectories that reflect the site's major sections. It is common to keep all of the graphics or images in an image directory. An image directory can be kept in each of the section subdirectories so all of the common information sticks together.

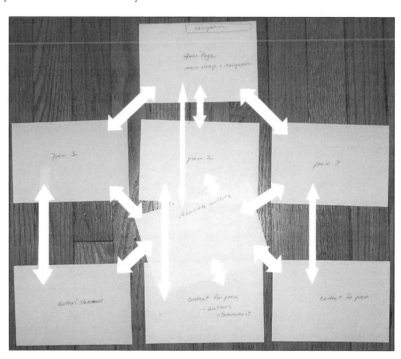

figure | 3-1 |

Example of Web site diagram

Alternately, if you plan to use the same images on multiple pages, you can have image directories organized by type—for example, logos and site branding in one directory, navigation images in another, and so forth.

Once you have determined the structure of your site, create sketches of each page. Develop a color scheme and choose images or sketch ideas for images. Again, remember that a picture says a thousand words so spend time creating the most powerful images imaginable for your site.

Once you have organized your information, create a folder on your hard drive which will be the root directory of your Web site. Have your subdirectories and image folders all in this root directory. Folder names do not include spaces or special characters and are limited to eight characters. This is where your prior organization will pay off.

SAVING FOR THE WEB IN ADOBE PHOTOSHOP AND ADOBE ILLUSTRATOR

Create your images either in Photoshop or Illustrator or both. (Remember to check the dimensions. In Chapter 2, we used the Image pull-down menu to gather the pixel size information of an image. Even though Dreamweaver will accommodate pixel information for you, it is good practice to write down this information. It may come in handy later.) Once your images are created, make them Dreamweaver-ready in Photoshop or Illustrator through the Save for Web feature. With the image open, go to the menu bar for File. Choose Save for Web. This will bring up a new window.

In the Save for Web window, choose the 2-up option. The image on the left will show you the original image at its original resolution. The image on the right will show you the image quality

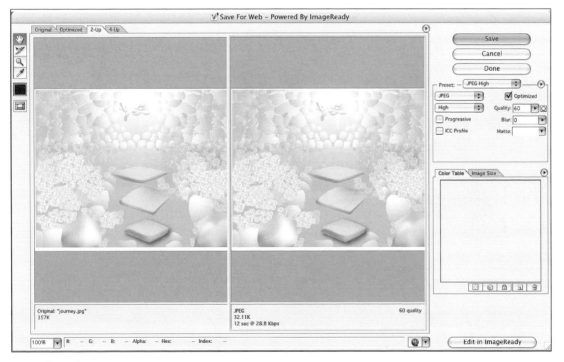

figure | 3-2 |

Save for Web Window in Photoshop and Illustrator

based upon your compression choices. In the right portion of the window you'll notice that there are different options in the Preset drop-down menu and below the menu. Explore the options here and notice how the image changes based upon your choice of settings. Also, just below the image, notice the download information. Make your choices by comparing image quality to download time.

You will also have choices of dither or no dither in some of these selections. Remember from Chapter 1 that we defined *dither* as the browser mixing the colors that are available to it in order to approximate the color in the image. It is best to stay away from dither unless you have a continuous tone image. Dithering creates larger files sizes.

Once you have made your choices, choose Save. This will bring up a dialog box.

At this point, just choose Images Only, Default Settings, and All Slices in the Save Optimized As dialog box. When bringing images into Dreamweaver, we don't need the HTML. We only need the images. In the next chapter, we'll learn how to change the default settings and slice choices and when it is important to distinguish these choices, but for now just stay with the default. Be sure to give your image file a short name and save it to the correct directory or folder. Create a logical naming so that images will be easy to locate.

Okay, you've organized your information, created your site design, and prepared your images for the Web. Let's try putting this all together in Dreamweaver and construct a Web page.

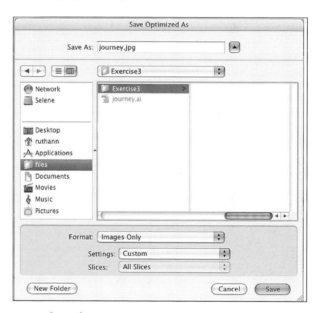

figure | 3-3 |

Save Optimized As dialog box

INTRODUCTION TO MACROMEDIA DREAMWEAVER

Macromedia Dreamweaver is a pixel-based, page-oriented layout, professional HTML editor for designing, coding, and developing Web sites. Dreamweaver allows you to work in HTML code only, HTML code and a visual editing environment, or just the visual editing environment. By *visual editing environment*, I am referring to Dreamweaver's ability to immediately translate HTML code into a visual result.

Let's take a look at this editing environment.

- Toolbar: Runs across the top of the work area and shows left to right: view (code and/or design), title of the document, browser support and error views and reports, file management, preview option, refresh option, and view option.

- Document window: Displays the current document as you create and edit.

- Floating panels: Includes the HTML Styles, Code Inspector, Layers, Frames, History, Assets, CSS Styles, Library, Template, Timeline, etc.

- Properties: Displays and allows you to modify information for the selected object or text.

- Tag Selector: Highlights a tag.

- Insert bar: Contains icons you click to insert various types of objects in your document, such as images, rollover images, tables, layers, and navigation bars. Alternately, you can use the Insert pull-down menu. The Insert bar layout tab allows you to change the way you work in a document through layout and view. In Layout view, you can design a page layout and insert graphics, text, and other media. In Standard view, you can insert layers, create frame documents and tables and apply other changes to your page.

- Preview: Under File, choose Preview in browser and select a browser in which to view your site.

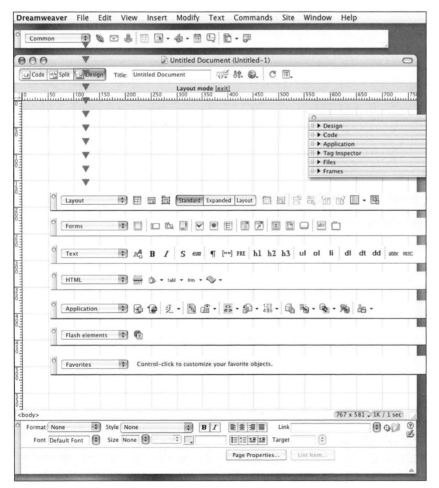

figure 3-4

Windows and panels overview of Dreamweaver

Defining a Local Site

A site is where you collect, store, and organize all of the files for a Web site. From the menu bar, select Site>Manage Site>New. When the Site Definition Wizard window opens, choose the Basic tab. In the Site Name field, type the name of your site.

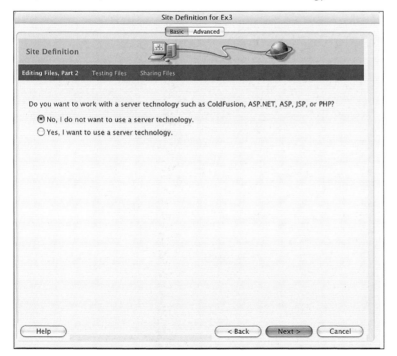

figure |3-5|

Site Definition Wizard window: Editing Files

Click the Next button. This will take you to a new window called Editing Files, Part 2. Here you can choose server technology such as Cold Fusion or other scripting technologies. For now, choose No, I do not want to use a server technology.

figure |3-6|

Site Definition Wizard window: Editing Files, Part 2

Again click the Next button. Stay with the Edit local copies on my machine option. You can then browse to the folder you have created for this site on your hard drive.

figure | 3-7 |

Site Definition Wizard window: Editing Files, Part 3

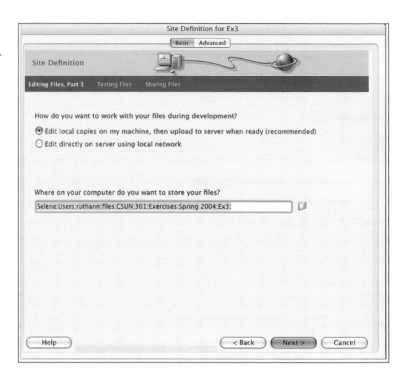

Click Next. For now, choose Local/Network and the same folder to indicate where you will store your files. When you are ready to upload the site to the Web and you have server space, you can change to the FTP option and name the folder created there by your host. (We will look more thoroughly at hosting and what it means in Chapter 7.)

figure | 3-8 |

Site Definition Wizard window: Sharing Files

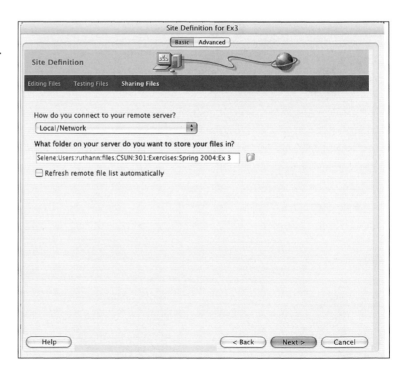

Click Next. Finally, unless you are working in an environment where a number of people are working on the same Web site, choose No, do not enable check in and check out. Check in and check out are primarily for use when more than one person is working on a Web Site. It is a convenient tool for companies that use teams to design and implement images, HTML, and scripting. It can keep two designers from working on images or authoring at the same time, as well as prevent overlap and confusion.

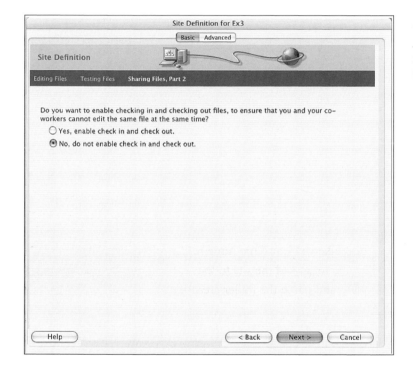

figure | 3-9 |

Site Definition Wizard window: Sharing Files, Part 2

Click Next. Now you will see a summary window that will show you all of the choices you have made.

You can move forward or backward through the Site Definition Wizard to make changes. You can also come back and edit the site at any time through the Site pull-down menu. Choose Site>Manage Sites, highlight the site you want to edit, and choose Edit. When you are sure everything is correct, click Done to close the manage sites dialog window. You will then be moved to a new window that will display a list of the root directory, subdirectories, and their included pages and images. This Manage Sites feature works as a file manager in the same way that you can work on your computer desktop to create folders and move files around.

figure 3-10

Site Definition Wizard window: Summary

figure 3-11

Manage Sites

CREATING THE SITE HOME PAGE

Once you have saved the site directory, a document window will open. If it doesn't, choose File>New. Begin by typing the Title of the document in the title field in the toolbar window. This title is what will show up in a browser window so make it informative, short, and concise. Next, save the document to save your site definition, title, and file. Choose File>Save. Now, let's move onward to the fun part—designing the page.

Think of your page as a grid. Check the sketch that you made. How do you begin to translate the sketch into Dreamweaver? Can you overlay a grid onto your sketch that will translate into an HTML table? Dreamweaver works with tables to create cells for images, text, and blank space, just like what you worked with in Chapter 2. You can work with tables in one of two ways. You can create a table in full or you can create with individual cells and let Dreamweaver complete and adjust the table as you work.

Let's begin by drawing individual cells and letting Dreamweaver add and adjust additional cells to complete the table as we work. This means that we'll start in Layout mode. It will help you to understand what is happening and how it is occurring in real time. You can access Layout mode view from the menu bar. Select View>Table View>Layout Mode or, on the Insert bar, Layout>Layout Mode.

Drawing with Layout Cells

figure | 3-12 |

Insert bar with Layout tab selected

Use layout cells to define the design areas of a document. Generally speaking, you'll be creating cells for each image and text group. You can add cells for blank areas. This is all, of course, made much easier if you have a sketched sample layout with a superimposed grid to work from.

Choose the Draw Layout Cell icon and move your pointer to the document window. Click in the upper-left corner and drag down and to the right to define a cell. You can resize a cell through two options. Click on the edge of the layout cell to activate it and drag the middle resize handle to modify, or type a new number in the Fixed field of the Properties window.

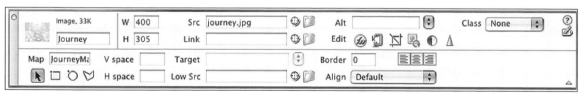

Once you've created cells in a general layout to match your sketched page, choose a cell into which you want to place an image. Back on the Insert bar, choose Common, select the Import Image icon, and click in the cell. A file browser window will open to allow you to browse to the appropriate image. Choose the image. It will then be inserted into the cell.

figure | 3-13 |

Properties window

As we learned in HTML, you need to make sure that the dimensions of your cell match the dimensions of your image. You can either drag the cell handles to snap into place at the edges of the image or you can type in the dimensions in the Properties window. Click on the image first to get the correct dimensions from the Properties window, then click on the edge of the cell and type these dimensions into the Properties window.

In the Properties window, with the image selected, notice that you can add a link to the image, target it, and choose how it opens in a browser. Let's take this one step further and look at how one image can contain several links.

IMAGE MAPS

An *image map* is an image that has been divided into regions, or *hotspots*. When a hotspot is clicked, an action occurs, like opening a new file or linking to a new HTML page. When a viewer clicks a hotspot in an image, the associated URL is sent directly to the server. Client-side image maps store the hyperlink information in the HTML document. Server-side image maps store the hyperlink information in a separate map file. Client-side image maps are now faster than server-side image maps because the server does not need to interpret where the visitor clicked.

To create a client-side image map, import the image into a cell and then select it. In the Properties window, make certain that all properties show. Type a unique name for the image map. Next define the hot spots. Select the circle, rectangle, or polygon tool and drag the pointer over the image to create a hotspot. When you use the circle or rectangle tool, click on the top left corner of where you want the hotspot to be and drag down and to the right until it is the size that you want. When you use the polygon tool, define each point by clicking as you draw. Do not overlap hotspot shapes.

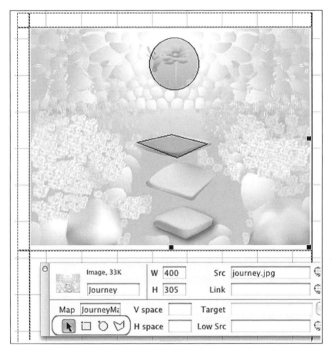

figure | 3-14 |

Drawing with the hotspot tools

When you are finished mapping the image, click a blank area in the document to change the Properties window.

To set the properties for the hotspots, click on a hotspot in the image. Then, in the Properties window, type the name of the map, the link, and the target. The link specifies the file or URL. The target specifies the frame (see Chapter 5 for a discussion of frames and framesets) or browser window in which the linked page should load. (This option will not be available until the selected hotspot contains a link.) For targeting, you can choose _blank, _parent, _self, or _top:

• _blank loads the linked file into a new unnamed browser window.

• _parent loads the linked file into the parent frameset or window of the frame that contains the link. If the frame containing the link is not nested, the linked file loads into the full browser window.

• _self loads the linked file into the same frame or window as the link. This target is the default.

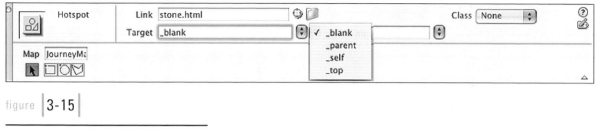

figure | 3-15 |

Properties window with Target pane

- _top loads the linked file into the full browser window, thereby removing all Frames.

These options will show up in the pull-down menu for the target.

Opening a new window (_blank) gives the viewer the advantage of not losing their location in your site. They will simply need to close this window to return to the previous page. Do, however, limit opening a new window to one or two levels.

To modify an image map or edit hotspots, simply use the pointer hotspot tool from the Properties window to select and drag any of the points of a hotspot or move an entire hotspot to a new area. `Shift+arrow` keys moves the hotspot by ten pixels at a time on a Mac. On a PC, use `Control+arrow` keys. An arrow key alone will move a hotspot by 1 pixel at a time.

SUMMARY

In this chapter, you've learned how to structure your site, create directories, and manage your files. You've also learned how to save images for the Web using Photoshop and Illustrator. You've explored the differences in image formats for the Web and how they translate to the issue of resolution versus download time.

Furthermore, you've learned the basic tools and work area of Dreamweaver. You now know how to draw layout cells, change their size, insert an image, and draw hotspots to create an image map. You've learned how to apply links and targets. With just this much information, you can begin to create dynamic Web sites.

in review

1. What is the importance of organizing information for a Web site?

2. Is Dreamweaver a vector-based or pixel-based Web authoring program?

3. How can you edit a site definition?

4. How do you draw a layout cell?

5. When do you use the Properties window?

6. What is an image map?

exercise 3

1. Create a root directory on your hard drive. Create a subdirectory called "images" inside of the root directory. From the Chapter 3 folder on the back of book CD, copy journey3.jpg into the images folder. Under the root directory, on the first level, copy boat.html and moon.html from the CD.

2. Open Photoshop. Find the folder you just created on your computer and open the file journey3.jpg. Choose Image>image size. Write down the pixel dimensions of the image. Close Photoshop.

3. Open Macromedia Dreamweaver. Take a look around. Study the Insert Bar. (Windows>Insert). Click the various tabs and familiarize yourself with the corresponding icons.

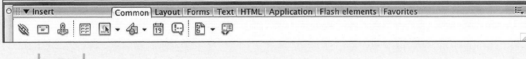

figure |3-Ex1|

Dreamweaver's Insert bar

Study the Properties window. (Windows>Properties).

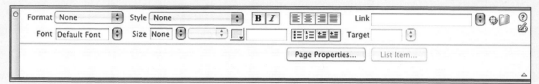

figure | **3-Ex2** |

Dreamweaver's Properties window

Find the floating panels. Click the triangles on the left side of these panels and note their functions.

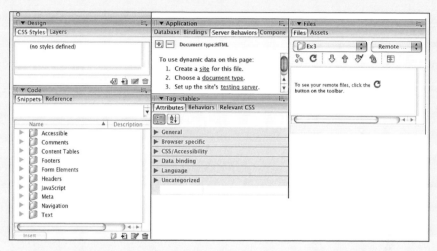

4. Under File, choose Preview in Browser and select a browser in which to view your site if one is not already selected.

figure | **3-Ex3** |

Dreamweaver's floating panels

5. Choose Site>Manage Sites>New Site. When the Site Definition wizard opens, name your site.

figure | **3-Ex4** |

Dreamweaver's Manage Sites feature

6. Click the Next button. Choose No, I do not want to use a server technology.

7. Click the Next button. Choose Edit local copies on my machine. Choose the folder you created to store your files by clicking on the folder icon and browsing to the folder.

8. Click the Next button. Choose Local/Network and the same folder as in the previous step to indicate where you will store your files on the server.

9. Click the Next button. Choose No, do not enable check in and check out.

10. Click the Next button. When the Site Definition Summary window appears, review what you have chosen and make sure that all is correct. If it is not, use the Back button to return to the menu that needs changing. Click Done. Then click done again to close the Manage Sites dialog box.

    Manage Sites will display a list of all the folders and files in the local site.

    If a blank document isn't already open, from the menu bar, select File>New>Create.

11. Begin your actual Web page by typing your name in the title Field in the toolbar window. Save the document as exer3.

figure | 3-Ex5 |

Site Title bar

12. Work in Layout view to begin. From the menu bar, select View>Table View>Layout Mode, or, on the Insert bar, choose Layout>Layout Mode.

figure | 3-Ex6 |

Insert bar with Layout tab selected

13. Now it's time to start drawing the layout cells. On the Insert bar, choose the layout tab, click the Draw Layout Cell icon and move your pointer to the document window. Click in the upper-left corner and drag down and to the right to define the cell.

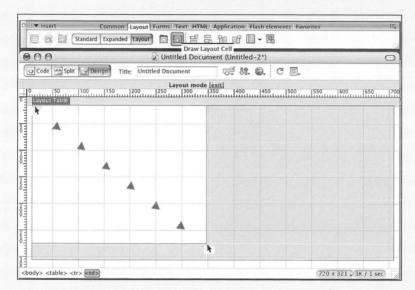

figure | 3-Ex7 |

Drawing a layout cell

14. On the Insert bar, choose Common and select the Import Image icon.

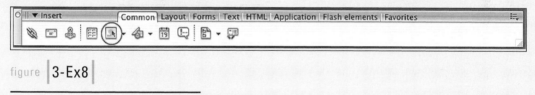

figure | 3-Ex8 |

Insert bar with Common tab selected

15. Import the image, journey3.jpg and then click on the image. In the Properties window, make certain that all properties show. In the far left of the window, type *journey* for the image map name.

16. Click on the edge of the cell. Resize it by typing in the pixel dimensions you copied down from Photoshop. This information goes in the Fixed Width and Height fields of the Properties window.

17. Define the link area hotspots for the image map. Click on the image and choose the drawing icons from the Properties window. Over the moonglow with the bird and flower, create a circular hotspot. Over the stepping stone, create a polygon hotspot.

figure | 3-Ex9

Journey image map with hotspots

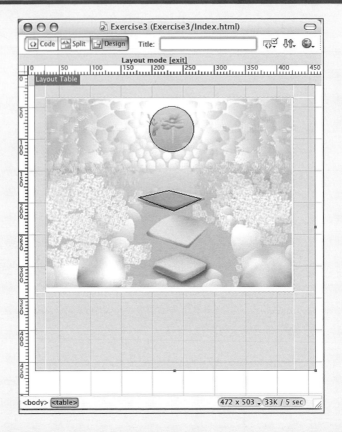

18. Choose the Select tool from the Properties window and click the circle hotspot. In the Properties window's Link field, click the folder icon to browse to the file moon.html. Choose Open or OK on a PC. To set where the linked file opens, choose _blank in the Target field.

19. Click the polygon hotspot and in the Properties window's Link field, click the folder icon to browse to the file stone.html. Choose Open or OK on a PC. To set where the linked file opens, again choose _blank in the Target field. When you are finished mapping the image, click anywhere on the document to change the Properties window.

20. Save and view the page in at least two browsers. (The keyboard shortcut to preview is F12.) Test your links. Do the poems open in new windows? Can you close a new window and still be on your page? Since different browsers look at HTML differently, you will want to have a full understanding of what your user might be seeing based upon their computer configuration and browser.

When everything looks correct, save and enjoy.

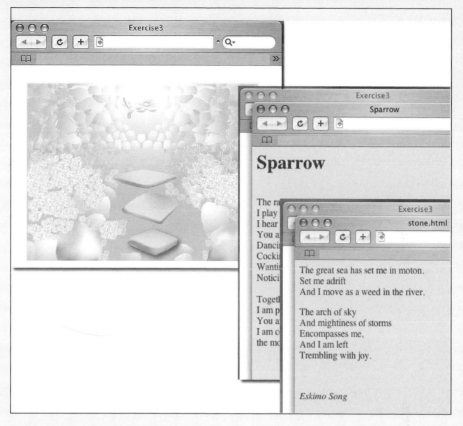

figure | **3-Ex10**

Exercise 3 displayed in browser window

on your own

Try creating your own link pages. In the exer 3 document, take note of the location of the top left corner of the Journey image cell. Open moon.html in Dreamweaver, select the text, and cut it. Draw a cell in the same location as the Journey image cell. Use the same coordinates of the top left corner of the Journey image cell exer 3. Paste the text into the cell. Repeat this for the second HTML document. This will give your Web site a more consistent look.

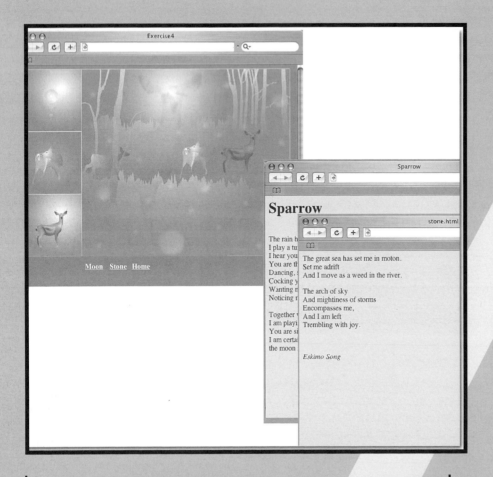

navigation, linking, and image slicing in Photoshop and Illustrator

Objectives

Learn about the conceptual process of navigation.

Explore creating links and targets to images.

Examine slicing in Photoshop and Illustrator.

Understand the Properties window in Dreamweaver.

Learn how to reassemble slices in Dreamweaver.

Introduction

While weaving our dreams, we need to successfully guide others. Dreamweaver has several options to guide you through the labyrinth, but you need to have a successful navigation scheme first. Once your structure is in place, the path to the inner circle of the labyrinth is easily enhanced through Dreamweaver's navigation tools.

NAVIGATION

Navigation is a system of signage intended to help visitors to your Web site find their way around. It is one of the most important elements of your site. A good navigation system must answer the questions "Where am I?" and "Where can I go from here?" Navigation needs to be clear, logical, consistent, efficient, concise, and easy to use. It is in your best interest to make the learning process behind your navigation as quick and painless as possible, by making your navigational tools intuitive and easily understood at a glance.

One of the main duties of a navigation system is to let users know where they are. Because a visitor may have landed in your Web site on a page other than your home page, it is important that every page in your site contains labeling that not only identifies the site, but also has a link back to the home page. The other primary duty of a navigation system is to clearly present the options for where users can go or what they can do next.

There are three key ingredients to a successful navigation system. They are clarity, consistency, and efficiency.

| **NOTE** |

Secondary Navigation and Consistency

If your site is divided into sections, you might choose to provide links to the main pages of the other sections as part of the consistent navigation bar, with an additional navigation bar containing the links to subsections. This is called *secondary navigation* or *section navigation*. Make certain that navigational options are consistent throughout all of the levels. For example, if there is a link to the home page on a second-level page, then there should be a link to the home page on *every* second-level page. It should look the same and be in the same location on each page. Also, if you offer a list of options, such as in a toolbar, keep the selections in the same order on each page.

- Clarity: Navigation should look like navigation. Label everything clearly. Use icons wisely. Icons are sometimes difficult to decipher and can be misinterpreted. Some icons, such as a globe, are so overused that they have lost their meaning. If you use icons, make certain that they are clear in their meaning and intent, and that they always answer the questions of "Where am I?" and "Where can I go from here?"

- Consistency: Navigational options need to be consistent throughout the site in availability as well as in appearance. Navigation elements should stay put throughout the site. Be tenacious. Navigation that jumps around is not only confusing but also annoying—a surefire way to lose your user.

- Efficiency: With every click into a Web site's hierarchy, you run the risk that the user will lose interest and leave. Be mindful of how many clicks it takes to get to content or to get a task done. Your goal is to efficiently get users to the information they want and to keep them engaged in the process. This is a case where less is indeed more. A maximum of three clicks is a useful rule of thumb.

Navigation Systems

There are several systems that can be used in designing navigation.

- Left navigation is a left column navigation system that remains in the same place throughout the site. It is a common navigation system. Top navigation is becoming more of an industry standard, as scrolling, which is more typical of left navigation, has become more annoying and less popular.

- Tabs across the top of the page are very popular but are often used arbitrarily without any logical metaphor. This system is sometimes combined with left navigation as a secondary navigation system, particularly for a complex site.

- Breadcrumb navigation leaves a trail as you click through a site's hierarchy, with each successive level indicated as a text link, allowing the user to easily return to an earlier page.

- Site maps are a useful tool if your site is large and complex. A site map is an overhead view of a site's logic and lists the contents of the site, reflecting the structure of the site by section and subsection. You may also wish to provide a site index, which is an alphabetical listing (like a book index) of all the topics available on your site.

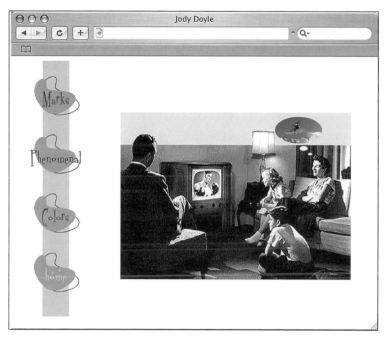

figure | 4-1 |

Example of left navigation by student Jody Doyle. (photo credit: Margaret Ewing/Camerique/Retrofile.com)

figure | 4-2 |

Example of a Site Index

Whatever system you use, be consistent, clear, and efficient. *Rollovers*—the term used for the change in a navigation element when a user rolls the mouse over it—can also add clarity and engagement. We'll take a deeper look at rollovers in the next chapter.

CREATING A COMPELLING USER EXPERIENCE

This all adds up to the notion of creating experience. Web design comes at a time when our common economic experience is shifting. This new economy prospers under the concept of intangible offerings and products, such as home delivery of groceries, reading environments, social settings for conversation, theme restaurants, or the creation of memories. Companies stage an experience whenever they engage customers, connecting with them in a personal, memorable way. An example of this is the very successful world of Starbucks. Starbucks doesn't just offer a cup o' joe. It offers an experience. Music is playing, live performances are frequently scheduled. You can sit down, enjoy a cup of coffee, and read a good book. An entire atmosphere appealing to the "educated cool" is created. Similarly, in the digital world of the Web, an experience must not only inform users but also thoroughly engage them. Value must be provided immediately. Because the Web is truly the most customized experience, it needs to be compelling and unique.

There are basically five disciplines involved in creating a Web site:

| NOTE |

The Digital Experience

The digital experience is like a jigsaw of individually created moments, engaging the individual emotionally, physically, intellectually, and even spiritually. The idea is not to create things that blink, honk, or beep but rather to create experiences that meld seamlessly with the momentary and unique needs of the individual user. From a solid knowledge of typography to faceless interface and transparent design, let your creativity blossom with imagination and innovation.

- Site and information design

- Interaction design

- Interface design

- Graphic design

- HTML engineering and programming

These must all come together successfully to create a dynamic user experience. A few reminders:

- Remember that color is a wonderful, magical element in any art form but especially on the Web. When we look at high-end monitors with millions of color, the detail and light can totally captivate us. However, when it comes to Web design, color can be overwhelming to the user who does a lot of surfing. A block of white type on a black background is very hard on the eyes. Don't assume that because you have a black background that your site looks cool looking. Pastel colors tend to imply the whimsical. Using too many colors is visually chaotic and makes it difficult to prioritize the information. It is better to choose one or two analogous colors and one complementary color as a highlight for a color scheme, then stick with them throughout the site.

- Again, don't use wild background tile patterns, as they make text very difficult to read. Background patterns should be as subtle as possible or avoided all together. And don't use rainbow dividers, especially animated rainbow dividers. This is a surefire indication of amateur Web design.

- Do everything possible to avoid the necessity of scrolling and scroll bars. It is a better choice to use a navigational element to take the user to a new page. Have this new page delight and reward the user. This method is much more likely to engage the user than scrolling.

- In your directory, you should only have your HTML files and your image directory. Have all other supporting files in an external folder.

DESIGNING A SPLASH/HOME PAGE

Let's talk more about what you may want to do with your home page. As always, begin by sketching. Design your page with a grid. This will help you to organize your elements. Give the navigation no more than one fourth of the page. Give your introductory image visual weight by having it occupy as much as 50% of the grid and making certain that it has plenty of breathing space around it. This initial image is your most important image. Your viewer's willingness to go deeper is lost or gained here. This image should not only give information about the site and add clarity to its intended content, it should also have some emotional impact—even with the driest of subjects. Try bringing something personal to this image. Be enthusiastic. Design from a desire to create. Color Plates 1, 2, 3, 8, 9, 11, and 12 include examples of great page design and powerful images.

You can design your entire site, one page at a time, in Photoshop and/or Illustrator. Remember all of the great design elements we have discussed so far. Don't be afraid of clean or empty space. This gives images and type air around them to breathe.

Choose a simple color palette (remember only two or three colors). You can access Web-safe colors in Illustrator from the menu bar of Window>Swatch Libraries>Web. In Photoshop, you can access Web-safe colors by opening the Swatch Palette (Window>Swatches) and then, in the top right corner, clicking the triangle and scrolling to Web-safe Colors. If you want to have a background color, be sure to use a Web-safe color and write down the number of that color so that you can use it in Dreamweaver.

Choose a readable, clear typeface, since type will lose some of its resolution when uploaded to the Web. San serif is always a good choice for the Web. Again, limit the choices to just one or two typefaces. Use an easy-to-read typeface for paragraphs and navigation. You can use a more

| NOTE |

A Few Checkpoints
for a Good Design

- Sketch, sketch, sketch.

- Create powerful images.

- Avoid chaos and clutter.

- Give your graphics breathing room.

- Use a simple color palette.

- Choose Web-safe colors.

- Design clean and efficient navigation.

- Choose a readable clear typeface.

complex type, fancy or funky, for titles and headlines. In Illustrator, turn your type into outlines before saving for the Web. You can also wait and create your text in Dreamweaver. It's preferable to create large blocks of type in Dreamweaver to save download time and ensure that the blocks more clearly translate to display in a browser window.

In Illustrator, you can create graphics, type, and placed images from Photoshop. If you are creating just a portion of your page in Illustrator, you can copy and paste into Photoshop. Conversely, you can create your page in Photoshop and import graphics, images, and text from Illustrator. The programs are entirely compatible and you can go back and forth between the two by exporting and importing or copying and pasting. Just remember that Photoshop is pixel based and Illustrator is vector based. Dreamweaver requires that all images have a pixel orientation, so you will find the interactivity between Photoshop and Dreamweaver to be plenty satisfactory.

Whether you are creating in Illustrator or Photoshop, you can save the entire page for the Web or you can slice the page into clear, logical divisions to be reassembled in Dreamweaver. (Slicing is discussed in the next section.) Take a look at Color Plate 12 for an example of a page created in Illustrator.

figure | 4-3 |

Page designed in Adobe Photoshop (site by student Theresa Paul)

SLICING

Slicing divides a Photoshop or Illustrator page into sections that can then be redefined as cells in an HTML table in Dreamweaver. Slicing a page offers the advantage of downloading smaller images. You can make decisions regarding GIFs and JPGs (as discussed in Chapter 2) so that your page downloads as quickly as possible for your user. You can also assign non-image space in Dreamweaver to further decrease download time. In other words, space that isn't part of an image can be redefined in Dreamweaver as a blank cell rather than bringing in an empty slice. The simpler the table, the faster the download.

In either Photoshop or Illustrator, the steps for slicing are the same. After creating the page(s), turn on rulers. In either Photoshop or Illustrator, from the menu bar select View>Rulers (Command-R on a Mac, Control-R on a PC). Now you can pull guides with the Select tool from either the horizontal or vertical ruler. Click in the ruler with the Select tool and drag the guide to the position you want. Use the guides to divide up your page. Be logical, clear, and concise. Divide according to need, interface, and visual logic, and keep the idea of a table in the back of your mind as you divide.

Next, use the Slice tool to create divisions. In Photoshop, it is located on the right side of the toolbar, third tool down from the top. Once you've selected the Slice tool, the toolbar at the top will have an option to create slices from guides. Simply click on this button to create slices all at once based on the guides.

In Illustrator, the Slice tool is located on the left side of the toolbar, second tool from the bottom. As in Photoshop, you can create slices from guides. From the menu bar select Object> Slice>Create from Guides. In either program, slices created from guides will be perfectly aligned.

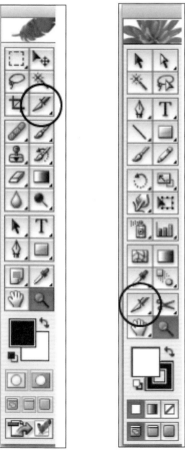

figure | 4-4 |

Drag a Guide to the desired position

To draw slices manually, turn on Snap to Guides (under the menu bar of window for a Mac, menu bar of view for a PC) so that the Slice tool will align with the guides. With the Slice tool, click in the top left corner of the image and drag down and to the right to the next guide to create the slice. Notice that when you draw a slice, both Illustrator and Photoshop will automatically fill in the rest of the page with slices based on a grid. The slices that you draw will be highlighted, while the slices that the software draws will be dimmed. As you continue to draw, the grid highlighting will be readjusted to accommodate your new slices. Also, in both programs, slices will automatically be numbered in the top left corner. As you continue to add slices, this numbering will be adjusted accordingly. If these numbers are not showing up in Photoshop, from the

figure | 4-5 |

figure | 4-6 |

Slice tool in Photoshop   Slice tool in Illustrator

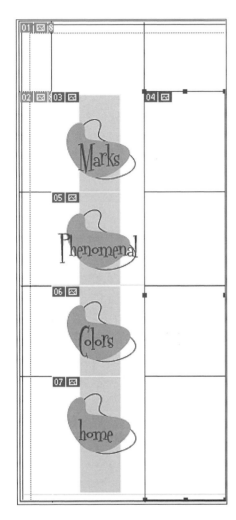

figure | **4-7** |

Illustrator page with completed slicing

menu bar, select Edit>
Preferences>Guides, Grid
and Slices. In the lower left
of the dialog box that
appears, you will see a box to select Show Slice Numbers.

Create all of the slices that you need on the page before going any further. Make certain that the slices do not overlap each other. Be sure that they line up precisely, make sense, and are logical. If you need to edit a slice, whether you drew it manually or created it from guides, the Slice Edit tool on a Mac, slice select tool on a PC in both Photoshop and Illustrator can be found directly behind the slice tool. Simply click on the small arrow on the bottom right of the slice tool to find it. Access the Slice Edit or slice select tool, click on the slice that you want to edit, and make any necessary adjustments. You can adjust the slice by grabbing the handle of the appropriate side and moving it to where you want it to be. When you make adjustments, be sure that all other affected slices are also adjusted. When you are adjusting a slice, you should be able to feel it snap to the adjacent slice. If you leave a gap between slices, it will cause a new slice to be created, so be very accurate here—you will be grateful later. Make certain to zoom in to double-check your accuracy.

Now you are ready to save each slice for the Web. From the menu bare, select File>Save for Web. When the optimize menu appears, choose 2-up. This allows you to compare the choices of compression to the original image. You can save all of the slices at once or

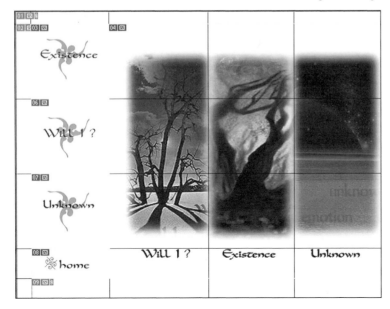

figure | **4-8** |

Photoshop page with completed slicing

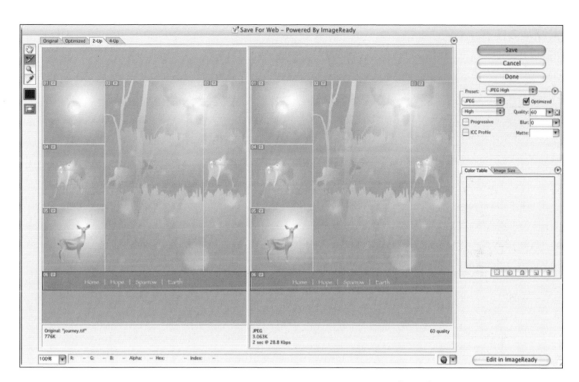

figure | 4-9 |

select one slice at a time. It is better to select one slice at a time and save. In doing so you can optimize slices according to flatness, color, and size, remembering the trade-offs of size versus resolution and download time.

Save for Web window with Slices

When the Save dialog box appears, you will have additional options. We briefly visited this in the last chapter but now let's look at it more thoroughly. In the Save dialog box, you will have three categories. The Format is a pull-down menu of HTML only, Images only, and HTML and Images. As long as you are working in Dreamweaver or another Web editor, you don't need the HTML. You just need the images.

The next concern is the Settings drop-down menu. Here you can choose Custom, Background Image, Default Settings, XHTML, or Other. (Other will generate a new dialog box.)

Here you can change how Photoshop will name your slices. This is an advantage. Choose other in the second drop-down menu, located under the Settings pull-down menu. When the next dialog box

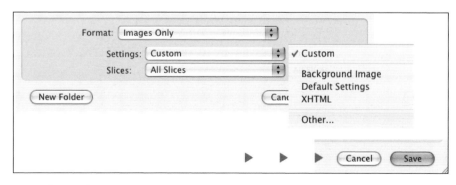

figure | 4-10 |

Settings dialogue window

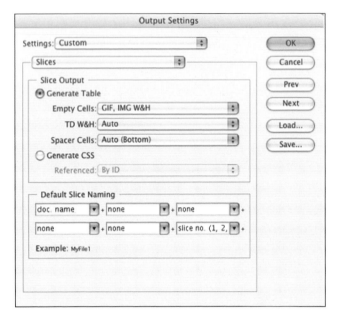

figure | **4-11** |

Naming slices

opens, choose slices from the second drop-down menu. This will open the Slices Naming window.

Keeping the names as simple as possible, under Default Slice Naming, choose doc.name in the first menu, none in the second, third, fourth, and fifth option boxes and slice no. (01, 02, 03, etc.) in the last option box. This will produce a slice name something like Journey01.

Next in the Output Settings window, choose the Saving Files option in the second drop-down menu.

Once again, logic combined with simplicity is best. Save files with just the slice name, number, and extension. The Put Images in Folder option is particularly important here. When saving individual slices, the first time you save a slice, select this option. For the rest of the slices, deselect this option. This way you will have one folder for all of the slices.

Obviously, if you are not using a background image, deselect the Copy Background Image when Saving option. Most likely, you will not need to use the Include Copyright option at this point either.

Once you have saved all of your slices, go to the desktop and make certain they all reside within one folder and it is the Image folder in the directory that you are expecting them to be in. If not, move things around into the logical hierarchy, making sure that you have one folder for all of the images.

figure | **4-12** |

Saving slices

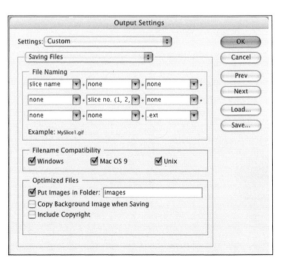

REASSEMBLING SLICES IN DREAMWEAVER

When you start any new project in Dreamweaver, you will need to go through the steps of defining a site that were covered in Chapter 3. Once these steps are complete, take a look at Page Properties. This is under the Modify pull-down menu. Here you can make universal page decisions about such things as background color, font choices, and link information. Additionally, it is in this menu that you can match the background color to the Photoshop or Illustrator Web-safe color you chose earlier when creating pages.

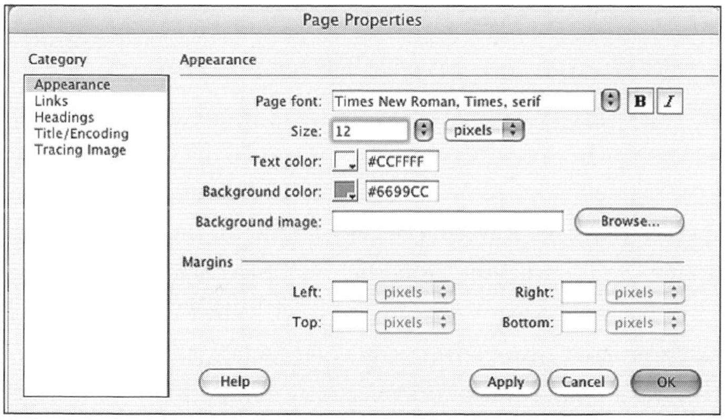

figure | 4-13 |

Page Properties Appearance dialog box

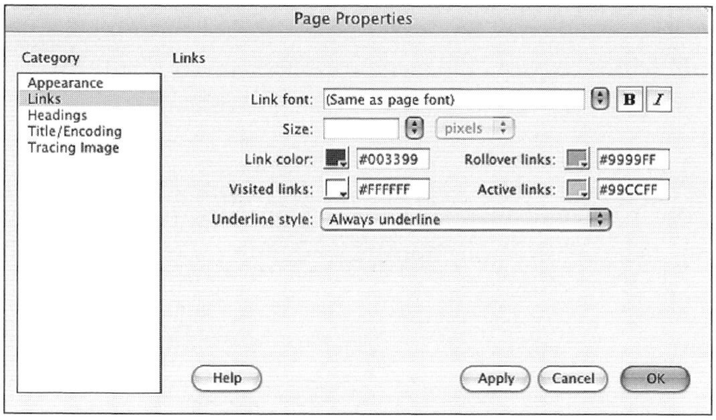

figure | 4-14 |

Page Properties Links dialog box

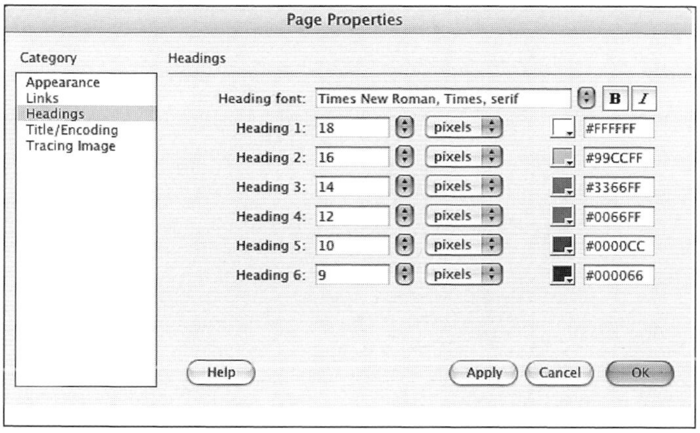

figure | 4-15 |

Page Properties Headings dialog box

figure | 4-16 |

Page Properties Title/Encoding dialog box

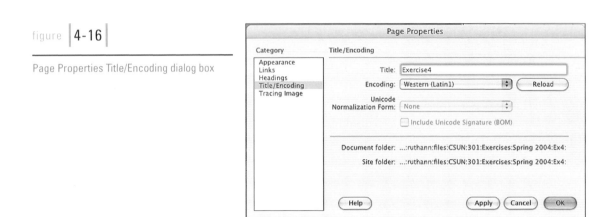

Make your choices as best as you can for now. You can always return to this menu and make changes.

Now it's time to reassemble your slices in Dreamweaver. Draw cells, importing images and matching the dimensions of the cells to the images using the Properties window. Remember that a cell is the table data information that you studied in Chapter 2 (<td>). When you draw a cell, Dreamweaver will automatically create the accompanying table and table rows coding. As you continue to draw additional cells, Dreamweaver will adjust these to accommodate your changes. You can add blank areas without importing images simply by drawing cells to match the size of the needed blank space. Add a non-breaking space, ( ) to an empty cell to ensure that the browser does not collapse the cell. To do this, from the menu bar select Insert>HTML>Special Characters>Non-Breaking Space. Create a cell for each sliced image and blank space.

You can also draw cells to hold text. Use the Type tool and click inside the cell to begin typing. You can change font face, size, color, and alignment in the Properties window. You can also apply links and targets to type. The cell size will automatically adjust to your typing. We'll look at type in depth in Chapter 6.

figure | 4-17 |

Completed Dreamweaver page with cells and images

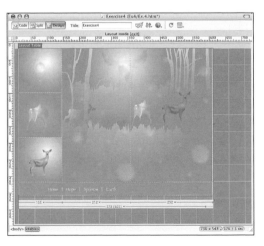

Finally, add links and targets to the navigation images.

Check your page in a browser frequently to make certain everything looks the way you expect it to, including links and targets. You can go back and make adjustments to your Photoshop or Illustrator files at any time. Dreamweaver will automatically update these changes as long as the file is correctly called out in the site definition. This is an especially great feature that saves a lot of time.

If you do feel the need to adjust an image, but don't want to return to Photoshop or Illustrator, there are additional limited options available in Dreamweaver. From the menu bar select Modify>Image. Here you will find options to crop, adjust the brightness or contrast, and sharpen.

figure | **4-18** |

Figure 4-17 displayed in browser

SUMMARY

In this chapter, you've learned how to slice an image in Photoshop and Illustrator in order to import larger images in sections that use less download time into Dreamweaver. You've also learned how to create your slices and save them for the Web in Photoshop and Illustrator. You've explored the differences in image formats for the Web and how those translate to the issue of resolution versus download time. You've increased your knowledge of cells and the Properties window that allows us to change the information for cells. You've examined linking and targeting and you've also explored the importance of clear, efficient, and consistent navigation.

in review

1. What are the three key ingredients for successful navigation?

2. What are three important considerations when designing a Web page?

3. What is slicing?

4. How do you create a slice?

5. How can you create a link that opens a new browser window?

6. How do you access the Page Properties window?

exercise 4

1. Create a folder on your desktop and name it Exercise 4. Copy the HTML files and the image journey.jpg from inside the Exercise 4 folder on the back of book CD into this folder.

2. In Photoshop, open journey.jpg. Determine how you want to divide or slice the image. Define several slices. Drag guides from the rulers marking those divisions.

3. Using your guides, select the Slice tool and slice your document according to your guides.

figure | 4-Ex1 |

Journey image showing slices

4. From the menu bar, select File>Save for Web. Choose the Optimized tab in the compression window.

figure | 4-Ex2 |

Journey image in Save for Web window

5. In the Save for Web window, save one slice at a time, using the Slice Select tool in the left portion of the window. Choose Selected Slices under the slices drop-down menu. Remember to deselect the Save to Images Folder in the Save for Web menu after the first slice is saved. Name the slices in a logical fashion (journ1, journ2, journ3, etc.). Use the Images Only format as you save. When you are done saving the slices make certain that they are all in the same images folder inside of the Exercise 4 folder. If not, go to the desktop and drag the folder of images into the Exercise 4 folder. This can be confusing, so make sure you are organized. Confirming your folder hierarchy now will save you time and hassle later.

6. Consider saving simpler images as GIFs, more complex images as JPGs—high, medium, or low. Consider the quality of the optimization versus the download time. Compare the compression options. These are critical points to understand. Make certain that you experiment with JPGs and GIFs. Determine the appropriate compression based on file size and acceptable image quality.

7. Open Dreamweaver and define a new local site as you did in Exercise 3 (Site>Manage Sites>New>Site). In the Site Name field, type the name of your site. Click the folder icon to the right of the Local Root Folder field and create a new folder. Follow the same steps as in Exercise 3 to finish creating your site.

8. In the document window, title your new file and save. Make sure you are saving in your Exercise 4 folder.

9. Click the Layout tab, click the Draw Layout Cell icon, and move your pointer to the document window. Click in the upper-left corner and drag down and to the right to define a cell. Continue drawing cells to approximate the slices you drew in Photoshop.

10. Return to the Common tab and choose the Import Image icon. Import each slice from your image folder into the appropriate cell. In the Properties window, note the pixel size of the width and height of the image. Click on the cell and resize it by typing the same dimensions in the Fixed field of the Properties window. You can also click on the handle bar of the cell and adjust it to snap to the size of the image. Check the dimensions and make sure that they match.

11. Repeat this procedure for all of your slices, reassembling the final page in Dreamweaver.

figure | 4-Ex3 |

Images reassembled in Dreamweaver

12. Add blank space as needed rather than importing it from the Photoshop or Illustrator file. This will save on download time. Add a non-breaking space, *" "* to assure the integrity of the cell. You can access this option through the Insert menu bar. Select Insert>HTML>Special Characters>Non-Breaking Space.

figure | **4-Ex4**

Insert>HTML>Special
Characters>Non-Breaking Space

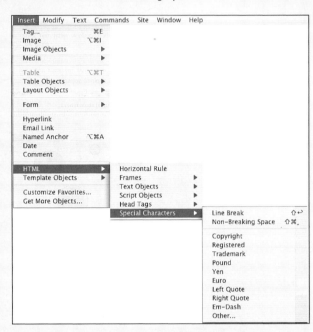

13. Consider adding text to each of the navigation images to help clarify them. You can also add a horizontal cell span at the bottom to add duplicate navigation. Both navigation elements should take the user to the same pages.

figure | **4-Ex5**

Properties window for text

14. Create links to the images to take the user to the poems. In addition to creating links in the Properties window, you can also find a Make Link option under the Modify pull-down menu. Target the links as _blank so that a new browser window will be generated. This will allow the user to close this new window after reading the poem and return to your main page, preventing the possibility of confusion. (In the next chapter, we'll learn about frames and targeting frames so that it will appear that the user is always on the same page. For now though, _blank is the best choice.)

15. Save and view your document in several browsers. Internet Explorer will show a border around a clicked Dreamweaver link even if you set borders as 0 in Dreamweaver. This is a browser function specific to Internet Explorer that you cannot delete.

16. When you are certain that everything looks great, save and enjoy.

figure | 4-Ex6 |

Completed Exercise 4 in displayed browser

on your own

Recreate the poem pages for the Exercise Web site. Modify the Page Properties background color of each poem page to match the home page. Create a grid that also matches the home page and place the poem in the same area as the main image. Recreate the title of the poem in Photoshop or Illustrator to give it more of an ethereal sense. Add images to the inside pages. Finally, match the font of the poem to the font on the home page. In other words, create a sense of unity and consistency throughout the Web site.

notes

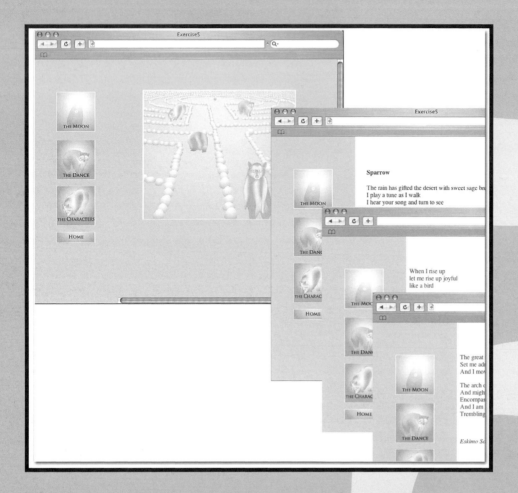

framesets, frames, and navigation with rollovers

Objectives

Learn about frames in Dreamweaver.

Understand framesets.

Explore invisible technology in Web design.

Examine rollovers and rollover images.

Create links and targets to rollover images.

Develop further an understanding of a compelling user experience.

Introduction

We've discussed the importance of the Web Design interface technology to be invisible and seamless. Buttons, boxes, and links are becoming less obvious. Web sites today are to be experienced instead of searched. For example, navigation now includes rollovers that hint at clickable content. Information *flows* to the viewer. In fact, the Web has materialized into a metaphor for how we currently experience the world. We simultaneously process multiple channels of information, and we usually demand more than one source of input to remain stimulated. We feed on simultaneous distractions.

With these concepts in mind, let's take at look at frames and rollovers. Frames and rollovers are important elements in the experience of invisible technology, multitasking, and seamless design. These tools offer opportunities to delight and entertain the user, while at the same time providing valuable information. They can be important components in creating a compelling user experience.

FRAMESETS, FRAMES, AND NAVIGATION WITH ROLLOVERS

FRAMES

What exactly are *frames*? Frames are an HTML organizational tool in which two or more individual HTML pages (*frames*) work together to look like one page in a browser. In other words, frames-based pages look and act like a single Web page, but in fact, each frame is a single HTML document that acts independently. Frames are held together and defined by a *frameset definition document*—the frameset HTML page. You can have any number of frames in a frameset, but two to three frames are most common.

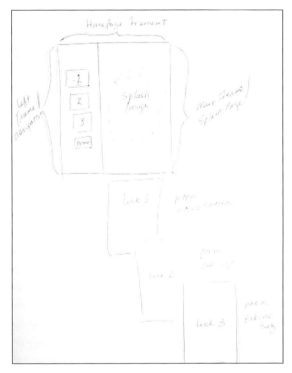

figure **5-1**

Sketch of a frameset with frame-based pages

Frames can be highly successful if you want to leave a navigation bar in place throughout your site. Navigation can sit inside of one frame while the other frames change information, visuals, and other elements, giving you a way to design an information-heavy Web site with consistency and grace. Frames can blur obvious borders, eliminate reloading, and offer an invisible interface. See Color Plate 13 for a beautifully designed frames-based Web site.

Frames are not to be confused with tables. Tables can function within a frame or a non-frame page. Tables have their own set of possibilities and rules and cannot create pages that act independently. Frames can be confusing because they sort of look like tables while you are working, but they function entirely differently.

A frameset page includes the <frameset> tag that defines the layout of the frames-based page. The <frameset> tag also includes the location and names of the initial HTML pages that occupy each frame, as well as details of overall appearance and actions. Dreamweaver will automatically create a frameset definition page when you divide a document with frames.

To access frames in Dreamweaver, make certain that you are in the Standard Layout mode of the Layout tab of the Insert bar. The icon to access frames is the second icon from the right on the Insert bar. Click the icon to view a submenu of 13 preset choices.

When you choose any of these preset options, Dreamweaver will automatically create the layout of frames shown in the icon in your work window. Alternately, you can access frames from the menu bar by selecting Insert>HTML>Frames. The same 13 choices will be in the submenu (by name only).

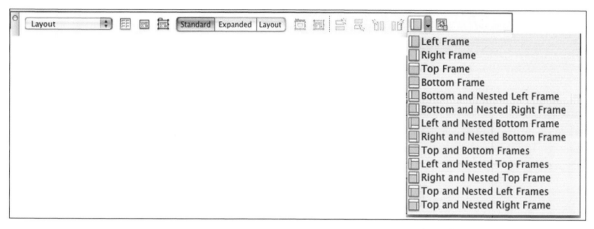

To view frames while you are working with them, turn on frame borders. From the menu bar, select View>Visual Aids>Frame Borders. Heavy outlines will appear around the frames in the document window. Mouse over one of the borders and the mouse pointer will turn into a double-headed arrow. Drag it to a new location and release the mouse button to reposition the border. You can continue this process until you have exactly what you want in terms of number and placement of frames. And you can always go back and adjust the frames later.

figure | 5-2 |

Frames icon on the Layout tab of the Insert bar

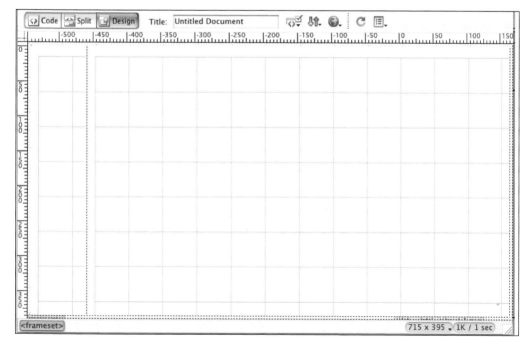

figure | 5-3 |

Document window with frames and view frame borders and grid showing

You can design within any of your frames by selecting the individual frame or the entire frameset. To select a Frame, hold down Shift+Option on a Mac, Alt Key on a PC, and click anywhere in the frame, or in the Frames panel, click on the frame. To view the Frames panel, select Window>Frames. You can also access a frame by clicking on its border. In any case, a dashed line will appear in the document window around the frame you selected, and the Properties window will display the frame's properties. The Properties window will also provide you with options to set the frame's width, source, name, borders and border color, and scrolling behavior, as well as the capability to resize the frame.

Creating and editing content within a frame is the same as doing so in a blank Dreamweaver window. You can create tables, draw cells, type text, and import images and multimedia objects. Setting the background color is also done the same way. Control-click on a Mac, right click on a PC the frame, selecting Page Properties from the pop-up menu. Or, from the Document window menu bar, select Modify>Page Properties. Either way, the Page Properties window will appear. From here, you can adjust page properties for that frame, including background color, background image, page margins, text colors, and link colors.

figure | 5-4 |

Properties window for frames

Saving the Frame

Saving pages with frames is a multistep process since each frame as well as the frameset is an independent HTML page. This is where it is easy to get confused, so be careful and pay attention to where you are. If you follow the usual step of Command+S or File>Save, you may not be saving what you think.

With your frames page visible in the document window, select File>Save Frameset. This tells Dreamweaver that you are saving the frameset definition document. In the Save As dialog box, type a meaningful name in the File Name text box. This file name will be part of the URL or path name.

figure | 5-5 |

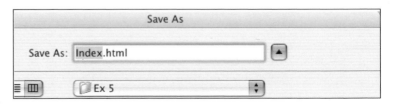

Save As File Name text box for saving a frameset

Once you have saved the frameset, then save each frame. Select the first frame you want to save by clicking it in the document window or in the Frames panel. (Clicking on the frame with the Shift and Option keys on a Mac or presing the Alt key on a PC will access the frame and the Properties window for that frame.) Select File>Save Frame.

Save As
Save As: left.html ▲
≣ ⫿⫿⫿   📁 Exercise 5   ⬍

figure | **5-6** |

Save As File Name text box for saving a frame

In the Save As dialog box, type a meaningful name in the File Name text box. You'll want to be able to distinguish one frame file from another when dealing with these documents later, so choose a name such as nav.html or main.html, or add a numbering system. Make sure that the Save In list box displays the folder in which you want to save the files. If not, browse through the folders on your computer and select the proper one. Click Save and return to the document window to repeat these steps for each frame.

Title each frame in the Title text box as you move through this process and be sure to name the Frame in the Properties window also. Be consistent, logical, and clear when naming and saving your frames and frameset.

Once all of your frames and frameset HTML pages have been correctly saved, you can then just choose File>Save All Frames as you continue working. It is important to save all of the documents in a frameset in the same folder.

The next step is to develop the content within the frames. You will need to create the cells of a table to import images and slices, create text, and generally design your page just as you did in the last chapter. Draw cells using the Layout tab and the Draw Layout Cell icon. Create blank cells to hold space as desired. Add the non-breaking space to blank cells. Continue designing your Web site using frames in the same way you would develop any independent HTML page. You can use image maps and import multimedia or any other design element into any frames page.

Targeting

Targeting can make all the difference when designing with frames. When you link a navigational element to an HTML page and then target the original main frame, the new page will only replace the main frame of the frameset. The other frames will remain the same and will

| **NOTE** |

The Tedious Part

Saving frames and framesets may seem tedious and sometimes unnecessary. There are a lot of steps to make certain that everything is correct, and the process isn't that much fun. However, if you take the time now to make sure frames are saved correctly, you will be able to avoid numerous problems that will be much harder to figure out later. And always check and double-check your work!

not need to be reloaded. Thus the interface becomes invisible to the user, download time is reduced, and the navigation remains clear and consistent. Once you have created a frameset and saved and named the frames, as well as any linked HTML pages, all of the frames and HTML pages in the directory will show up in the Properties window when you are linking and targeting. To link and target a navigation element, click on the element and link it to the HTML page. Then click the triangle to the right of the target to access the frames that you created. Choose the frame that you want to target (most likely the Main Frame) using this window. By choosing the frame through this window, you will eliminate the risk of misspelling or misnaming frame names.

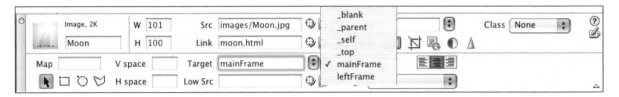

figure | 5-7 |

Properties window showing link targets

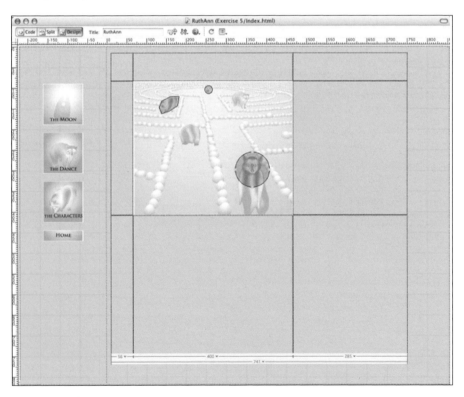

figure | 5-8 |

Document window showing frameset, frames, cells, and images

ROLLOVERS

Rollovers let you seemingly stack two images on top of one another to create the appearance of button highlighting. A simple image rollover makes three things happen. First, the corresponding images preload when the Web page loads so that the rollovers are ready to go. Second, when the user mouses over the specified image, a different image file is displayed. Finally, when the user mouses away from the image, the original image is restored.

Rollovers can add clarity to navigation, even if they just add an image to a word or vice versa. In any case, the two images for a rollover need to be exactly the same pixel size. If they are not, the second image will be distorted into the size and shape of the first by Dreamweaver when you import it. Take this into account when you are creating these images. If the second image needs to appear larger than the first, create the extra space around the first image in pixels.

You will need to create separate images for the navigation elements and their rollovers in Photoshop or Illustrator. In either program, create the navigation image on its own layer. Duplicate the layer to make certain the dimensions remain the same. Now you can alter the image or add text to create the rollover image.

If you are working in Photoshop to design a frames-based page, create all of your elements except the rollover images. Then, using the Layers palette, make certain that all of the navigation, and only the navigation, is on one layer. Name this layer *Navigation*. Have other images on

| NOTE |

Rollovers

Rollovers are a fantastic way to delight and enchant users. Not all rollovers need to be buttons or provide any further function. On my Web sites, I like to incorporate rollover images simply to add a burst of stars and music. A user may not even know that the rollovers exist until they accidentally move the mouse over one—they don't even have the appearance of a button. This can be an important ingredient in creating a compelling user experience. Entertain your viewer with these surprise elements.

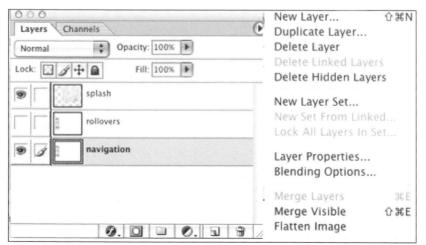

figure | 5-9 |

Duplicate layer in Photoshop

different layers. Highlight the Navigation layer, then access the pull-down menu in the top-right corner of the Layers palette. Duplicate the layer and name it *Rollovers*. Make changes to this new layer, remembering to consider clarity, surprise, and delight when you are designing these rollovers. As you alter the images, think about what has delighted and engaged you and/or what has added clarity to navigation when you have visited other sites.

The beauty of treating the navigation elements as one layer and the rollover elements as another layer is consistency. Even though you will separate these elements into individual slices later, you can treat them consistently now by working with them on their respective layers.

Next, as we did in Chapter 4, create guides to divide the page into logical, clear divisions to be sliced. Make sure that each navigation element has its own slice. Hide the Rollovers layer by clicking on the eye icon to the left of it in the Layers palette. Save the slices using the directions in Chapter 4. Be sure to take into consideration compression versus image quality versus download time.

Now reveal the Rollovers layer and hide the Navigation layer. Using the same slices, save each slice in the Rollovers layer. It's a good habit to get into to name these slices with the same names as the navigation, adding an "R" to the end of the name. This will help keep you from getting confused later when you are importing the images into Dreamweaver. Making certain that the correct rollover image is connected to its corresponding navigation image is so much easier if the names match.

Finally, check once again to make sure that all of your image slices ended up in the same image folder.

figure | 5-10 |

Folder with all navigation and rollover images

Importing Rollover Images into Dreamweaver

Once you have saved all of your slices, you are ready to import the images into Dreamweaver. Open Dreamweaver, create a new site, then open a new document. From the menu bar, select Insert>Images(Image Objects on a PC)>Rollover Image or simply click on the Image button on the Common tab of the Insert bar. This will access the drop-down menu. Select Rollover Image.

In either case, the Insert Rollover Image dialog box should appear.

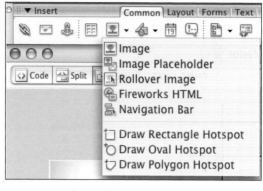

figure | 5-11 |

Image button on the Common tab of the Insert bar

figure | 5-12 |

Insert Rollover Image dialog box

Select the source of the original image and the rollover image by typing the file names in the respective text boxes or clicking Browse to use the Original Source and Rollover Source dialog boxes to select a local image. If the rollover image is to link to another Web page, then type the URL in the When Clicked, Go To URL text box or click Browse to select a page from your local site. Leave the Preload Rollover Image box selected.

Click OK to close the Insert Rollover Image dialog box and return to the document window. Repeat this step for each navigation element.

Make certain that you preview in a browser to check that everything looks correct. Remember that it is always best to check your pages in several browsers.

SUMMARY

In this chapter, you've learned how to implement frames and framesets. You've been introduced to methods for invisible technology and seamless interface. You've also learned about rollovers and how they can provide additional clarity to navigation, as well as how to create images for rollovers in Illustrator and Photoshop. Additionally, you've discovered how to import rollover images into Dreamweaver. You are now well on your way to creating a compelling user experience.

in review

1. What is a frame-based document?

2. How do you access frames?

3. What is the difference between Save and Save Frame As in Dreamweaver?

4. How can you access a frameset in the Dreamweaver document window?

5. What is a rollover?

6. How can you create a rollover image?

exercise 5

1. Create a folder on your hard drive and name it *Exercise 5*. Copy the files from the Exercise 5 folder on the back of book CD into this folder.

2. In Illustrator, open the file navLinks.ai

figure | 5-Ex1 |

NavLinks Illustrator file

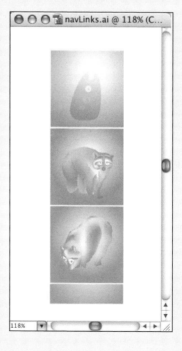

Add the text *The Moon, The Dance, The Characters*, and *Home* to the appropriate buttons. Turn the type into outlines (Type>Create Outlines). Make any additional changes you like and export as a TIFF, with a screen resolution of 72 and Color Model as RGB.

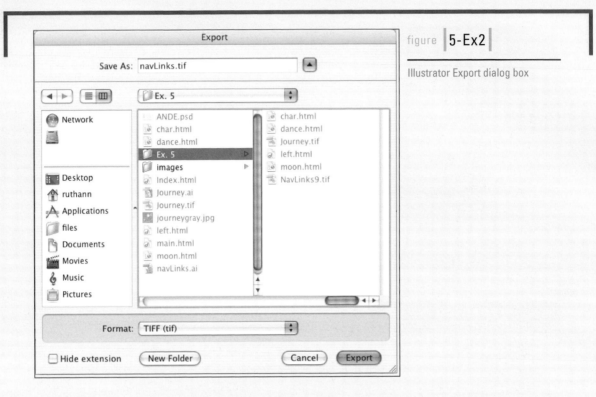

figure 5-Ex2

Illustrator Export dialog box

3. Open this new TIFF file in Photoshop and enlarge the document. From the menu bar, select Image>Canvas Size. Click the left center square of the anchor box and change the width to 640 pixels and the height to 480 pixels. Click OK.

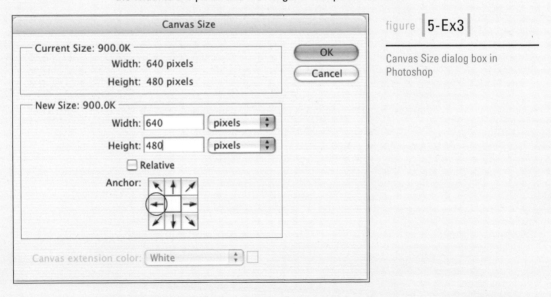

figure 5-Ex3

Canvas Size dialog box in Photoshop

4. Duplicate the default layer and name it *Navigation*. Highlight the default layer and select Edit>Select all and select Edit>Clear. Name this layer *Background*. Return to the Navigation layer and with the Marquee tool, select the navigation image. Change

to the move tool and move the navigation image to where you want it, making sure to stay in the left third of the document.

5. Next, duplicate the navigation layer. (Layers>Duplicate Layer). This layer will contain the rollover images. Name it *Rollovers*.

6. Change the look of this layer in some way. You can make changes by selecting Layer> Layer Style, Image>Adjustments, or by selecting Filters from the menu bar, just to name a few ways. You can also use any combination of these methods. Just make sure that you have highlighted the Rollovers layer when you are making changes. The following example was created by altering the color by selecting Image>Adjustments>Hue/Saturation and then applying the Ocean Ripple filter with settings of Size [6] and Magnitude [3].

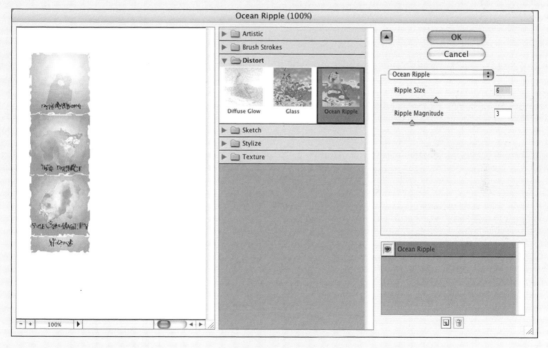

figure | 5-Ex4 |

Photoshop Ocean Ripple filter
Window

figure |5-Ex5|

Rollovers layer after changes

7. Save the file as
exercise5.psd in your Exercise 5 directory.

8. Open journey.tif in Photoshop. Using the Select tool,
choose Select All. (You can also Select all with Command-
A on a Mac, Control-A on a PC or use the Select pull-
down menu and choose All.) Copy (Edit>Copy or
Command-C on a Mac, Control-C on a PC) the selection
and return to your PSD file. (You can use the Window pull-
down menu to get back to the PSD file.) Paste (Edit>Paste
or Command-V on a Mac Control-V on a PC) the copy.
With the move tool, move the journey.jpeg copy to the
right-hand side of the navigation image in your PSD. In the
Layers palette, name this layer *Splash*. (Often, a home
page is referred to as a splash page.)

9. Make any changes you want. Return to the Background
layer and choose a background color analogous or
complementary to your images. Select all.

10. Now you can fill with the foreground color (Edit>Fill). Make sure Mode is Normal and
preserve transparency is not checked. Try different foreground colors by clicking
inside of the foreground square of the toolbox. A swatch dialog window will open.
Select different Web-safe colors until you find a color that looks good with the rest of
the image. Write down the number of this color
to use later in Dreamweaver.

11. When you are satisfied with your page, save.

| NOTE |

Choosing Colors

You will have a better sense of
colors when you are working in
Photoshop or Illustrator. These
programs are designed to offer
you the best, most accurate
display of onscreen color.
Dreamweaver, however, isn't
known for its ability to closely
portray colors.

12. Draw guides where you want to create slices.

Create the slices, knowing that you will save only the ones that you will reuse in Dreamweaver. Create a slice for each navigation element in addition to the splash image slice(s). Be logical and create as tight of a grid around the images as possible. Remember that the slices for navigation need to accommodate the rollover images as well.

figure | 5-Ex6 |

PSD Image with guides

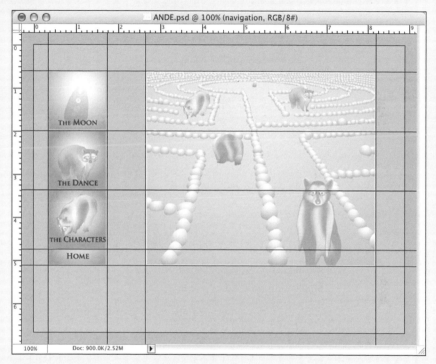

13. In the Layers palette, click the eye icon to the left of the Rollovers layer to hide it. With only the original Navigation layer eye icon open, save each slice for the Web choosing appropriate compression and extension.

14. Name the slices appropriately—for example, moon.jpg. Save the slices in a folder you name *images* inside of the Exercise 5 Directory, following the same guidelines that you learned in the last chapter.

15. Return to the Layers palette. Click the eye icon to the left of the Navigation layer to hide it and click the Rollovers layer eye icon to reveal this layer. Using the same slices as in Step 13, save each rollover slice to the same folder of images. Name these slices with the same names as in Step 14, adding the letter "R" to each name. Save the Splash slice.

figure **5-Ex7**

Layers palette

16. Once you have saved all of the Photoshop Images that you will need, save the file, close Photoshop and open Dreamweaver. In Dreamweaver, use the same steps that you have followed in the last two chapters to develop a local site. Use the Exercise 5 directory to define this site.

17. After you have developed a local site, select Modify>Page Properties. Change the background color to the color you chose in Photoshop.

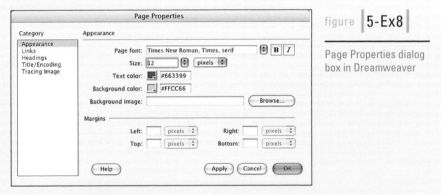

figure **5-Ex8**

Page Properties dialog box in Dreamweaver

18. Now develop a frameset. One frame will be on the left to accommodate the navigation. The other frame will be on the right to accommodate the main image and additional pages. Begin by selecting the Frames icon on the Layout tab of the Insert bar. Click on the first frameset icon (Left Frame)—it will automatically display two frames in your document.

figure **5-Ex9**

Frame Selection button on the Insert bar

19. From the menu bar, select View>Visual Aids and make certain that Frames Borders is selected. Mouse over the inside borders of the frameset so that the mouse pointer turns into a double-headed arrow. Click on the border and drag it to a position of your choice. Release when you are satisfied. You can always go back and change this.

20. Begin the save process by saving the frameset. Title the document with your name. With your frames page visible in the document window, from the menu bar, select File> Save Frameset. (If Save Frameset is grayed out, then you need to return to the document window and click the outside border of the frameset.) Once the Save As dialog box appear, name this initial frameset *exer5.html*.

21. Next, save each frame. Name and title each one. Select the left frame by clicking inside of it in the document window. In the Title text box, type *Navigation*. From the menu bar, select File>Save Frame. In the Save As dialog box, type *left.html* in the File Name text box. Click Save.

    Return to the document window to repeat these steps for the other frame. In the Title text box, type *Splash*. Save the file as main.html.

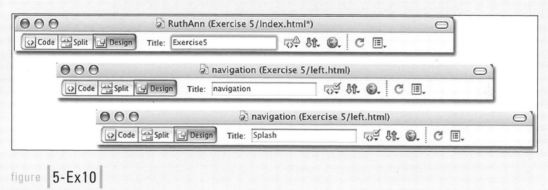

figure | 5-Ex10 |

Title Text boxes for frameset and
main and navigation frames

22. Access the Frames panel by selecting Window>Frames. In the Frame panel, choose either frame by clicking on it.

figure | 5-Ex11 |

Frame panel

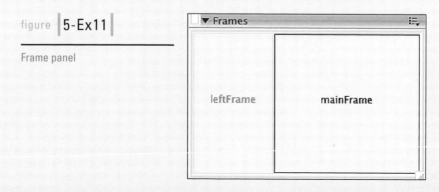

The Properties window should display for the selected frame. Name the frames here also. Once all of your frame pages have been named and saved, you can then select File>Save All Frames (save all on a PC) for all future changes.

figure 5-Ex12

Properties window showing title and frame source

You will now need to create tables to import the slices as you did in the last chapter's exercise. Create tables by drawing cells, using the Layout tab and the Draw Layout Cell icon. Create cells for images and text as well as blank cells to hold space as desired. Insert the non-breaking space into blank cells.

Pay attention to the table created and adjusted by Dreamweaver as you draw cells. Draw the cells to import images in both the navigation frame and the main frame. Then import the slices appropriately, matching the cell sizes to the sizes of the images.

23. Begin in the navigation frame. Click inside and draw a cell. Click inside the cell. On the Common tab of the Insert bar, click on the Image icon. Scroll down to the Rollover Image choice. (See Figure 5-12.)

24. When the dialogue box appears, browse for each navigation image, rollover image, and HTML link. The HTML pages are those from the Exercise 5 folder that you copied into your directory. The HTML page names will match the navigation names.

Repeat these steps for each navigation element. Name each link in this window. Be consistent.

25. Back in the document window, click on each navigation image. In the Properties window, target each link to the main frame. (This will not show up in your Target dialog box if you have not saved your frames properly.) By targeting main, each poem will open up in the main.html frame, creating that invisible technology.

For the home link, browse to main.html and again target main frame.

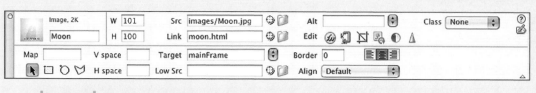

figure **5-Ex13**

Properties window showing links,
titles, and targets

26. Next, click inside the main frame and draw a cell for the splash image. Use the Insert Image icon on the Common Tab. Import the journey.jpg slice(s). Make adjustments as you deem appropriate.

27. Test the page and its functionality in several browsers. Test the links to verify that they work and open in the proper frame. If a targeted link opens in the navigation frame, most frequently the problem is with the target. If the target is called out correctly and you still cannot figure out the source of the problem, go back and make sure that your frames are saved correctly.

When you are satisfied with your Web site, be sure to choose File>Save All.

on your own

Just for fun, in the Splash image, create hotspots on those parts of the image that match the poem titles. Link the hotspots to the same pages as the corresponding navigation bar elements. Again target the main frame.

Add a third frame across the top to create a header. Click inside the main frame and from the menu bar select Modify>Frameset>Split Frames Down. This will add an additional frame to the right section of the frameset. Title and save the frame and any changes to the frameset. Change the Page Properties to match the background color. Draw a cell inside of this frame and write down the pixel width and height.

Create a new document in Photoshop, giving it the pixel dimensions of the cell you just created. Create a new image for this cell. It can be a title image; for example, you could use the word *Journey*. Or it can be a collage of different raccoons copied and pasted from the original image. Back in Dreamweaver, import the image into the new frame. Save all frames and show your friends.

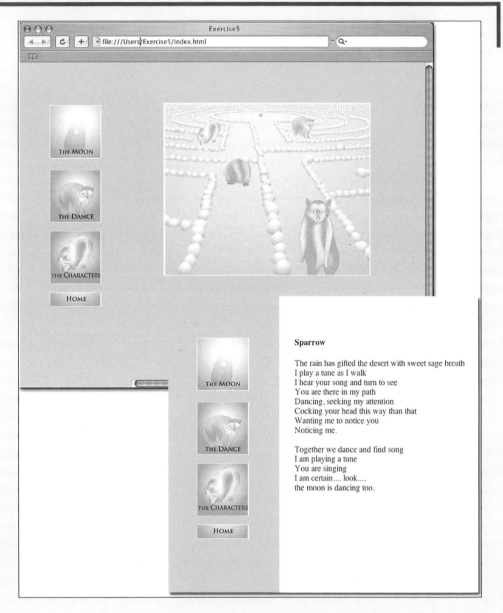

figure

5-Ex14

Completed Exercise 5 displayed in browser with both stages of rollovers

notes

navigation in four parts, gesture, and type

Objectives

Examine the use of metaphors, icons, the concept of less is more, and human gesture in creating navigation images.

Understand four-part navigation.

Explore type settings in Dreamweaver.

Uncover paragraph formatting, and styles.

Introduction

Navigating your way through a complex Web site can be far more interesting with four-part navigation, and Dreamweaver hands this to us on a silver platter. With four-part navigation, user viewing can be enhanced with surprises, additional clarity, and something that works similar to breadcrumb trails. We'll take a look at developing images for this type of navigation and then accessing them in the Dreamweaver environment.

We'll also take a more in-depth look at type in Dreamweaver, checking out formatting possibilities for both text and paragraphs, spell checking, and style developing. Dreamweaver facilitates HTML text codes to make formatting easy to access and utilize, as well as visually instant. You can see the results of your formatting immediately, rather than jumping to the browser to view changes.

NAVIGATION IN FOUR PARTS, GESTURE, AND TYPE

FOUR-PART NAVIGATION

Four-part navigation refers to the states of the mouse cursor. The Up State refers to the navigation image that sits on the page when it loads into the browser. The location of the cursor is not important at this point as long as it is not over the image. The Over State refers to the image that appears when the user rolls the cursor over the Up State. The Down State refers to the image that appears when the user clicks on the Up State. Finally, the Over While Down State refers to the image that appears after the navigation image has been clicked. The Over While Down State can actually add a visual element that works similarly to breadcrumb trails.

All of these images should relate to one another. They can offer surprising changes or they can be subtle. They should be informative and engaging.

figure | 6-1 |

The four states of a navigation bar with linked images by student Chelsea Jenkins

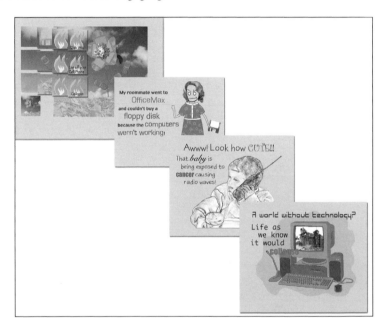

Let's take this opportunity to consider the notion of the human gesture as it relates to technology. The human gesture here is the user moving the mouse cursor over a button. The result of this human gesture is an interaction with technology. This is an interesting design theory. We are creating an experience between human cause and technological consequences. Think about the avante-garde art movement beginning in the late 1800s. Artists were interested in the imprint of the creator, the mark of the artist. They began to explore the notion that the gesture is the art. Take a look at some of Kandinsky's, Pollock's, or Van Gogh's paintings. Pollock's paintings were created by splashing paint on the canvas from a dripping paint-filled brush with a repetitive movement of the arm. The result is reminiscent of the deep texture of a forest floor or an intimate view of a spiritual practice. Van Gogh elevated the texture of the brush stroke to such an important prominence that artists 100 years later are still influenced by his work. Or look at the art performance movement beginning in the sixties. Again, the art was about the gesture of the artist.

These movements had a lot to do with reactionary theory. Artists were reacting to the hyper-realism of French Academic painting as well as the emergence and eventual dominance of mass media. All of these explorations elevated the handprint, the gesture, or the movement of the artist to define art. The results of their explorations can feed our thinking in approaching the various states of navigation. The gesture is the user's arm, hand, and mouse movements. The results of these gestures can follow the same theoretical concepts.

Perhaps the Up State of your navigation is an image or icon that visually describes the link. The Over State may add additional information about the link, such as descriptive text. The Down State may be a metaphor or type responding to an imagined swipe by the user. The Over While Down State may be the image responding to an imagined click. In other words, when you are creating the four states of navigation buttons, consider the action of the user as a gesture that influences how the design is altered.

figure | 6-2 |

Using metaphors to develop navigation states

Another approach to four-part navigation is the concept of *less is more*. Simplifying an image to its basic components or zooming in on the image to show only a small portion are all ways to visually describe an image in a reduced fashion. Reducing the image to the simplest visual possible while maintaining clarity is the process of creating an icon. Using the concept of less is more allows the viewer to visually finish the image. This is another good method to engage a viewer even further.

figure |6-3|

Using the concept of less is more in
navigation states by student Natalia Wehba

figure |6-4|

The Over State adds clarity to the link by
student Annalee Bird

Above all, avoid those overused icons of rotating globes, blinking whatevers, and prebuilt buttons. Be creative. Build your own images in Photoshop or Illustrator using conceptual theories of metaphor, less is more, and gesture.

Begin by conceptualizing the four states of each navigation link. Be consistent with the four states, using the same style for each category for each navigation link. You want the style—including the color of each state—to inform the user as to their whereabouts. This offers the user some breadcrumb navigation.

Think metaphor, think gesture, think emotional uses of color. Then develop your images, making certain that each state utilizes the same dimensions. Be logical when saving and naming images. For example, if a link is named moon.html, name the states of the navigation to this link moonU, moonD, moonO, and moonOWD. Take the time now to be consistent and logical.

Whether you are creating in Photoshop or Illustrator, develop a layer for each state of navigation and name the layer appropriately. Put all of your Up State images on the Up layer, all of your Over State images on the Over layer, all of your Down State images on the Down layer, and all of your Over While Down State images on the Over While Down layer. You want to make certain that each state is directly on top of the other states so that when you create the slices they won't jump around in Dreamweaver. You can use the transparency bar to reveal the layers below. Temporarily change the transparency to about 40%. This will allow you to see through the layers and verify precise placement. Remember to change the transparency back to 100% before moving on.

Work with your Photoshop or Illustrator document to create your navigation and your splash look. Consider your design. Is it engaging? Is it

| NOTE |

Pixel Space for All Parts of Navigation Needs to Be the Same

When developing the four states for navigation images, you need to design within the same amount of pixel space. In other words, if your Up State is 40 pixels wide by 10 pixels high, then all of the additional states need to be 40 pixels wide by 10 pixels high, even if an image does not use all of the area. This will avoid later distortion of the image by Dreamweaver or a browser.

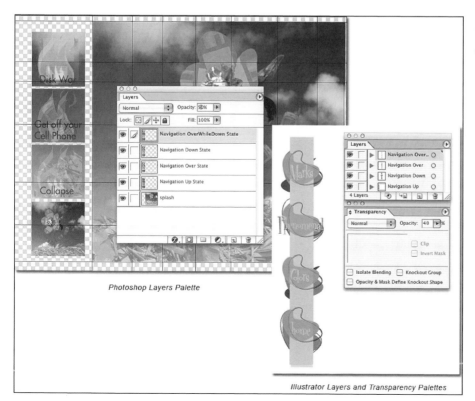

figure | 6-5 |

Photoshop and Illustrator Layers palettes showing all of the states of navigation and the Transparency bar

Photoshop Layers Palette

Illustrator Layers and Transparency Palettes

clear? Have you considered all of the design elements that we have discussed? Are you creating a compelling user experience?

The next step is to create the guides and slices of each state of each link and image. Once you have sliced your images, click off the eye icons to the left of the layers that you won't need in order to save the slice states one layer at a time. Save each slice for the Web choosing the appropriate compression and extension. Give each state of each category of the navigation an individual slice. Save all slices into a folder named *images*.

In the Save Optimized As window, change the drop-down menu of Settings to other. This will bring up a new window. There are four choices in the second drop down menu. The HTML choice gives options for tags, attributes, and other HTML information. The Slices choice allows you to change the way slices are named as does the Saving Files option. In both of these options, simplify the naming to just reflect a name and extension. The Saving Files option also allows you to deselect Put images in Folder. This will avoid creating a new folder for each image saved. Deselect Copy Background Image in this same window. See Figures 4-10, 4-11 and 4-12.

Go to your desktop and look in your images folder. Make certain that you have named your slices logically and that everything that you expect to be there is there . . . and nothing more.

REASSEMBLING NAVIGATION IMAGES IN DREAMWEAVER

Once your four-part navigation images are complete, you are ready to reassemble them in Dreamweaver. Since you are using four-part navigation, it makes sense to put all of the navigation into a frame. Choose a frameset icon that best fits with your design and then modify it as necessary. Be sure to save the frameset and each frame with names and titles that precisely follow the guidelines in the last chapter. Name the frames in the Properties window also. Again, all of your frame pages have been named and saved, from the menu bar, select File>Save All for your future changes.

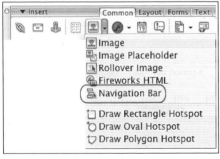

figure | 6-6 |

Four-Part Navigation Bar icon

Click in the frame you have created for the navigation. Choose the Insert Nav Bar icon on the Common Tab of the Insert bar. This is found when you click and hold on the image icon to reveal the choices available.

In the Insert Navigation Bar dialog box that appears, name each button by typing in a new name, then browse for each of the four states, the HTML link, and the target frame. When you name the elements, be consistent and logical. In the When clicked, Go to URL window, browse to the appropriate HTML page. Target each link to the splash or main frame.

This arts Web site is well designed, easy to navigate, and incorporates critical thinking about the World Wide Web. Developed and sponsored by Adhocarts. Executive Director: Andrew Bucksbarg. Technical Director: Lara Bank, Produced and Designed by Lara Bank and Andrew Bucksbarg.

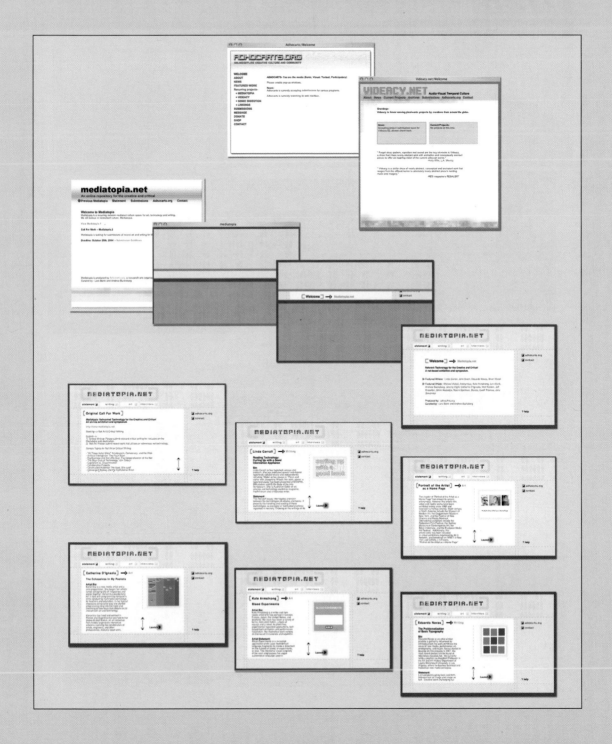

Students Cheri Hierbaum and Jared Miller created these two nicely designed Web sites to feature their portfolios. Simple color schemes allow the portfolio work to grab the attention of the viewer.

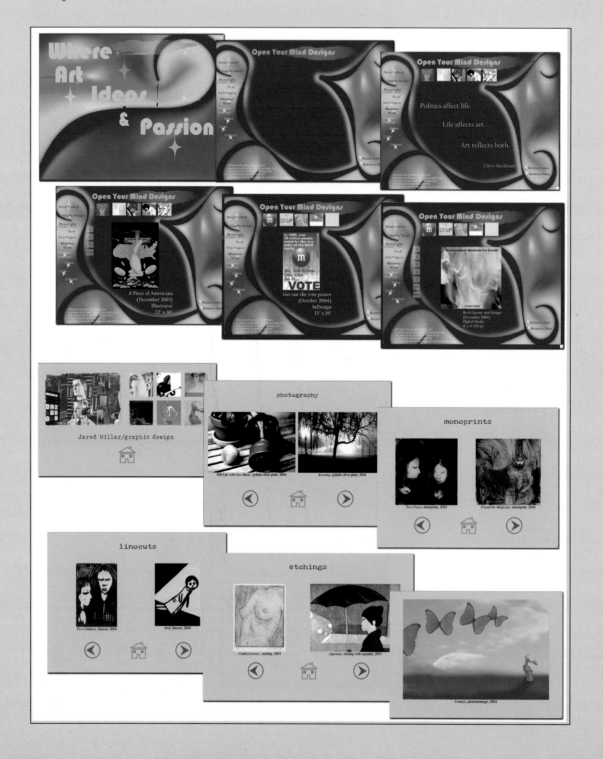

This nicely designed portfolio Web site by student Nick Rickenbach features a clean and dynamic layout. The great color scheme allows for the color of the portfolio artwork to dominate the page.

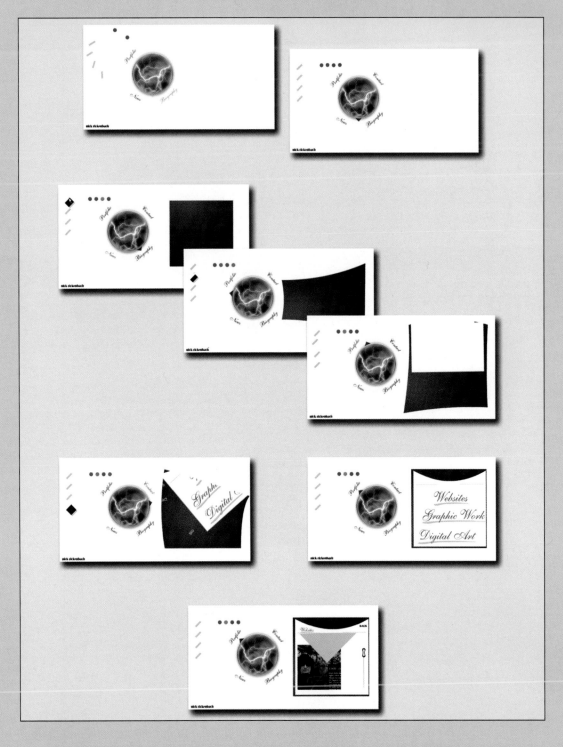

CMYK color wheel

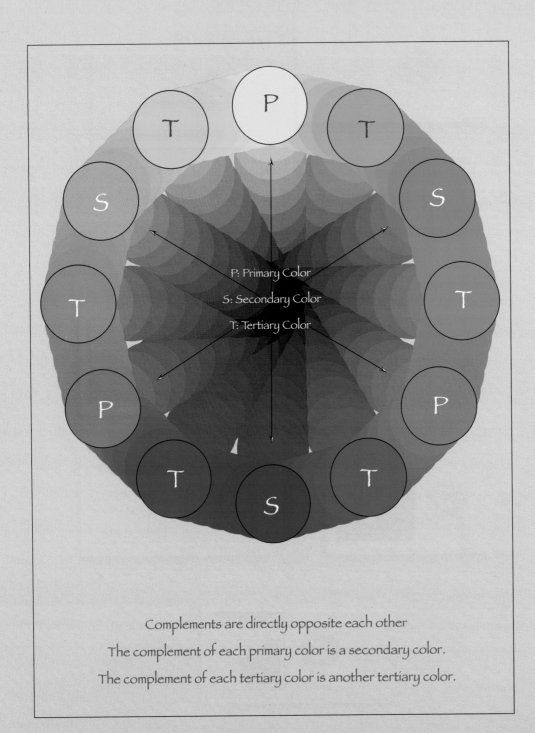

P: Primary Color

S: Secondary Color

T: Tertiary Color

Complements are directly opposite each other

The complement of each primary color is a secondary color.

The complement of each tertiary color is another tertiary color.

Web-safe color chart

FFFFFF	FFFFCC	FFFF99	FFFF66	FFFF33	FFFF00	FFCCFF	FFCCCC	FFCC99	FFCC66	FFCC33	FFCC00	FF99FF
FF99CC	FF9999	FF9966	FF9933	FF9900	FF66FF	FF66CC	FF6699	FF6666	FF6633	FF6600	FF33FF	FF33CC
FF3399	FF3366	FF3333	FF3300	FF00FF	FF00CC	FF0099	FF0066	FF0033	FF0000	CCFFFF	CCFFCC	CCFF99
CCFF66	CCFF33	CCCCCC	CCCCFF	CCCCCC	CCCC99	CCCC66	CCCC33	CCCC00	CC99FF	CC99CC	CC9999	CC9966
CC9933	CC9900	CC66FF	CC6666	CC6633	CC6666	CC6633	CC6600	CC33FF	CC33CC	CC3399	CC3366	CC3333
CC3300	CC00FF	CC00CC	CC0099	CC0066	CC0033	CC0000	99FFFF	99FFCC	99FF99	99FF66	99FF33	99FF00
99CCFF	99CCCC	99CC99	99CC66	99CC33	99CC00	9999FF	9999CC	999999	999966	999933	999900	9966FF
9966CC	996699	996666	996633	996600	9933FF	9933CC	993399	993366	993333	993300	9900FF	9900CC
990099	990066	990033	990000	66FFFF	66FFCC	66FF99	66FF66	66FF33	66FF00	66CCFF	66CCCC	66CC99
66CC66	66CC33	66CC00	6699FF	6699CC	669999	669966	669933	669900	6666FF	6666CC	666699	666666
666633	666600	6633FF	6633CC	663399	663366	663333	663300	6600FF	6600CC	660099	660066	660033
660000	33FFFF	33FFCC	33FF99	33FF66	33FF33	33FF00	33CCFF	33CCCC	33CC99	33CC66	33CC33	33CC00
3399FF	3399CC	339999	339966	339933	339900	3366FF	3366CC	336699	336666	336633	336600	333366
3333CC	333399	333366	333333	333300	3300FF	3300CC	330099	330066	330033	330000	00FFFF	00FFCC
00FF99	00FF66	00FF33	00FF00	00CCFF	00CCCC	00CC99	00CC66	00CC33	00CC00	0099FF	0099CC	009999
009966	009933	009900	0066FF	0066CC	006699	006666	006633	006600	0033FF	0033CC	003399	003366
		003333	003300	0000FF	0000CC	000099	000066	000033	000000			

A few examples of Photoshop's color cube palette

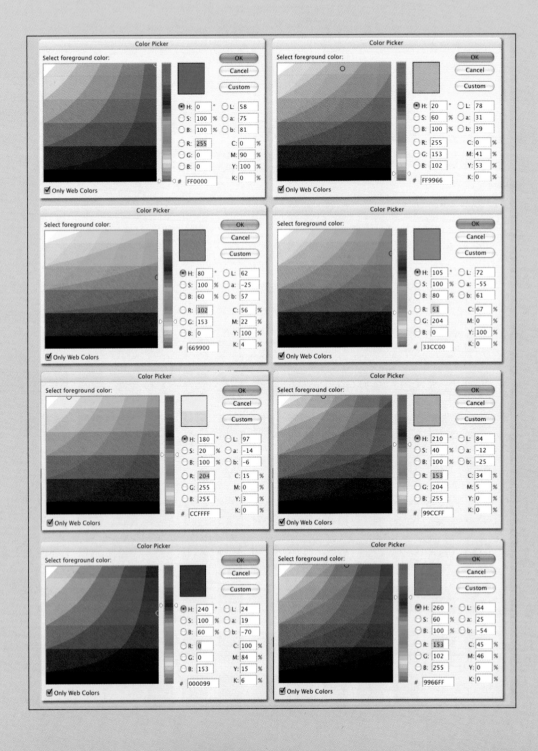

Basic HTML codes

Body Codes:
```
<html>
<head>
<title>title of page</title>
<Meta name="keywords" content="search engine identifying words">
</head>
<body>information that is to be displayed in the Browser</body>
</html>
```

Code Qualifiers:
```
<body bgcolor="#FFFFFF">
<body text="#000000">
<body background="image.gif">
```

Font Tags:
```
<font color="#000000">
<p>paragraph</p>
<h1>header</h1> Header styles number 1 through 6 with the text getting larger as the number gets
smaller.
<i>italicize text</i>
<b>bold text</b>
<blockquote>Indents text together in a block</blockquote>

<br>line break tag and is one of the few tags that doesn't need a closing tag.
<hr>is a horizontal rule and also doesn't need a closing tag.

<img src="graphicname.ext" width=pixels height=pixels border=pixels align=left valign=top
hspace=pixels vspace=pixels>
```

Links:
```
<a href="url"><img src="bird.jpg" width=120 height=120></a>
<a href="http://www.name.com/pathname.html/subpathname"><img src="bird.jpg" width=120
height=120></a>
<a href="mailto:name@server.com">linked text or image</a>
```

Tables:
```
<table border=0> (no border) a number=pixel thickness of a border
<table width=number height=number>
<table cell padding=number>pixel space held between the contents of the CELL and the CELL border.
<table cell spacing=number>pixel space between CELLs
<table bgcolor="#number">
<td colspan=number>CELL</TD>
<td rowspan=number>CELL</TD>
<tr> <td> </td ></tr>
```

This image by Milton Lee was developed to meet the requirement of a student project to "transcend the world", to defy the laws of nature in some way and use metaphor to reinterpret the world.

This image by Erik Wong was also developed to meet the student requirement of the project to "transcend the world."

This Web site was developed in HTML using tables.

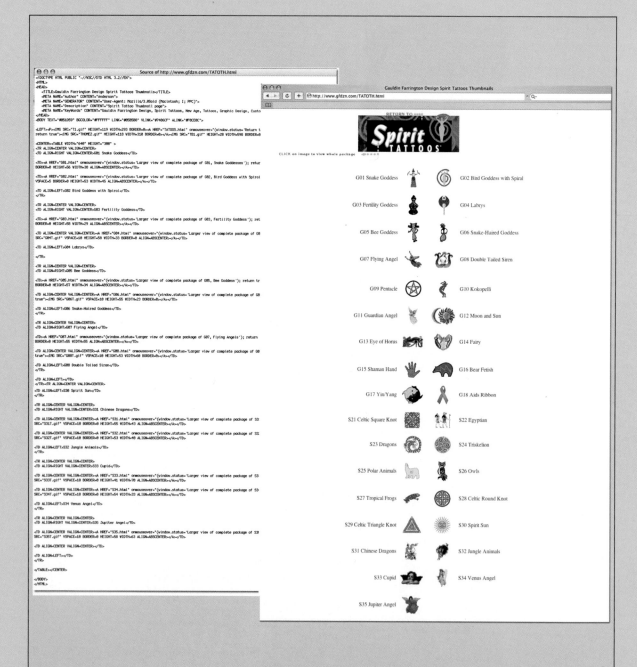

color plate | 11 |

These two Web sites by Daniel Echeverri and Mike LeMay were developed for a student project using the concept to "Reinvent the World." Students were to think about the relationship between technology and human experience and then reinvent the world. Abstract expressionism, the richness of human gesture, movement, and/or dream-like images were encouraged. These projects encouraged fantasy and dreams.

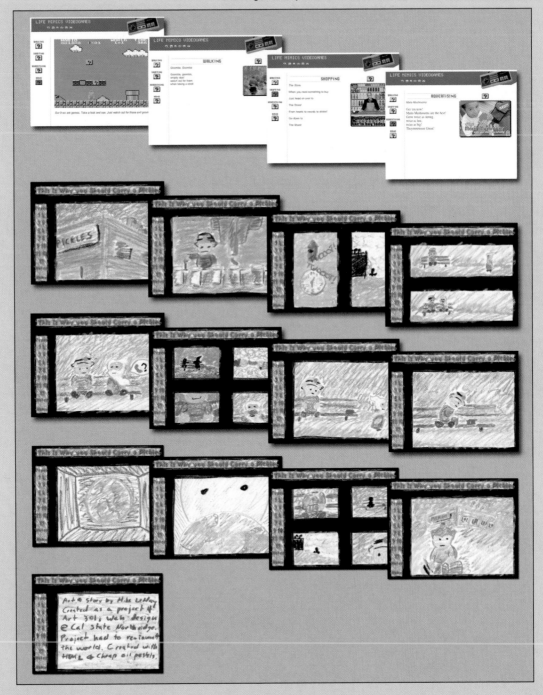

These two Web sites by students Richard Hogge and Keith Kocka were also
developed using the concept "Reinvent the World." Students were to consider
the user's movements as an element of human gesture and the individuality of
each user's experience. The rollovers in these projects reveal surrealistic and
challenging images.

The Barker and Associates Web site is an example of a beautiful site designed with frames (http://barker-publicart.com/index.html).

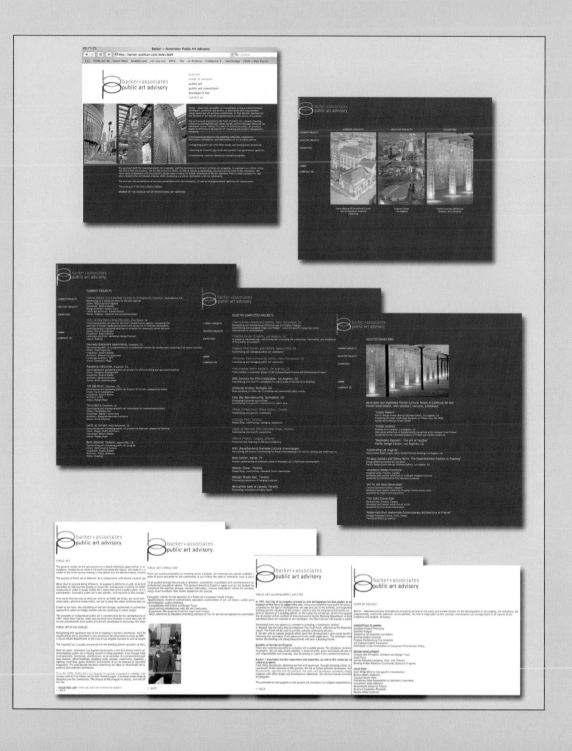

Exercise 6

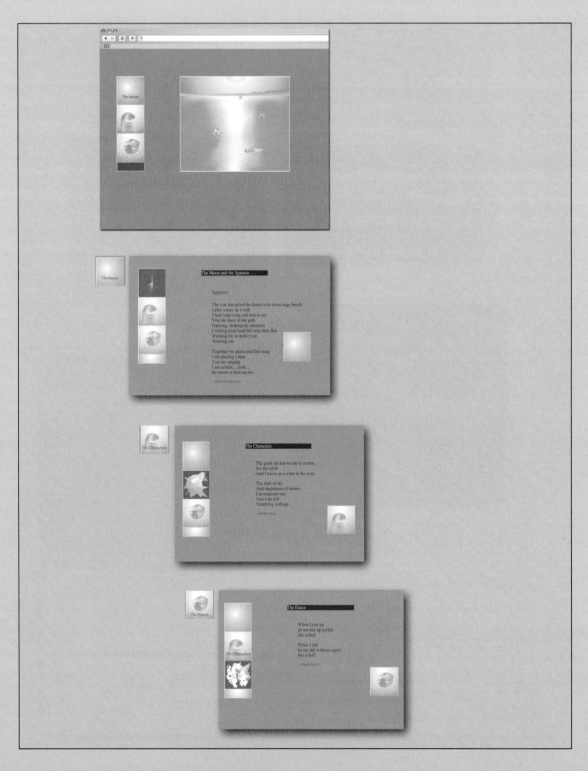

Ricardo Trujillo's Web site, designed in Dreamweaver, includes portfolio pieces, philosophy, and music preferences

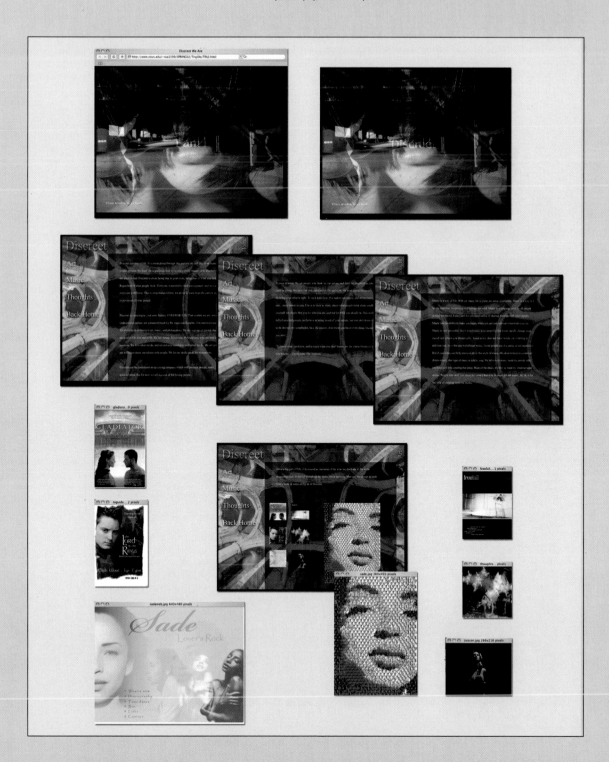

These files were developed in Illustrator prior to exporting AI Files to Flash files.
Drawings by the author for Flash poem dialogue "Site." Poem by Starr Goode.

These Web sites by students Orly Osman and Rachelle Franco were created in Flash.

These Web sites by students Jody Doyle and Jay Kim were created in Flash.

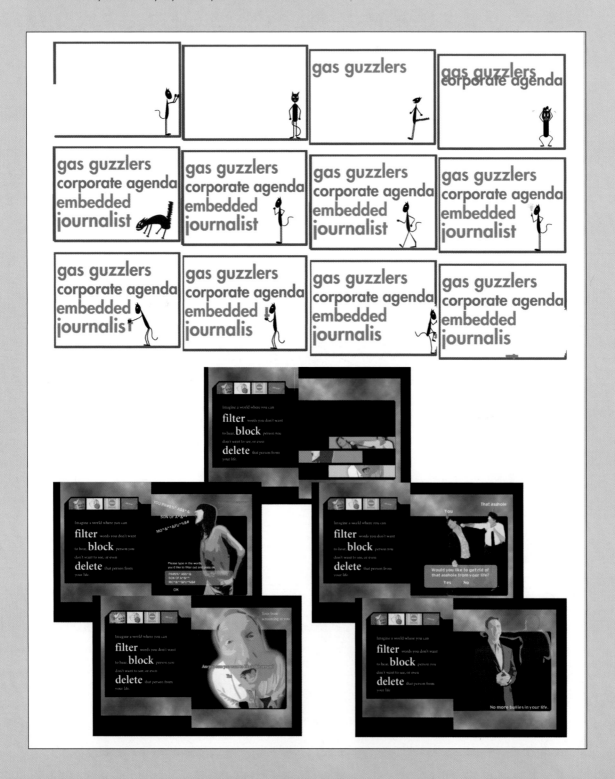

Drawings by the author in Illustrator for "Remember," a poem by Rose Marcario. The drawing of the pieta and the gardenia were created with the Pen tool. The background was created using a gradient mesh.

do you remember how we walked along the shore at sundown
how the tide was drawn so far out the sand we walked on was
like reflective glass and I watched your shadow emanate
my darling, do you remember how I held you to me and
kissed you hard on the mouth

darling, do you remember how I fell away
like Icarus and singed my whole body
rain drops fell on my tears
and you held me like Mary
holds the Christ in the Pieta
sycamores shadowed pattern
on the sky above us
and in one moment of wholeness
twenty years of that half-life ended

These graphics were developed in Illustrator and exported as SWF files to be imported into Flash. Cat graphics by student Jody Doyle and domestic scene by Jason Faraci.

Movie clip timeline and stage

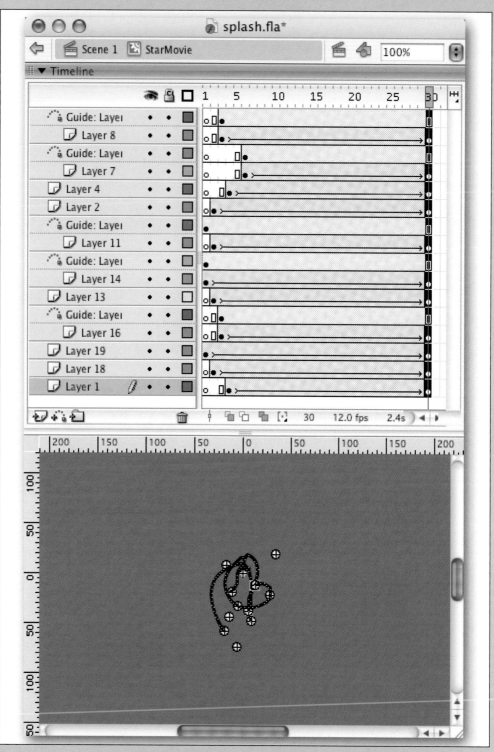

This wonderful Web site created in Flash explores the symbolic attributes of color. "Color in Motion: An Animated and Interactive Experience of Color Communication and Color Symbolism" was developed and created by Maria Claudia Cortes, a graphic designer/animator/programmer from Colombia. She explains the Web site this way: "One of the main goals I had in mind for my thesis was that it had to have an educational purpose, a source for the end user to gain new knowledge or skills. Color provided a great opportunity since there are many disciplines that use color as a tool and that include color courses in their programs, whether it is color theory, color symbolism, or color reproduction. Another goal was that it had to show the information in a non-traditional way-it had to provide the user with an experience that was fun and would make the user retain knowledge. Color, along with motion and music, would help me achieve those goals." See color plate 23 for more "pages."

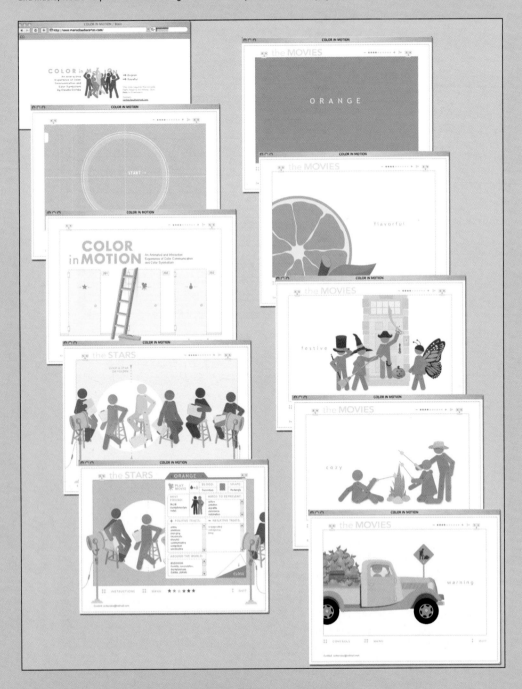

See color plate 22 for a description of these pages.

Student Francisco Ruiz created his beautiful portfolio Web site using the loadMovieNum ActionScript. See color plate 26 for more pages.

See color plate 24 for a description of these pages.

Exercise 14

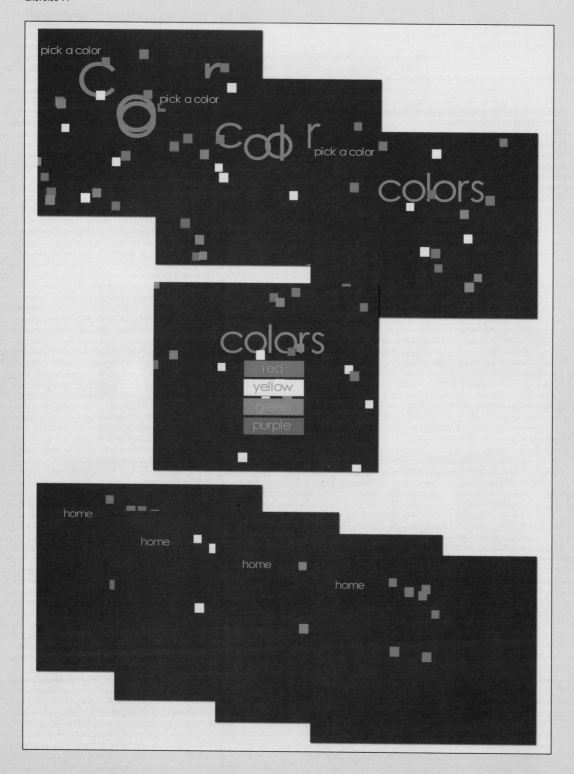

The author's portfolio Web site uses the loadMovieNum ActionScript.

Mary Peterson's portfolio Web site uses a clean, logical page layout that allows for maximum clear viewing of images with plenty of breathing room and easy navigation.

Student Natalia Wehba used a very nice color scheme to develop this Web site about flowers.

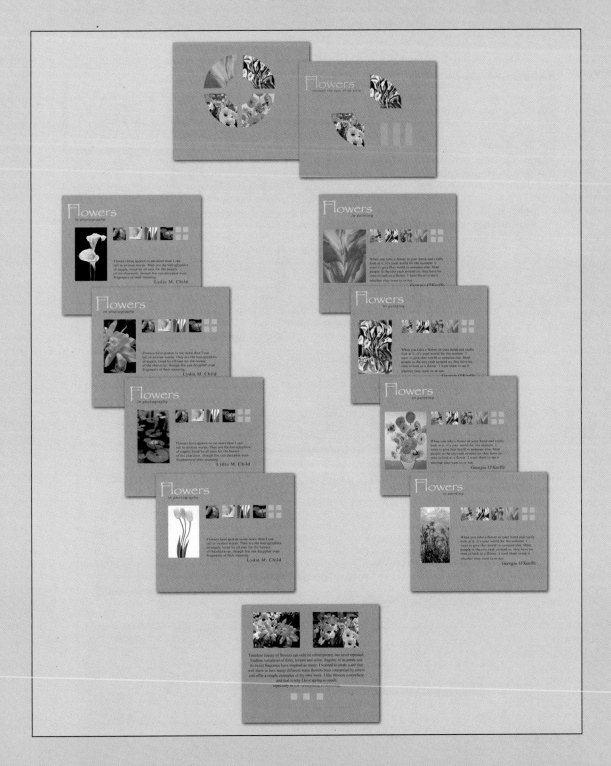

http://www.distibutive-justice.com. This Web site project is a part of Distributive Justice. It focuses on a global dialog for Americans and non-Americans to stimulate critical reflection on prevailing beliefs. The project is beautifully created in Flash by Andreja Kuluncic, visual artist, and co-authored by Gabrijela Sabol, Ivo Martinovic, Neven Petrovic, Dejan Jankovic, Trudy Lane, Matija Puzar and Mono Kuzmarovic. The Web site originates from Croatia. (See figure 1-2)

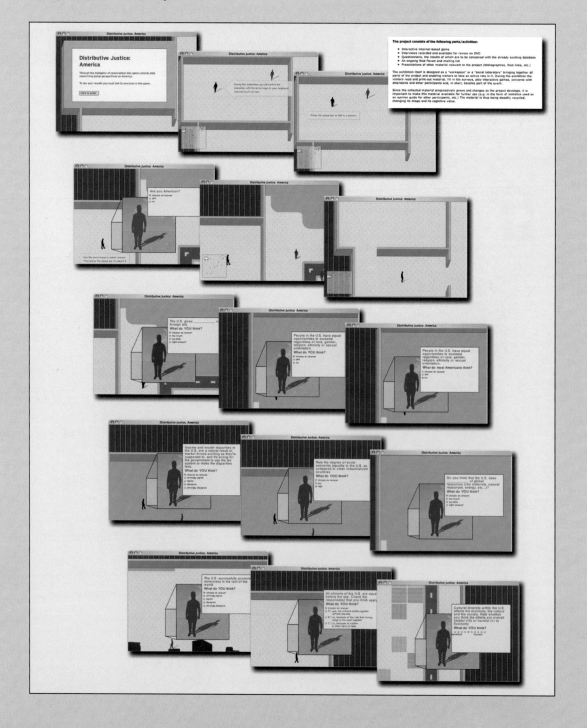

These two Web sites developed by students Nick Rickenbach and Lori lindland combine portfolio images and commercial goals.

Students Lucero Paniagua and Iris Kim interpreted Exercise 15 in their own way.

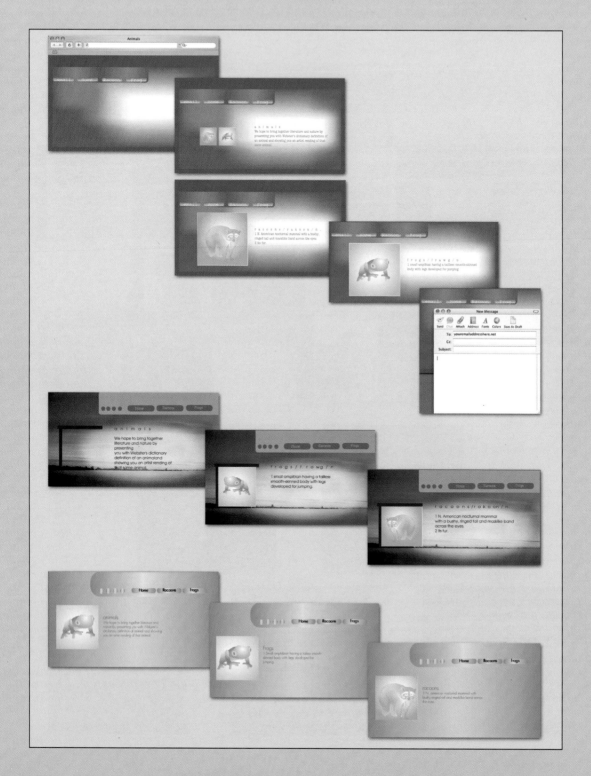

Wait! Don't press OK yet. You must press the plus sign to add all of the buttons and then follow the earlier steps for each state of each button, HTML page, and target. Finally, choose Vertical or Horizontal for the Insert and select Use tables. This allows you to arrange the buttons vertically or horizontally.

If you need to return to this dialog box to correct or revise a link or target, you can always access it by clicking on the navigation bar and from the menu bar, select Modify>Navigation Bar.

When you have added all of the Navigation buttons with their respective states and links, you will want to make certain that in the Properties window each button link is targeted to splash (or main) frame. Remember to select File>Save All.

figure | 6-7 |

Insert Navigation Bar dialog box

figure | 6-8 |

Completed Navigation Bar dialog window with highlighted options

ADDITIONAL TYPE AND PARAGRAPH FORMATTING

Let's poke around the text commands a bit more. This will give you additional options for designing your text. Although you've already studied most of these commands in HTML, it's essential to know how Dreamweaver facilitates the process and makes formatting visually instant, allowing you to make your decisions based upon seeing the design rather than guessing at the results of the code.

Fonts

Let's start with the Properties window for type. Click in the splash (or main) frame to display this window.

figure | 6-9 |

Properties window for type

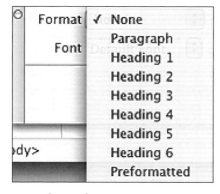

figure | 6-10 |

Formatting options in the Properties window for type

There are drop down menus for format, font, style, size, and color. Additionally, there are icons to easily add bolding, italicizing, justification, and list features, as well as browsing options for linking and targeting.

The Format drop-down menu includes Headings 1 through 6, Paragraph, and preformatted options that we studied in HTML. Remember that Heading 1 is the largest and Heading 6 is the smallest. (Heading 6 is so small it is rather useless.)

The Style drop-down menu gives you options of Styles that you create. We'll discuss this menu shortly.

The Fonts drop-down menu shows the basic combination of fonts that are available on most systems.

Additionally, you can edit this font list to add fonts from your sytem. You have to be careful here though, because if you use a font from your systems and your user does not have that font, then your user's system will revert to its default font over which you will have no control.

figure | 6-11 |

Fonts drop down menu

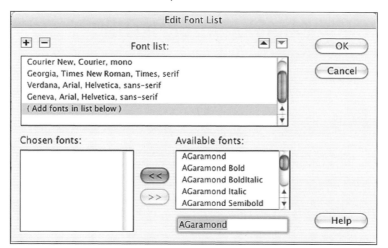

figure | 6-12 |

Edit Font List dialog box

Finally, you have one more menu in which you can assign font choices. This is the Page Properties choice in the Properties window. There are five categories in this menu. In the Headings option, you can customize Headings 1 through 6 with font, font size, bold, italic, and color.

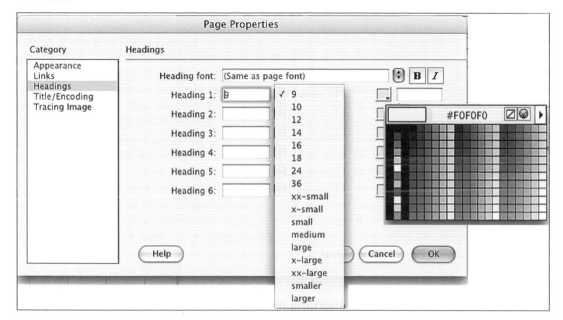

All of the options discussed here are also available through the Text pull-down menu.

figure | 6-13 |

Page Properties window showing heading font size and color options

Alignment

In the Properties window for type, the four alignment icons are, from left to right, left alignment, centered, right alignment, and justified. If you are writing a paragraph, the easiest format to read it in is left alignment. Large blocks of text are best designed with a left alignment. Justified is going to be problematic because you won't necessarily see what the user sees and there could be unwieldy space between words and letters and/or odd line breaks. Use caution with this option. Centered text is best used only in headlines, points of interest and paragraph headers.

Lists

In the Properties window for type, the list icons include bulleted (unordered), numbered (ordered), hanging outdent, and indent. Clicking on any of these icons will turn your typed returns into the corresponding icon parameters. In other words, whenever you hit RETURN, a new bullet or number or a new indent or outdent will occur when you apply one of these four choices.

figure | 6-14 |

Different alignments in the Properties window

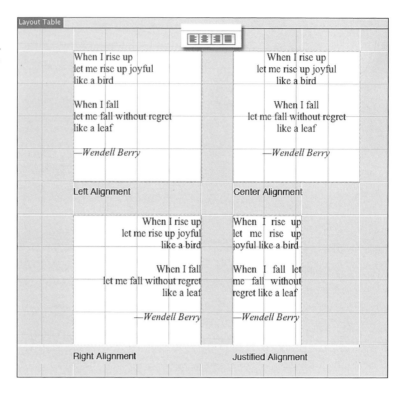

All of the text options through the Properties window are also available under the Text pull-down menu.

figure | 6-15 |

Various list options in the Properties window

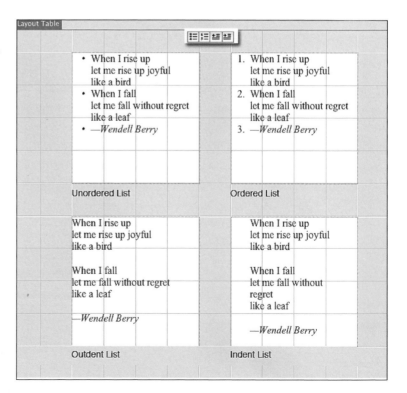

Styles

Some of the uses of Dreamweaver styles have already been presented. You create a style when you change the Headings pane of the Page Properties window (select Modify>Page Properties). These styles are universal when applied; however, if you change an instance of a heading style that you created through the Properties window or the Text pull-down menu, you will only change that one instance.

You can create a style by highlighting the text and then modifying it in the Properties window. As soon as you apply a font, Dreamweaver automatically assumes that you are creating a new style and will display *Style1* in the Style drop-down menu. You can change the name of the style to a more meaningful name simply by scrolling down to rename in this pane.

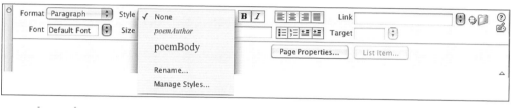

figure |6-16|

Properties window for type showing style names

Once created, you can apply a style to any type.

Open the Design pane to view the styles you have created on the CSS Styles tab. CSS refers to *cascading style sheets*. A single-page style will show up under a style code. A CSS style will show up under a CSS style code. These styles function differently. For now, let's continue working with single-page styles.

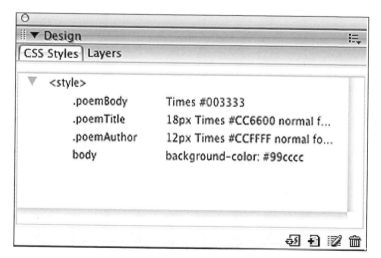

figure |6-17|

CSS Styles tab of the Design pane

You can also create a new style before you type. Open the Manage Styles window and click New.

figure | 6-18 |

Style pane

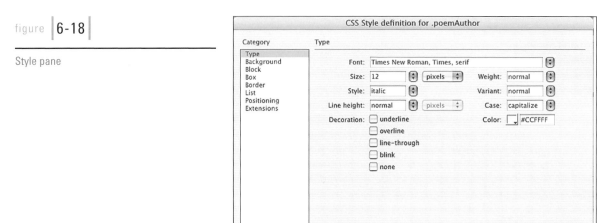

You will see a list on the left side of this pane that you can access to make any variety of changes. Once you have named the style, Dreamweaver will insist upon saving it as an accessible HTML document.

Export the style so that it is accessible to other pages you will create within a site. From the menu bar, select Text>CSS Styles>Export. In the dialog box that appears, name the export *Styles* and save it within the site folder.

You can then access this Style in a different HTML page. Select Text>CSS Styles>Manage Styles>Attach. From the dialog box that appears, choose link in the window and notice that the Styles shows up in the Design pane and the Properties window. Also notice that the page properties have been brought into the new HTML document. However, to apply the style, you must first highlight the text and then choose it through the Properties window.

figure | 6-19 |

Naming and saving a style and Export Styles As CSS File dialog box

You can also edit a style through the Design pane. The icon to the left of the trash can is the Edit Style icon. Select a style, click on this and it will return you to all of the style panes. Whenever you make a change here it will show up in the document. If you change a style in a document, it will make the change only in the document in which you are working. Even though the style may be exported, changes will not be made in any other documents. To remove a style from a document, simply highlight it in the Design pane and click on the trash icon.

Again, a CSS style is a group of styles that covers all of the functions listed in the CSS Style window that we just looked at. CSS styles may or may not be of interest to you. Some people find them frustrating. Others find them helpful. Fool around with them and decide for yourself. You can learn more about cascading style sheets at the Macromedia Web site, http://www.macromedia.com/support/dreamweaver, and Thomson/Delmar Learning's Dreamweaver book, *Exploring Dreamweaver MX 2004*, by James L. Mohler and Kyle Bowen.

SUMMARY

We have covered a lot of material in this chapter. Four-part rollovers in Dreamweaver are easy to use, fun to work with, and add true potential and usability to a navigation system. You've reviewed how to create the elements in Photoshop and Illustrator and save them for use in Dreamweaver. You've also learned how to use slices in a four-part navigation system and how to link and target the elements.

Additionally, you've learned how Dreamweaver facilitates the creative use of text. You now know a bit about using styles and how to edit and access them for different documents. And, staying true to our mission of the art of Web design, we've discussed concepts, this time as design relates to navigation. We looked at the use of gesture and metaphor as inspiration for creating navigation elements. We also examined the concept of less is more as a design theory in creating icons for navigation.

in review

1. What are the different states in four-part navigation?

2. How is gesture considered when designing navigation?

3. What is one consideration when using the concept of less is more?

4. What is a style?

5. How can you access a created style?

6. Where is Edit Style located?

exercise 6

1. From the back of book CD, copy the Exercise 6 folder onto your desktop. Save all your work for this exercise into this directory.

2. In Illustrator, open the navigationU.eps document. Note that all four buttons are in one file. You will continue to work with all four buttons in a document for each of the four states. You'll end up with four documents, one for each state.

figure | 6-Ex1 |

NavigationU.ai document

3. Save the file three more times, one for each state. Name the four Illustrator documents Up.ai, Down.ai, Over.ai, and OverDown.ai. Make changes to each state. You will end up with four states of navigation buttons and four Illustrator documents, one document for each state, each document containing all four buttons for that state. This will help you keep the style consistent for each state.

figure | **6-Ex2** |

Illustrator documents creating
four states of navigation

4. Consider the four states as you create your documents, making certain that they relate to one another and are clear, consistent, and engaging. Remember to consider gesture, metaphor, and less is more when creating these states. The states should be consistent, for example, all of the Up States should have a certain look, all of the Down States should have a certain look, etc.

5. Export each document as a TIFF, using a screen resolution of 72 dpi, a color model of RGB, and anti-alias.

6. Open Photoshop and create a new document. Set the width to 640 pixels and the height to 480 pixels, choose the RGB color model and 72 pixels/inch resolution. You will create the look of your splash page in this file. Save as exercise6.psd into your Exercise 6 Directory.

7. Open the Up.tif file in Photoshop. Select all, copy, and paste into exercise6.psd.

8. Move the layer with the Select tool to where you want to place it, making sure to stay in the left third of the document. This layer will be the Up state. Name it *Up State* in the Layers palette.

9. Open the Over.tif file. Select all, copy, and paste into the exercise6.psd document. Position the second layer on top of the first layer, naming it *Over State*. Use the Transparency bar to reveal the layer beneath. Temporarily change the transparency to about 40% to see through the layers in order to make certain that you precisely line up the navigation states. Remember to change the transparency back to 100% before moving on.

    Repeat this procedure for the Down State images and the Over While Down State images.

10. Open journey.tif. Select all, copy, and paste into the right-hand side of exercise6.psd. Name this layer *Splash*.

11. Make changes to the entire "page" (PSD document) as desired. Consider your design. Is it engaging? clear?

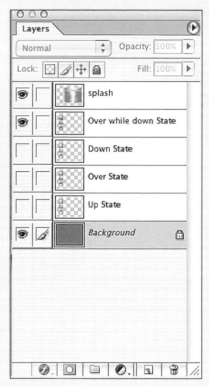

figure | 6-Ex3 |

Photoshop Layers pallete window

figure | 6-Ex4 |

Photoshop file with Over While Down State showing

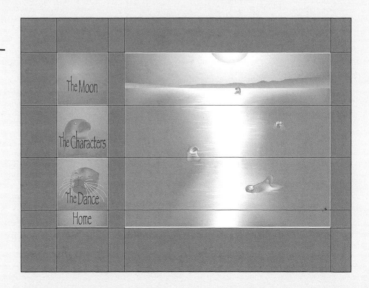

If you want to choose background colors, do so here, where you can really see the colors. Write down the formula number for any chosen colors. When you are satisfied, save.

12. Draw guides where you are going to create your slices.

13. In the Layers palette, click the eye icons to the left of the Down State images, Over State images, and Over While Down State images to hide these layers.

14. Using the steps you followed in Exercise 5, with only the Up State images and Splash eye icons open in the Layers palette, create slices and save each slice for the Web, choosing an appropriate compression and extension.

    Give each category of the navigation bar an individual slice. Save all slices into a folder named *images*.

15. In the Save Optimized As window change the settings to other and simplify the file naming. Finally, choose Selected Slices and click OK.

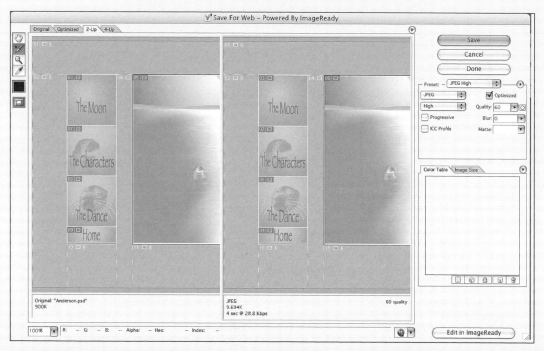

figure | 6-Ex5 |

Photoshop Save Optimized As Window

16. Name the Up navigation images *moonU.jpg, charU.jpg, danceU.jpg,* and *homeU.jpg.* (They can also be gifs.)

17. In the Layers palette, click the eye icon to the left of the Up State image layer to hide it and click the Down State image eye icon to reveal the Down State navigation bar.

    Using the same slices, save each of these slices to the same folder of images. Use the same names as in Step 17, replacing the letter U with D.

18. Repeat these steps for the Over and Over While Down States, naming the slices appropriately.

19. Go to the desktop and look in your images folder. Make certain that you have named your slices logically and that everything that you expect to be there, is there, nothing more.

20. In Dreamweaver, use the same steps that you have followed in the last three exercises to develop a local site. Name the site and save as excer6.

21. Once again you will create frames. Choose the Layout tab and the Frames icon with a smaller frame on the left and a larger frame on the right. The frame on the left will accommodate the navigation bar. The frame on the right will accommodate the main image and linked files.

22. In the Properties window, set the borders to No and border width to 0.

23. Mouse over where the two frames come together and the mouse pointer will turn into a double-headed arrow. Drag the division to the right and release the mouse button when you've positioned it, allowing enough room for your left navigation bar.

24. Begin the save process by saving the frameset. With your frames page visible in the document window, click on the frameset to select it and title it with your name. Name and save the frameset and both frames following the directions from Chapter 5. Make certain to save these documents into the Exercise 6 directory that you created.

25. Make certain that your Frames panel shows. Choose each frame and name it in the Properties window. (See Figure 5-Ex11.)

    Once all of your frame pages have been named and saved, you can then choose File>Save All for your future changes.

26. Create a table to import the Journey slices into the main.html (splash) frame. Choose the Layout tab and click inside the splash page. Choose the Draw Layout Cell icon

and draw cell(s) to accommodate the journey image. Import it, making certain that the cell size matches the image size. Create blank cells to hold space as you deem appropriate. Click File>Save All.

27. Before adding the navigation bar to the index frameset, you'll need to create the three HTML pages to which the navigation will link. Open a new document in Dreamweaver. Create a basic HTML page. From the menu bar, select Modify>Page Properties to change the background color to match the background color of the frameset or the main frame.

28. Use Layout mode and draw a cell in the middle-left area of the document. Type the poem provided or one of your choosing.

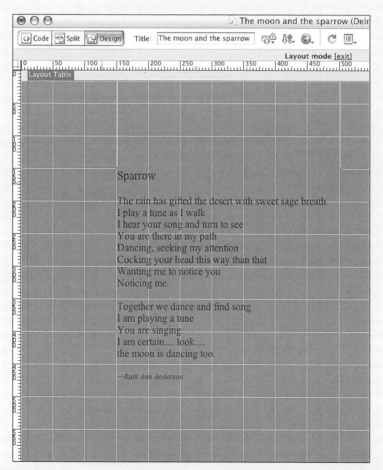

figure | **6-Ex6**

Poem typed in cell

29. Highlight the body of the poem. In the Properties window, change the font to Times New Roman, Times, Serif. Change the size to 16 and the color to 003333. Click on the Style options and then click Rename. Change the style name to *poemBody*. Note that Dreamweaver will not allow spaces in this name.

figure | 6-Ex7 |

Properties window for style specifications

30. Repeat these steps for the title and author of the poem to change the name of the style, using a larger font for the title and a smaller, italicized font for the author name.

31. Save the file as moon.html. Export the styles. From the menu bar, select Text>CSS Styles>Export. Name the export *Ex6 Style* and save it in your Exercise 6 folder.

32. Create two more new HTML documents. Save the HTML documents as *dance.html* and *char.html*. These names will match up with the navigation and will be easy to organize when you are creating links. Import the style document that you created in moon.html. From the menu bar, select Text>CSS Styles>Manage Sites>Attach into each of these new HTML documents.

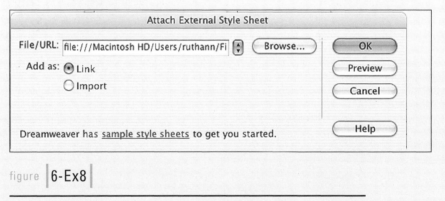

figure | 6-Ex8 |

Attaching the style document Through the Attach External Style Sheet dialog box

33. Apply the styles to the title, body, and author of each document through the Properties window.

34. Save each document. You now have three HTML documents to match up with the first three navigation buttons. Copy and paste the poems from the back of book CD into your respective HTML files. The fourth HTML document will be the splash.html (or main.html) from the index frameset to respond to the fourth navigation button—home.

35. Return to exer6. Click in the left frame and choose the Insert Navigation Bar icon on the Common Tab of the Insert bar. When the Insert Navigation Bar dialog box appears, name the first button moon and browse for the Up State, Over State, Down

State, and Over While Down State images in your images folder. Name each button, staying consistent with the names of the slices and HTML page. (See Figure 6-7.)

36. In the When clicked, Go to URL dialog box, browse to the moon.html page. Target the page to splash (or main).

37. Press the plus sign to add the second set of buttons. Name these characters and browse to their four states of navigation. Browse to the char.html page you created in the above step.

38. Repeat these steps to link dance.html and browse for its four states of navigation. Be sure to target each HTML page to splash (or main).

39. Finally, repeat these steps for the home link. Browse for each state of Home. In the When clicked, Go to URL dialog box, choose the splash.html (or main.html) page from the index frameset and target it to itself.

40. Before closing this window, review the different states of each button and make sure that everything is correct. Highlight a button name in the pane and you'll see the four states of navigation and linked HTML page. Your navigation must be in the same order as what you created in Illustrator. Dreamweaver will assign the buttons accordingly. If a link is in the wrong order, you can use the small triangles at the top of the dialog box to move a highlighted name up or down in the list.

Choose Vertically in the Insert pull-down list and select Use tables. The dialog box should look something like this:

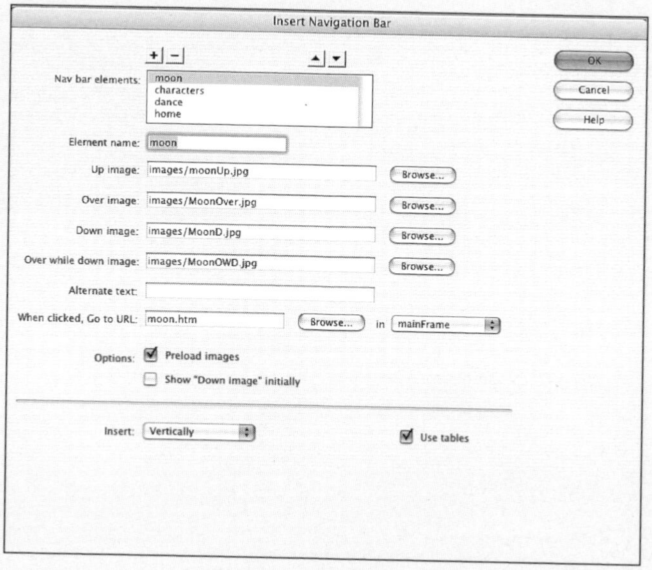

figure |**6-Ex9**|

Completed Navigation Bar window

When everything looks correct, click OK.

41. Return to the Properties window, click on the navigation bar, and make certain that each button link is targeted to main.

42. Embellish as desired. View in several browsers to make certain that the links work correctly and everything looks the way you want it to. Make adjustments as needed.

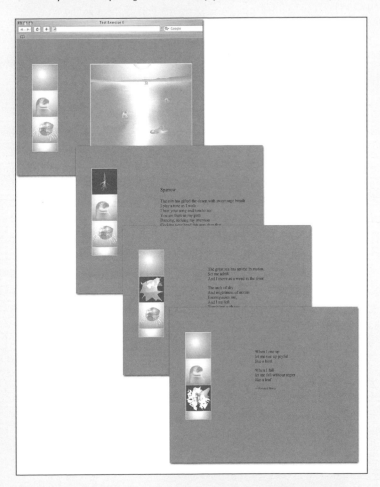

figure | 6-Ex10 |

Complete Exercise 6 displayed in browser showing additional links

When you are certain that everything looks correct, save and share with your friends. You are going to build on this exercise in the next chapter so be sure to keep it. See Color Plate 14 for a full-color, final version of this exercise.

on your own

Play around with the linked poem pages. Change the background color to match the frameset. Try revisiting the Over State layer in Photoshop. Duplicate the layer and name it *Poem Images*. Give the layer a transparency of 20% or 30%. Make other changes as desired. Save the slices for the three images and import images into the appropriate poem pages, on the left of the title of each poem. Alternately, place the images where you think they look good, staying consistent between poem pages.

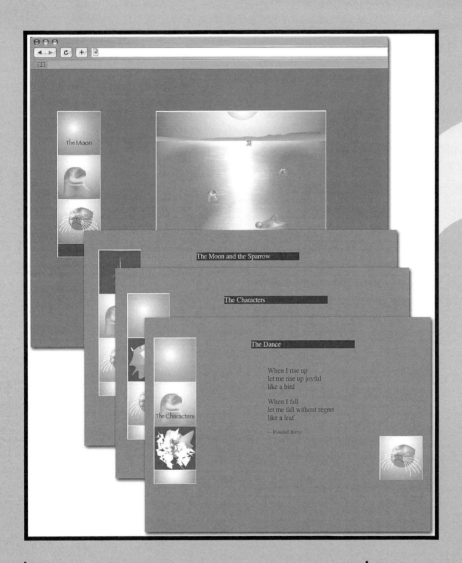

layers, media files, ftp, and uploading to the internet

Objectives

Explore layers in Dreamweaver.

Re-examine the element of surprise.

Discover how to import media files.

Explore FTP.

Learn how to upload files to the Internet through Dreamweaver.

Introduction

Well, we're almost there. In this chapter, we'll take a brief look at the design capabilities of layers. Layers are a dreamy feature, giving the designer the additional ability to stack graphics, images, and text. We'll also explore importing media files and take a look at adding a few final touches.

Then we will move on to that final step: uploading to the Internet. We'll learn about FTP and uploading through the site definition dialogue box. This is it: from here on in, your design is out there for all of the world to see.

LAYERS

Dreamweaver offers an easy way to produce layers, something we did not explore in HTML. Layers are a nice addition to page layout design and operate similarly to graphic design software for print. Layers offer the ability to add graphic elements that are not limited to the grid of cells, tables, or imported images. Once a layer is drawn, you can import images into it, add text, simply use it as a graphic element by giving it a background color, or any combination of the above. You can also convert tables to layers and vice versa.

You can access layers in Dreamweaver through the Insert pull-down menu. Scroll down to Layout Objects, then over to Layer. This will place a layer on the page where the cursor is sitting. Alternately, and more precisely, from the Layout tab of the Insert Bar, choose the Draw Layer icon, the third icon from the left.

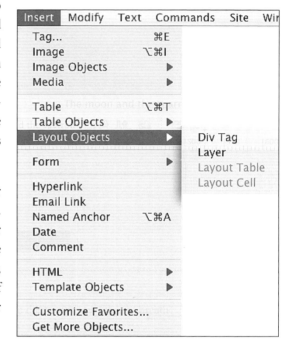

figure **7-1**

Insert pull-down menu

figure **7-2**

Draw Layer icon on the Layout tab of the Insert bar

| NOTE |

Expanded Mode

The Expanded mode choice on the Layout tab of the Insert bar allows you to view and select layers, tables, and frames more easily. However, this mode does not display layers, tables, and frames the way a browser would. Be sure to switch back to Standard or Layout mode before you resize or move any of these objects.

(This icon will not be available if you are in Layout mode. You must be in Standard or Expanded mode.)

Once you have clicked on the Layer icon, you will be able to draw a layer of any size in any location on your page. Click in the top left corner of where you want the layer to start and drag to the desired height and width. You can click on the edge of the layer shape to access the Properties window, where you can type in the x and y coordinates, (measured from the left and top), width and height, color, and so forth. Also, it is good practice to name the layer in the Properties window.

It may seem a little difficult at first to select a layer's boundaries. You will see the hand symbol on a Mac, the four way arrow symbol on a

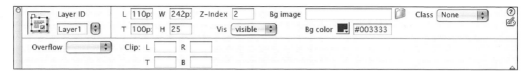

PC, when you are on the edge of a layer rather than the pointer. Go ahead and click—this will access the layer boundaries. Clicking *inside* the layer will not access the layer boundaries, but it will generate the layer handle. You can then click on the handle to access the boundaries. Adjust the boundaries by dragging on the vertical or horizontal boundaries or on a corner handle to adjust in both directions.

figure | 7-3 |

Properties window for a layer

You can type in a layer, import images, add color, and center text and images. In other words, you can do anything in a layer that you can do on a page.

If you need to align multiple layers or make their widths or heights the same, you can do so through the Properties window by selecting each layer and setting the x or y coordinates, width, or height. Alternately, you can select multiple layers by holding down the `Shift` key and accessing the Modify pull-down menu. Choose Align and the desired alignment.

figure | 7-4 |

Modify pull-down menu

There is a third coordinate for layers: This is the Z-index. The Z-index is the stacking order. The lower a layer's Z-index, the further it is from the top. In other words, a layer with a Z-index of 1 is below a layer with a Z-index of 2 or 3. The Z-index for a layer is shown in the Properties window.

| NOTE |

Further Exploration of
Dreamweaver

Dreamweaver has so much to offer, we have just barely begun to scratch the surface in this book. If you find this approach to Web design appealing, investigate the Macromedia Web site, http://www.macromedia.com/support/dreamweaver, and/or Thomson/Delmar Learning's Dreamweaver book, *Exploring Dreamweaver MX 2004*, by James L. Mohler and Kyle Bowen.

Layers can respond to Behaviors. Behaviors are Java Scripts that combine events, objects and actions such as 4-part navigation. Dreamweaver cana help you with Behaviors through the Behavior panel. Behaviors are a bit tricky in that they are subject to the combination of event, browser version and the object. We won't tackle Behaviors in this book but you may want to poke around in the panel and see what you can figure out. What Behaviors can do for layers is to make them visible or invisible and move them around the page.

IMPORTING MULTIMEDIA

You can import Flash files, Shockwave files, applets, and sound files into Dreamweaver documents through the Common tab of the Insert bar. The sixth icon from the left is the media icon.

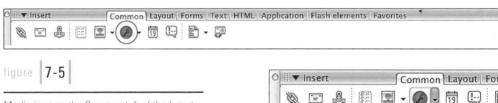

figure | 7-5 |

Media icon on the Common tab of the Insert bar

Alternately, you can import files from the menu bar. Select insert. Scroll to Media and over to the type of media you want to import. This will bring up a files window from which to choose your file.

Importing a media file is as simple as importing any image. Like an image, you will need to create the file first, save it into your site directory, and then import it. In the Flash section of this book, we will learn how to create SWF files. SWF animations can also be imported into Dreamweaver.

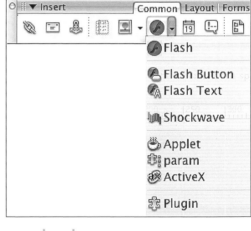

figure | 7-6 |

Insert pull-down menu with media

Media files will show up on your page only as an icon matching the dimensions of the imported file. In other words, if you import a 300 x 100 pixel SWF file, you will see a 300 x 100 plain rectangle in your document window with a small SWF icon in the center of it. You won't be able to see the actual animation until you view the Dreamweaver document in a browser. To adjust the dimensions of any of these files, it is best to return to the original application and make the adjustments there rather than resizing in Dreamweaver. Resizing any media file in Dreamweaver will distort its quality.

Be sure to keep your imported files within the same color scheme as your Web site. You don't want to have these files stand out like a sore thumb just because they can perform something cool. Also, stay away from clever or cool just for its own sake. Use imported media files for a reason. Do they add functionality? Do they add clarity or delight? Don't add media files just because you know how or because it is easy. Make sure they integrate into your page visually and theoretically.

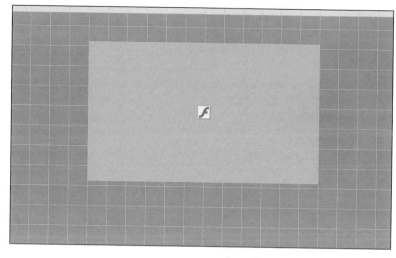

figure | **7-7**

Inserted SWF file in Dreamweaver

You can link or embed sounds. The sound files must first be in your site directory. Use the ActiveX from the Media option of the Insert pull-down menu or click the Media icon on the Common tab of the Insert bar. Either method will place an icon on your page and give you the Properties window for the ActiveX option.

In the Properties window, you can browse for your sound file, choose to embed, and name and test the sound. The sound file will show up in your document window as a small square showing only the ActiveX icon. You can place the sounds anywhere you like but keeping them at the top or bottom of your document may help you locate them and stay organized more easily.

figure | **7-8**

Properties Window for ActiveX

If you are attaching a sound to a link, click on the link and in the Properties window browse to the sound file just as you would an image.

Be careful when adding sound files. Sound files will definitely slow the download of your Web site, creating that potential for user boredom. Ask yourself if you really need the sounds. If the answer is yes, explore how to create sounds so that the files are as small as possible. Chapter 13 explores sound in more depth, including finding and creating sounds.

A FEW FINAL TOUCHES

Let's explore just a few final touches. Remember back in Chapter 3 when we discussed image maps and hotspots? Hotspots are a great way to delight the curious user, the user who will move the mouse around just to see what happens. This is yet another notion of keeping the user engaged: Surprise them. Treat them to something unexpected. Use a hotspot not to present important information, but rather some bit of trivia that isn't necessary to the Web site but does enhance it. For example, if you are creating a corporate Web site, you could use hotspots to display testimonials or employee photographs. If you are creating a portfolio Web site, you could use hotspots to give a glimpse of a small portion of a painting or a photo of you in the process of creating. Finally, if you are developing a Web site for a small business, you could use hotspots to show photographs of the employees at work. Have hotspots open up new browser windows so that the user can just close them when finished. Be creative with hotspots but use them sparingly and effectively.

Other ideas to explore in Dreamweaver include forms, behaviors, draggable layers, scripts, and actions. There is far more than we have room for in this book. Poke around the sample pages that Dreamweaver offers. This will give you some idea of further possibilities as well as how to go about them. Experiment. Be courageous.

In Chapter 1 you were encouraged to surf the Web. Now when you are surfing you should be able to tell if you are looking at a frames-based Web site. Try looking specifically for this and when you think you have found one, check the source of the site. In the browser, from the menu bar, select View>View Source. Choosing this when you are on a specific Web page will show you a new window with code. Exercise 6 viewed as source through a browser looks something like this:

```
<!DOCTYPE HTML PUBLIC "-//W3C//DTD HTML 4.01 Frameset//EN"
"http://www.w3.org/TR/html4/frameset.dtd">

<html>

<head>

<title>Exercise 6</title>

<meta http-equiv="Content-Type" content="text/html; charset=iso-8859-1">

<style type="text/css">

<!—

body {

    background-color: "#669999";}
```

—>

</style></head>

<frameset rows="*" cols="182,*" framespacing="0" frameborder="NO" border="0">

 <frame src="left.htm" name="leftFrame" scrolling="NO" noresize>

 <frame src="main.htm" name="mainFrame">

</frameset>

<noframes><body>

</body></noframes>

</html>

The first two lines of the source tell you that the document is indeed produced with frames. <style type="text/css"> tells you that the document has cascading style sheets. The <noframes></noframes> code refers to the layer created.

So now that you know what to look for, try surfing the Web some more. What becomes trite due to overuse? What stands out to you? Chances are that if a Web site impresses you, there are some solid design principles behind the construction of it. Which sites offer you compelling experiences? Which sites enchant you and make you want to explore them even more? Learn from these. It's back to that notion of educating your eye. Surf, surf, surf.

THE LAST STEP

The final step we need to discuss is uploading to the browser. You've come a long way to be ready for this step. You've finished your site and it all looks perfect. Now it's time to test the waters.

To begin, rename your frameset *index.html*. Update all pages. Clean up your folders. Discard all unused images or image prep files and any unused HTML files.

Next, purchase Internet space from a Web hosting service. This is the company that hosts or stores your files and makes them available to the Internet. Spend some time researching what is available to you. Independent Web hosting services with substantial reputations, a good amount of storage space, 24-hour support, and quality service are worth the money. See Chapter 16, *Hosting and Uploading,* for a thorough discussion of how to find a Web hosting service.

| NOTE |

Index.html

Index.htm or index.html is the default page in a folder on the Web server that a browser will recognize. You must have the opening page of your Web site by this name.

| **NOTE** |

FTP

FTP stands for *File Transfer Protocol*. In Chapter 1, we discussed the definition of protocol as a set of rules by which transactions can take place. FTP is a set of rules by which files can be transferred to and from the Internet. There are numerous FTP programs that help you with this process. Dreamweaver has its own FTP set-up menu.

Once you have chosen a service, you will need to ask them for the host information and a user ID. You create your own password. (If you are uploading a Web site for a client, you will need this information for their Web Server.) Then go back and configure the server information for uploading through Dreamweaver. Return to the Site Definition Wizard. From the menu bar, select Site>Manage Sites. When the Manage Sites dialog box appears, click Edit. This will return you to the series of panes in which you originally defined your site.

In the first pane, click the link that reads "create an FTP or RDS server connection."

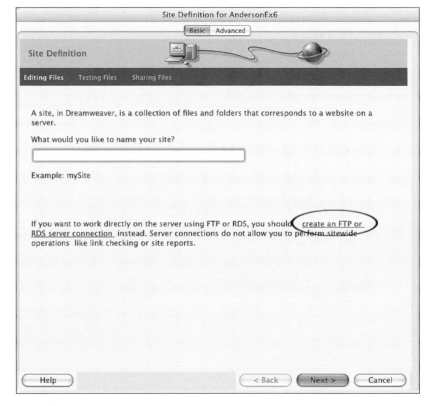

figure | 7-9 |

Site Definition Wizard window with link to create an FTP or RDS server connection

This will take you to the Configure Server dialog box. You will need to input the information from your Web hosting service. Use Access type: FTP. The FTP host, host directory, and login name are all supplied by your service. You'll choose your password when you are setting up your account with your server. It will stay the same every time you use the protocol. The host directory is your folder on the server that will house all of your files. Remember that you must have a document named index.htm or index.html for the browser to recognize. This is the initial page of your Web site.

Once all of the information is correctly entered, click the Test button to see if the connection is active. If the test is successful, files will be uploaded to the remote server. This will be indicated in the remote server window. Click OK to exit the dialog box.

Access the Remote and Local Site window through the docked panels. Choose the Files tab. On the far right side is an icon to expand the window to give you both the remote and local site information.

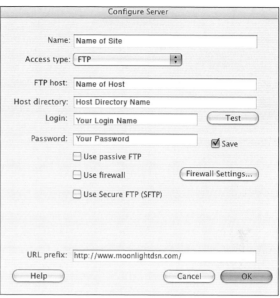

figure | 7-10 |

Configure Server dialog box

figure | 7-11 |

Files tab showing icon to expand the window

The icons in this window from left to right represent Connect, Refresh, Site Files, Testing Server, Site Map, Get Files, Put Files, Check Out Files, Check In Files, and Expand/Collapse. Choose the Connect icon to access the remote site information and connect to the Web server. Once connected, the Connect icon will change to a Disconnect icon and a remote file list will appear. To upload your files, select what you want to upload from the local files and click the Put icon. You can upload multiple files by holding down the Shift key while selecting files.

figure | 7-12 |

Expanded window showing remote and local site information

figure | 7-13 |

Put icon

You can also upload a page directly from the document window. Make sure that you are connected and choose Put from the File Management pull-down menu on the document toolbar. That's it. Dreamweaver does the rest!

SUMMARY

In this chapter, you've learned how to put the final touches on your Web site, examined layers, and learned about FTP and how to upload your files. Web sites can be so wonderfully creative and fun. Even if you are designing a corporate Web site, be sure to bring to the table all of the artistic concerns, creativity, delight, and fun that we have discussed throughout the last five chapters.

That's all the time we have for Dreamweaver in this book but there is oh so much more. Explore, experiment, surf, learn, engage yourself and others, and enjoy! Remember: If you are having fun, allowing your creative juices to flow and engaging yourself, chances are that your Web site is going to be a compelling user experience.

in review

1. Why use layers?

2. How can you access layers?

3. How do you make changes to layers?

4. What is FTP?

5. When can you upload to the Internet?

6. What must be the name of the first page in your Web site?

exercise 7

Let's continue with our exercise from Chapter 6. We'll add layers and a few surprises, then upload to a Web server.

1. Start by opening all of the Exercise 6 files. Begin by resaving the frameset as *index*.

   The advantage to using layers for this Web site is that it allows you to put graphic elements in exactly the same place on each page regardless of the length of the poems. This creates a visual consistency that is pleasing to the eye and connects otherwise visually unrelated pages to each other.

2. Open moon.html. Click the Layout tab of the Insert bar and select the Draw Layer icon. Begin dragging in the upper-left corner and to the right and down creating a title bar shape above the poem.

3. Select the boundaries of the layer to access the Properties window.

In the Properties window, enter 225 pixels for width, and 25 pixels for height. In the background color box, change the color to #003333. Write down your x and y coordinates. Leave as visible.

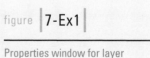

figure | **7-Ex1**

Properties window for layer

4. Click in the layer and type *The Moon and the Sparrow*. Change the text color to white.

5. Return to the Draw Layer icon and draw a new layer at about 400 (L) and 235 (T) so that it is to the right of the poem. Draw this layer 100 pixels wide and 100 pixels high. Leave the layer at no color and click inside the layer and choose the Image icon from the Common tab of the Insert bar. Import moonU.jpg. Center the image using the Properties window Text icon.

6. Test moon.html in a browser, then return to the index file. Test this file in the browser and click on the moon icon. Does it look correct in the browser? It should look something like this:

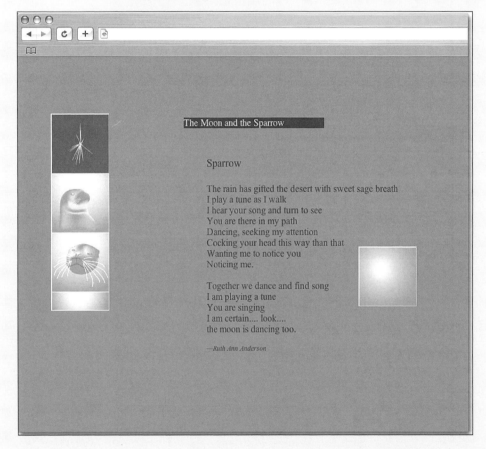

figure | 7-Ex2 |

index.html in displayed browser
with moon.html linked

Layers can be a little squirrely sometimes. If the layers jump around, check the codes to make certain that it reads something like this.

```
<div id="Layer3" style="position:absolute; left:400px; top:388px;
width:100px; height:100px; z-index:3; visibility: visible;"></div>
```

You want the code to be a <div> code and the position to be absolute.

7. Create the same layers (using the exact coordinates) for char.html and dance.html.

8. Return to index.html and test it in the browser. Do all of your links work correctly? Do all of the poems open with the layers in the same place?

   Now, let's add some surprises to the Splash image by adding hot spots.

9. Draw a hotspot over the image that matches the character image in the navigation. In the Link text box of the Properties window, with the hotspot selected, browse to char.html and target Splash (or Main).

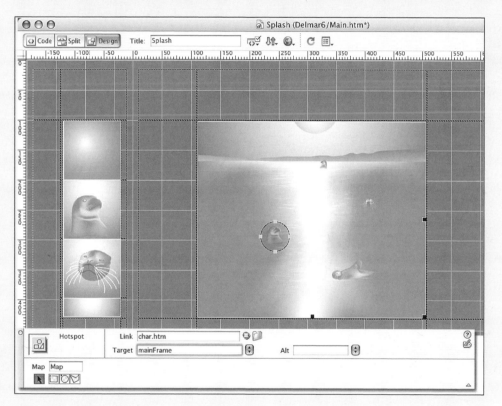

figure | 7-Ex3

Index frameset with hotspot over the seal image and Properties window for a hotspot

10. Draw another hotspot over the image that matches the dance image in the navigation. Link the hotspot to dance.html and again target splash. These two links will obviously match the navigation links.

    Let's have a little fun with another hot spot.

11. Return to Illustrator or Photoshop. Create a new document 200 pixels by 200 pixels. Draw a bubble much like you would see over a cartoon character. Type something surprising in the bubble. For example, "Oh how I love to swim under the path of the moonlight as it sparkles on the water's surface."

figure | 7-Ex4 |

Bubble drawn in Illustrator

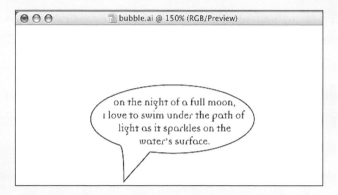

on the night of a full moon,
I love to swim under the path of
light as it sparkles on the
water's surface.

12. Save for the Web using the steps you know like the back of your hand by now. Name the file something like bubble.jpg. Back in Dreamweaver, create a new HTML document within your Exercise 6 folder. Type a title and modify the background color to match the rest of the documents. Draw a cell, import bubble.jpg, and save as bubble.html.

13. Back in the index frameset, draw a hotspot over the seal lying on its back in the foreground. Link the hotspot to the new bubble.html page that you just created and target the link to blank. This will cause a new window to open that can be closed after the user has a good chuckle.

   Feel free to create a couple of more hotspots like this. Be creative. Have fun.

14. Finally, it is time to upload your project. By now you need to have chosen a service provider and have the necessary information. From the index frameset, return to the Site Definition Wizard windows. From the menu bar, select Site>Manage Sites. When the Manage Sites window appears, click Edit. This will return you to the series of panes in which you originally defined your site. In the first pane, click Next three times until you reach the remote server window. Click on the pull-down menu and select FTP.

figure | 7-Ex5 |

Site Definition Wizard window
with link to create an FTP or RDS
server connection

15. Here you will need to input the information from your Web hosting service. Use Access type: FTP. The FTP host, host directory, and login name are all supplied by your service. Type in your password. Once all of the information is correctly entered, press the Test button to see if the connection is active. If the test is successful, the files will load into the Files window. If the test is not successful, you will be given a dialog box stating the reason why. When the test is successful, click Next twice and then Done. This should return you to the index frameset.

16. Access the Remote and Local Site window through the docked panels. Choose the Files tab. Expand the window to find the remote and local site information. (See Figure 7-11.)

17. Click the Connect icon (if not already connected) to access the remote site information and connect to the Web server. Once connected, the Connect icon will change to a Disconnect icon and a remote file list will appear. To upload your files, select what you want to upload from the local files and click the Put icon. You'll need to upload all of the HTML pages for this Web site, plus the Images folder.

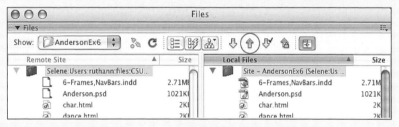

That's it. You're on! Check it out! Your browser window should show something like this:

figure | **7-Ex6** |

Local and Remote Sites window showing Put icon

figure | **7-Ex7** |

Index frameset displayed in browser

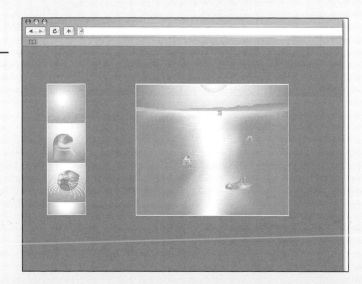

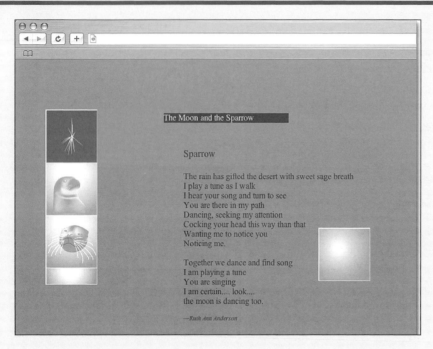

figure | 7-Ex8 |

moon.html in the splash frame

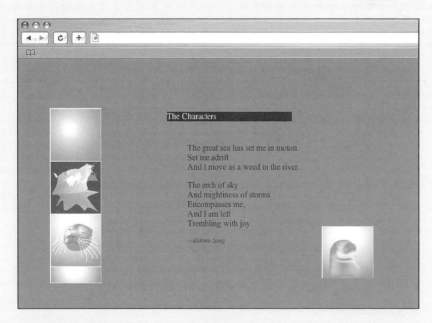

figure | 7-Ex9 |

char.html in the splash frame

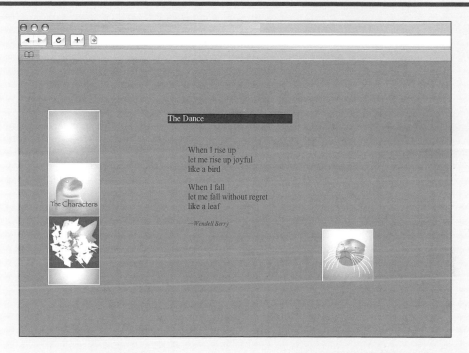

figure | 7-Ex10 |

dance.html in the splash frame

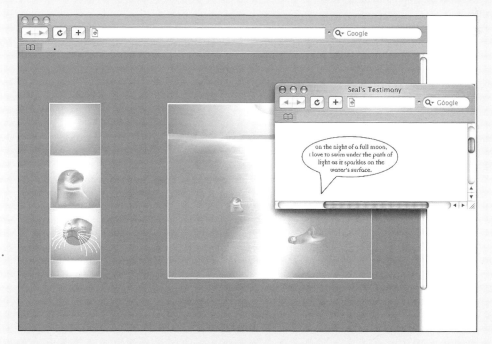

figure | 7-Ex11 |

Index frameset with bubble.html displayed in a new browser window

See Color Plate 14 to view this Web site in full color. See Color Plate 15 for cover artist Ricardo Trujillo's Web site designed in Dreamweaver.

on your own

Try revising one of the exercise files other than the index file. Make some sort of change and then return to the document site window. Find the HTML file that you want to replace and highlight it. Delete the old file and click the Put icon to upload the new file.

Return to the browser and refresh. Notice your new changes. If they do not show up, you may have to empty the browser cache.

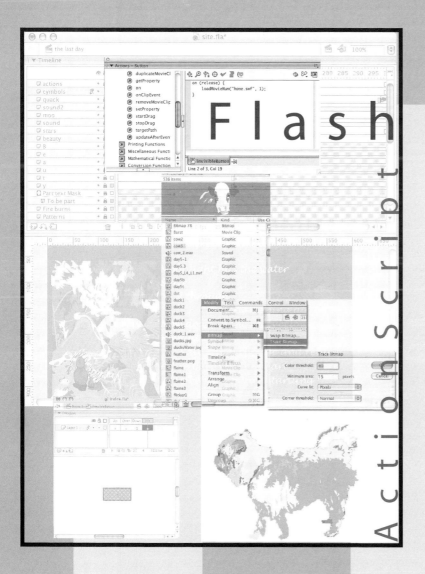

Flash

ActionScript

SECTION

| onstage: flash |

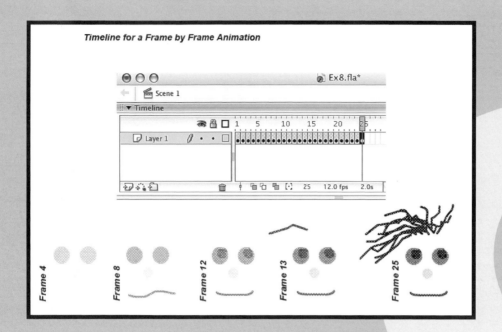

Timeline for a Frame by Frame Animation

an introduction to the Flash environment, frame-by-frame animation, and symbols

Objectives

Learn about Macromedia Flash.

Explore the Flash environment.

Discover how Flash frames are different than Dreamweaver frames.

Introduce some Flash tools.

Examine frame-by-frame animation.

Understand Flash symbols and their functions.

Introduction

Most Internet users think that Macromedia Flash is strictly for the advanced programmer who wants to do jazzy, razzle-dazzle animations to knock users' socks off. There is truth to this. Flash does provide a vast array of programming possibilities and since its introduction into the market, artists and programmers alike have used it to experiment and create delightful user experiences. However, Flash has become a desirable program for Web designers as well because it provides the ability to deliver vector images over the Web. Vector images download faster, display more clearly, and do not lose resolution when scaled up or down. Additionally, Flash offers streaming capabilities (we'll learn more about those soon) as well as scripting and animation.

Flash embeds all images into the published file so that when you upload, you need only upload the HTML file and the SWF (Flash) file. You do not need to upload images separately. This offers the advantage of never having an image that doesn't display, and eliminates the possibility that someone will hijack your images.

Flash Web sites can look as traditional or as animated and wild as you want. Only your imagination will limit the possibilities. What you need to know now is that Flash is as friendly to a novice as it is to the most advanced. So, gather all of your confidence and courage and let's go.

AN OVERVIEW OF FLASH

Again, Flash has become a desirable program for designers primarily because it provides the ability to deliver vector images over the Web. It is the first software to really achieve this successfully. Vector images keep file sizes down and are scalable, which means that you can maintain control of what your images look like when your user resizes the browser window. The entire window will stay in proportion as it grows or shrinks without losing image quality. Whereas bitmap instructions break a graphic into little dots and must tell the computer about each dot, vector instructions describe the graphic mathematically as a series of lines and arcs. This not only results in more rapid communication, it also provides consistent image quality.

Adobe Illustrator is also vector-based software. The two programs are very compatible, allowing the drawing capabilities of Illustrator to be used to full advantage in Flash. We'll examine this further in the next chapter. For now, examine Figure 8-3. Adobe Illustrator tools were used to draw these graphics before exporting them as SWF files. The SWF files were then

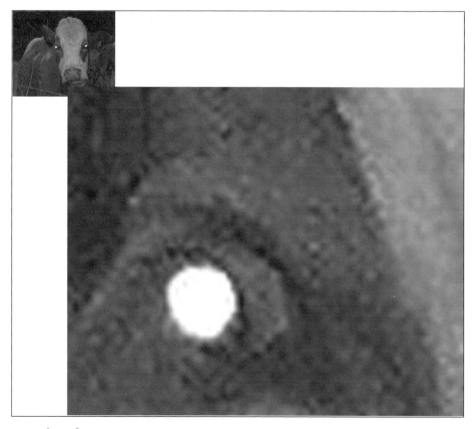

figure | 8-1 |

Scaled bitmap image

imported into Flash. See Color Plate 16 to view some of the files and a few Flash frames in color.

Additionally, Flash provides streaming capability. This means that once some of the vector art on your site has downloaded, Flash can display it while the rest of your data continues to download. As Flash plays the first frames of your movie, subsequent frames become available to your user's computer. Flash feeds them out at the specified frame rate. If you plan your movie right, the frames coming in stay caught up to the frames being displayed and your viewer sees a continuous flow of images—hence the word *streaming*. We'll continue to explore this with both images and sound.

figure | 8-2 |

Scaled vector image

In Flash, the word *frame* refers to a single unit of a layer in a document's timeline. In Dreamweaver, the word *frame* refers to a single unit of an organizational tool that divides an HTML document into two or more HTML documents viewable as one. Flash uses frames like pages in a book, displaying one frame at a time, 12 frames per second. Flash frames are displayed sequentially. Dreamweaver frames are displayed simultaneously. It is important to understand this major difference in the use of the word. Still, in both cases, *frame* can be understood by Oxford Dictionary's definition of a case or border enclosing a picture, etc., or basic rigid supporting structure.

Flash uses a scripting language called ActionScript. ActionScript codes interactivity, animation, and linking. Over the next few chapters, we'll learn some of the basic functions of ActionScript. You don't need to be nervous about ActionScript, even if you are completely frightened by computer programming. Flash makes it clear, simple, and easily understood at a beginner level, while offering very advanced features to the tech nerds among us.

It is as simple as this: Flash files are often referred to as *movies* and use the extension .SWF. (pronounced *swif*). Flash also includes a publishing feature that creates the necessary HTML

figure | 8-3 |

Illustrator-created SWF files imported into Flash

code to display your SWF in a Web browser. When uploading to the Internet, you will upload these two files via an FTP program.

See Color Plates 17 and 18 for great examples of student Flash Web sites.

STARTING AT THE BEGINNING

The Flash editing environment creates a new blank document when you enter it. Each document consists of three basic items:

- Timeline: a record of every frame, layer, and scene that makes up your document
- Stage: the actual area in which your images display
- Work area: the space that extends beyond the stage on all sides but is outside the visible frame of the final, published document

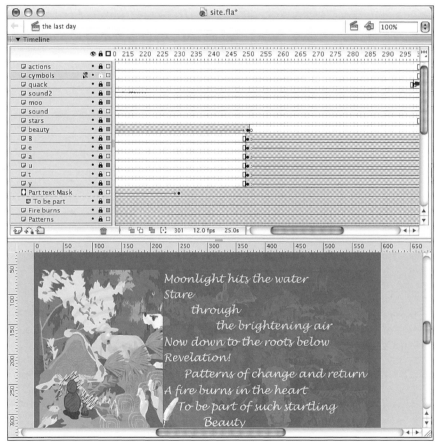

figure | 8-4 |

Flash Web site by the author (text by poet Starr Goode)

Think of a Flash movie as a book with each scene as a chapter and each frame as a page. Each page/frame may have transparent sheets stacked one on top of the other. In Flash, when you are editing, the frame that you click on in the timeline will be the frame that appears in the document window. The transparent sheets are called *layers*. Just as in Illustrator or Photoshop, you can hide, lock, and view outline only in any given layer.

The timeline is a vital and complex organizational and navigational tool. You can dock the timeline by clicking the bar at the top of the timeline or click any of the draggable window edges and drag the timeline to the edge of the document window. Release the mouse button when the pointer is at the edge of the win-

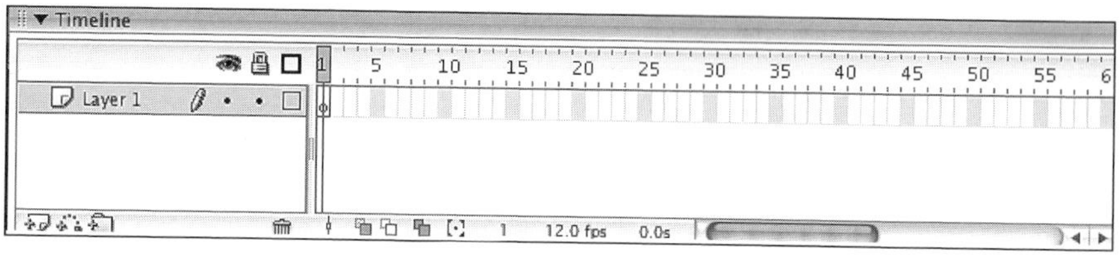

figure 8-5

Timeline

dow. You can dock the timeline vertically, which gives you easy access to several layers at a time, or horizontally, which increases the number of easily accessible frames. You can also hide a floating timeline simply by clicking the Close box. Finally, you can return the timeline to its standard position by dragging it back to the Scene bar.

The small red rectangle with a line extending down from it in the timeline is called the *playhead*. You can position the playhead where you want it to be simply by dragging it to that location. The position of the playhead will determine what you see on the stage.

Now let's briefly discuss the stage. This is the area where all of the graphic elements that make up your Flash document reside. Think of it as the screen on which you will project your movie. You control how big the screen is, what color it is, and all other parameters for viewing the Stage through the Document Properties dialog box. You can access this from the menu bar, select Modify>Document, press Command-J on a Mac, Control-J on a PC, or double-click on the Frame Rate icon in the timeline's status bar.

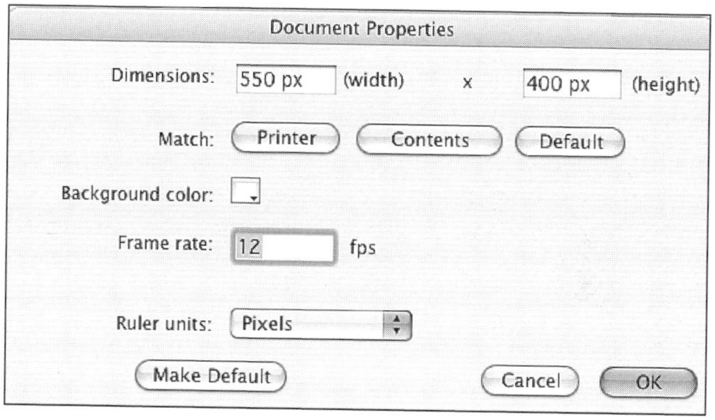

figure 8-6

Document Properties dialog box

It is in this dialog box that you set the size of your document, its background color, and the units of measure. You can access the units of measure by selecting the Ruler Units pop-up menu.

You also set the frame rate in this dialog box. Frames are the lifeblood of your animation and the frame rate is the heart that keeps the blood flowing at a certain speed. The default frame rate is 12 frames per second (fps).

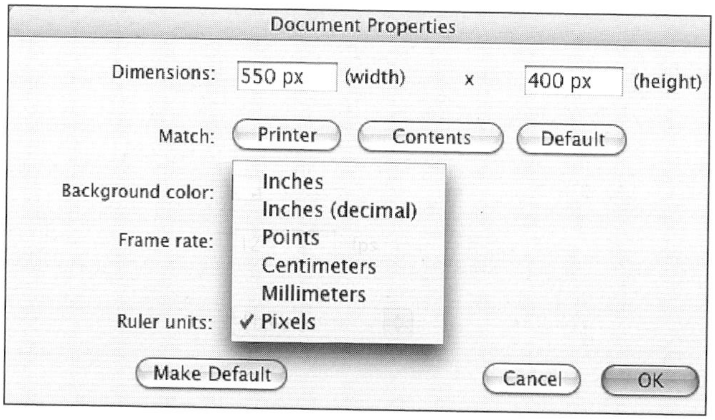

figure 8-7

Ruler Units pop-up Menu

THE FLASH TOOLBOX

As in Photoshop and Illustrator, Flash displays a toolbox on the left side of the document window.

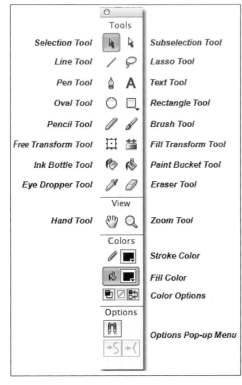

figure | 8-8 |

Flash toolbox

The first row of tools includes the Selection tool and the Subselection tool. These function in the same way as Illustrator's Select and Direct Select tools. The second row contains the Line tool and the Lasso tool. When you click on the Lasso tool, notice that new icons appear in the lower portion of the toolbox. These icons represent the Magic Wand, the Magic Wand Properties, and a Polygon mode. Click on the Magic Wand Properties icon to access a dialog box to change the settings.

Next are the Pen tool and the Text tool. These tools function much the same as in Illustrator or Photoshop. The Pen tool can be used to draw freehand and the Text tool is used to type or alter text. The fourth row contains the Oval tool and the Rectangle tool. Notice on the bottom-right corner of the Rectangle tool there is a small triangle indicating another tool is hidden beneath. When you click on the Rectangle tool, you will notice a change in the lower portion of the toolbox. This is the display for the corner radius settings for the rectangle. Click on the icon and the Rectangle Settings dialog box will display. Here you can type in the radius for the corners of the rectangle.

figure | 8-9 |

Lasso tool with icons for setting properties and setting dialog box

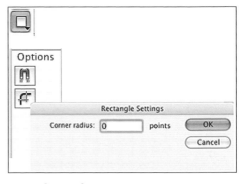

figure | 8-10 |

Toolbox Rectangle tool with icon for corner radius settings and Rectangle Settings dialog box

The fifth row of tools contains the Pencil tool and the Brush tool. Click the Pencil tool to access the Pencil options in the lower portion of the toolbox. Smoothness settings will show. Your choices are straighten, smooth, and ink. Click the Brush tool to access brush options. They include painting attributes, size and style of brush tip, and if you have a drawing tablet, whether or not the brush will respond to a drawing tablet pen's pressure and tilt.

The sixth row of tools contains the Free Transform tool and the Fill Transform tool. When you have drawn an object, be it graphic or text, you can select the object and then click on the Free Transform tool. This will then apply handles to the object that will allow you to scale in any direction, rotate, and adjust the object.

In the seventh row of tools are the Ink Bottle tool and the Paint Bucket tool. Change the colors in the toolbox, click on the Paint Bucket tool, and then click on the object. This will change the colors of the object. Similarly, the Paint Bucket tool has additional options that allow you to change the fill gap settings. Change the colors in the toolbox, click on the Ink Bottle tool, and then click on the line. This will change the colors of the line.

The last row of tools includes the Eyedropper and Eraser tools. These function pretty much the same as in Photoshop or Illustrator. Click on the Eraser tool to access additional settings, including brush tip size.

After all of these rows of tools, the next section in the toolbox is the View section. Select the Hand tool to move the document stage around in the document window. Select the Zoom tool to zoom in or out.

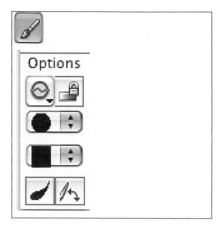

figure | 8-11 |

Brush tool options

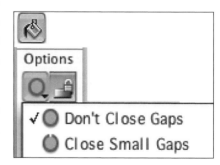

figure | 8-12 |

Paint Bucket tool options

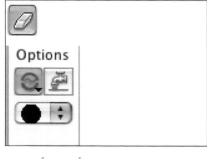

figure | 8-13 |

Eraser tool options

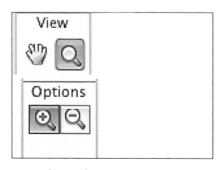

figure | 8-14 |

View section of the toolbox showing Zoom tool options

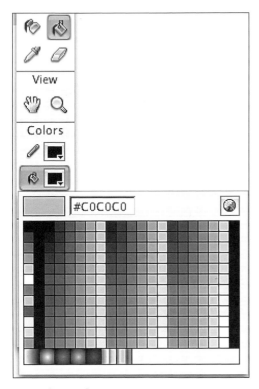

figure | 8-15 |

Paint Bucket icon with color palette

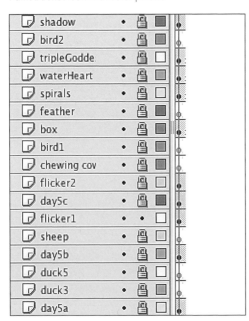

figure | 8-16 |

Layers in a Flash frame

The final section of the toolbox is the Colors section. The pencil icon is for strokes and lines. The paint bucket icon is for fills. Clicking on either of these icons will bring up a Web-safe color palette. Below these two icons are three smaller icons. The first is for a black stroke, white fill. The second is no color and the third swaps the stroke and fill colors. Just select the appropriate icon to apply.

You can access additional color options fom the menu bar. Select Window>Design Panels>Color Mixer or Window>Design Panels>Color Swatches.

FRAME-BY-FRAME ANIMATIONS

Traditional animators paint individual characters (or parts of characters) and objects on transparent sheets called *cels*. They stack the cels to create the entire image for the frame. The cel technique allows animators to save time by reusing parts of an image that stays the same in more than one frame. In Flash, you can also make frame-by-frame animations by placing different content in different frames. Flash calls the frames that hold new content *keyframes*, and what traditional animators referred to as *cels* are called *layers*.

You can create frame-by-frame animations by adding keyframes and making changes to the existing object. With each change, you need a keyframe.

figure | 8-17 |

Frame-by-frame animation (by student Paul Powers)

CREATING KEYFRAMES

In Flash, from the menu bar, choose Insert>Timeline>Blank Keyframe to define a keyframe that is empty. Select Insert>Timeline>Keyframe to define a keyframe that duplicates the content of the preceding keyframe in that layer. Select Insert>Timeline>Blank Keyframe when you want to change the contents of the Stage. Use Insert>Timeline>Keyframe when you want to duplicate the content of the preceding keyframe.

A dark bullet in a frame in the timeline indicates a keyframe with content. A hollow square indicates the last frame of that content; the gray tint on the frames in between indicates the continuing content. To add frames with no change in content, select Insert>Timeline>Frame.

figure | 8-18 |

Insert pull-down menu

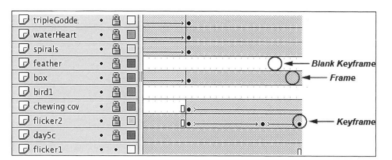

figure | 8-19 |

Blank keyframe, keyframe, and frame in timeline

SYMBOLS

Both Flash and Illustrator work with elements that are identified as *symbols*. Any element can be converted to a symbol, or you can create a symbol as such at the outset. A symbol automatically becomes part of a document's library. It can then be reused as many times as you need without adding to the file size. Defining an element as a symbol helps to keep a file size small. Converting a pixel image to a symbol will reduce the size of the image dramatically. Consider the trade-off between resolution and file size. Whenever possible, choose the file size as more important than the resolution.

Symbols have three behaviors: graphic, button, and movie clip.

Graphic symbols are static. A Graphic symbol operates in sync with the timeline of the current document, taking up one frame of the document in which you place it. You can use a graphic symbol for frame-by-frame animation. For example, a three frame-animated graphic symbol will take up three frames of the document.

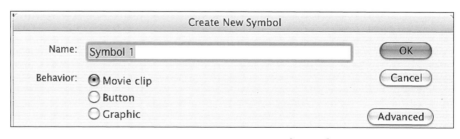

figure | 8-20 |

Create New Symbol window

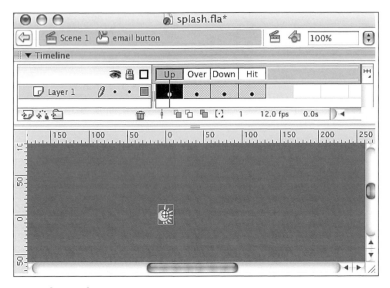

figure | 8-21 |

Button symbol timeline

Button symbols have their own four-frame timeline and sit in a single frame of the document.

Movie clip symbols have their own multiframe timeline. A movie clip symbol will take up one frame of the document's timeline but will play independently. It can also be multi-layered.

Symbols can be nested in any order. For example, a button symbol may have a movie clip in its Over State, or a graphic symbol may have a button symbol with a movie clip nested inside of it. There is no limit to the nesting. Some Flash Web site designers use movie clips as an organizational tool with each Movie Clip representing a "page" in the Web site.

figure | 8-22 |

Movie clip symbol timeline

As mentioned previously, you can create your graphics in Illustrator and export them as Flash (SWF) files. When you export, Illustrator will give you three choices: AI File to SWF File, AI Layers to SWF Frames, or AI Layers to SWF File. You can then import that SWF into a Flash movie. It will import as separate pieces. You then need to marquis the entire object in Flash and choose Modify>Convert to a Symbol or Modify>Group in order to keep the pieces together.

The beauty of symbols is that you can use them as often as you want without adding to the file size. Each time you use a symbol, it is called an *instance*. You can drag a symbol from the library onto the stage anytime you want to use it. If you want, you can change the properties of each instance. For example, you can change the tint or alpha. You change the properties of a symbol's instance through the Properties window. Access this window simply by clicking on the symbol once you have dragged it onto the stage.

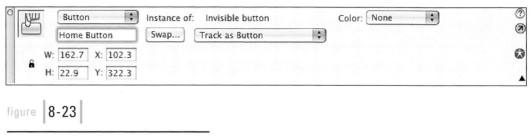

figure | 8-23 |

Properties window of a symbol's instance

SUMMARY

This is only your first venture into Flash and already you've learned how to create a cute little movie. You've explored the tools and work environment of Flash. You've learned how to draw shapes, lines, and how to alter them. You've also learned how to move around the timeline and create an animation using frame-by-frame animation.

in review

1. What is the document work area called?

2. How do you draw a circle with a Flash tool?

3. What is the timeline?

4. What is the playhead?

5. What is the difference between a keyframe and a blank keyframe?

6. What are a few ways to alter a shape or line?

exercise 8

1. Open Flash.

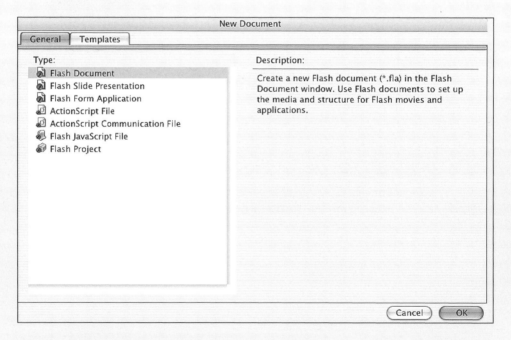

New Document

General | Templates

Type:
- Flash Document
- Flash Slide Presentation
- Flash Form Application
- ActionScript File
- ActionScript Communication File
- Flash JavaScript File
- Flash Project

Description:

Create a new Flash document (*.fla) in the Flash Document window. Use Flash documents to set up the media and structure for Flash movies and applications.

Cancel   OK

figure | 8-Ex1 |

New Flash document

Take some time to look around the timeline, the stage, the toolbox, and the palettes. Familiarize yourself with the pull-down menus.

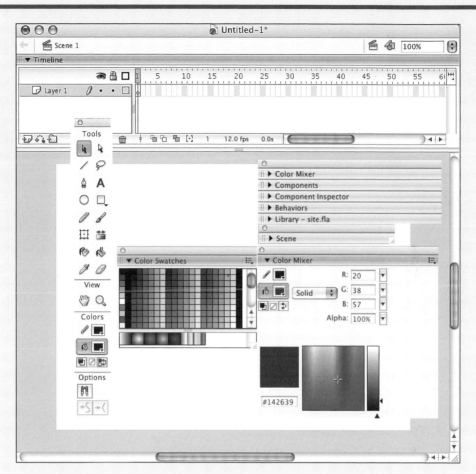

2. In the toolbox Color section, change the fill and stroke to a medium blue. On the stage, in Frame 1, use the Oval tool to create a solid circle (holding down the Shift key while drawing will constrain the oval to a circle).

figure 8-Ex2

Timeline, stage, tools, and palettes

figure 8-Ex3

Frame 1 circle on document stage

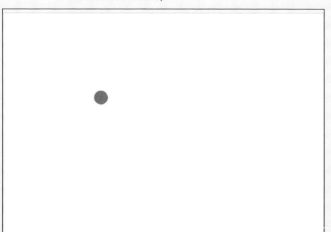

3. In the timeline, click in Frame 2. From the Insert pull-down menu, choose Timeline and Keyframe. This will insert a keyframe in Frame 2. With the Selection tool, marquis the circle and move it slightly up and to the right.

4. Click in Frame 3 and again add a keyframe. Marquis the circle with the Selection tool and move it slightly down and to the right. You can use your arrow keys to accomplish this.

5. Click in Frame 4 and add a keyframe. Again marquis the circle. Hold down the Shift key and the Option key on a Mac, Control key on a PC, as you copy/drag the circle to the right. You will now have two circles on the stage that are on the same horizontal plane.

figure | 8-Ex4 |

Two circles on document stage

6. Click in Frame 6 and add a keyframe. Change the fill and stroke colors to peach. Draw a smaller circle between and below the two blue circles.

figure | 8-Ex5 |

Two blue circles and one smaller peach circle on document stage

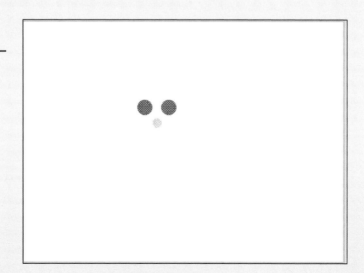

7. Click in Frame 7 and add a keyframe. Choose the selection tool and click on a blank area of the stage to deselect all objects. Change the stroke color to a deep red. With the Pen tool, draw a crooked line to the right of all three circles and slightly below the peach circle.

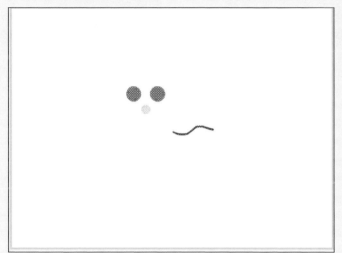

figure | 8-Ex6 |

Three circles and crooked line on document stage

8. Click in Frame 8 and add a keyframe. With the Selection tool, marquis the line and move it to the left but still to the right of the smaller circle. Return to the Pen tool. Zoom into the crooked line so that you can see the individual points in the line. With the tool, alter some of the points to change the line in some way. Also, delete a few points simply by holding the Pen tool over the points. Notice that the Pen tool now has a small minus next to it. This indicates that if you click, you will delete the point.

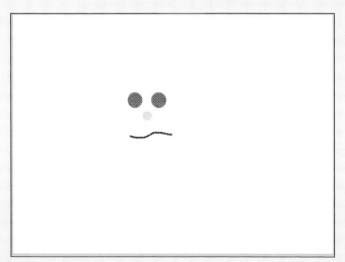

figure | 8-Ex7 |

Three circles with line adjusted on document stage

9. Click in Frame 9 and add a keyframe. Again move the line to the left but not completely under the three circles. With the Pen tool, alter the line in some way. You can alter with the Pen tool by clicking on existing points to delete them, or click on a segment to add a point. Use the Subselection tool to move a point or change the curve of a point.

10. Click in Frame 10 and add a keyframe. This time move the line so that it sits under the three circles. With the Pen tool, delete most of the points. Choose the Subselection tool and grab the handles of either end and curve the path upwards to form a smile.

figure | 8-Ex8 |

Three circles and line as a smile on document stage

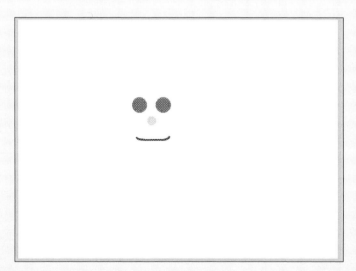

11. Click in Frame 11 and add a keyframe. Click in a blank area of the stage to deselect all. Change the fill and stroke colors to black. In the top left circle, draw a smaller circle in the upper-right section. Move the Playhead to Frame 12 and add a keyframe. Carefully marquis (or double click) the black circle and Shift-Option on a Mac, Shift-Control on a PC, and drag it to the same position in the right circle.

figure | 8-Ex9 |

Frame 12 with competed face on a document stage

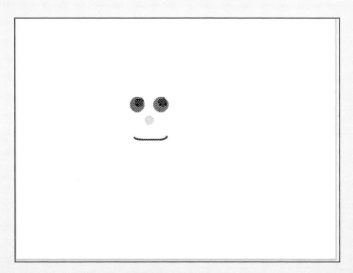

12. Click in Frame 13 and add a keyframe. Set the Pencil tool to Smooth in the Options window.

Use the Pencil tool to draw a line of hair.

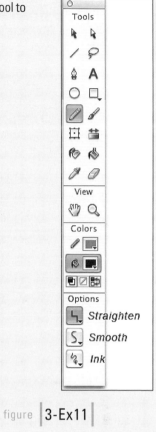

figure | 8-Ex10 |

Frame 13 with completed face and a line of hair on document stage

figure | 3-Ex11 |

Settings for pencil tool

13. Move the playhead frame by frame, adding keyframes in each one. Continue to draw new lines of hair in each keyframe until you reach Frame 25 and have a relatively full head of hair.

figure | 8-Ex12 |

Completed drawing in Frame 25 on document stage

14. Save the file as exer8. Choose Control>Test Movie. Watch the drawing appear step by step. When the frame-by-frame animation meets your satisfaction, save and show your friends.

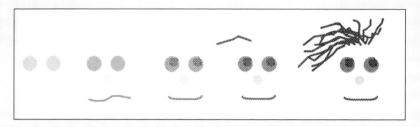

figure | 8-Ex13 |

Completed Exercise 8 in player window

on your own

You can stretch out the animation of a frame-by-frame movie by extending the action with frames in between the keyframes. Return to the timeline of the exercise. In Frame 3, from the menu bar, select Insert>Timeline>Frame. You can repeat this several times throughout the timeline, adding only one frame to a keyframe, or you can add several frames. Try adding five frames for most of the keyframes and only one frame for others. There will be longer periods between the actions when you add more frames.

Varying the timing creates a more realistic illusion. Experiment to see how adding frames can affect your playback.

notes

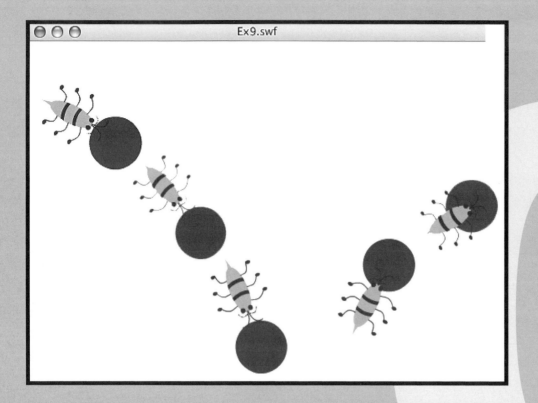

creating motion tweens, motion guides and illustrator swfs

Objectives

Learn about motion tweens.

Discover the Motion Tween Properties window.

Examine motion guides.

Explore guide paths and onion skinning.

Create an object in Illustrator and export as a SWF for use in Flash.

Examine the interactivity between Illustrator and Flash.

Introduction

In this chapter, we'll explore animation created by Flash motion tweens. Because only the keyframes on either end of a motion tween add to a file size, motion tweens create substantially smaller files than frame-by-frame animations. We'll learn how to create motion tweens and have them respond to a motion guide. We'll then learn how to draw a guide path, snap objects to it, and view progress through onion skinning. We'll also delve more deeply into Illustrator's ability to interact with Flash and the various export options that Illustrator offers.

MOTION TWEENS

When you apply a motion tween to a graphic, Flash creates in-between frames, breaking the motion into a series of small changes through a mathematical process. This in effect accomplishes frame-by-frame animation with a formula. Keyframes are required on either end of a motion tween. You create a motion tween by selecting Insert>Timeline>Create Motion Tween from the menu bar.

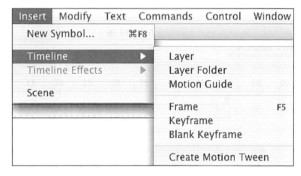

figure | 9-1 |

Insert pull-down menu

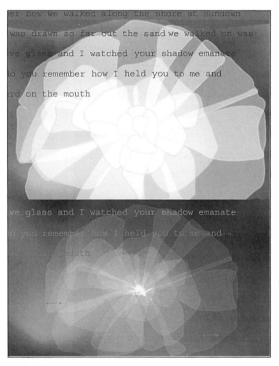

figure | 9-2 |

Example of a motion tween changing from an 80% alpha to a 10% alpha

Applying a motion tween to a graphic immediately converts it to a graphic symbol. Flash can only create motion tweens from symbols or grouped objects.

You must begin by defining the frames in the timeline. Start with the opening frame and position the object where the animation is to begin. From the menu bar, select Insert>Timeline> Create Motion Tween. A dashed line will appear in the layer of the timeline. Move the playhead to where you want to close the animation and insert a second keyframe. Move the symbol to where you want the animation to end or change the beginning. Either way, Flash will create the in-between frames. You can also change the properties of either the first frame or the final frame of the motion tween by clicking on the symbol and changing the properties in the Properties window. Accordingly, Flash will add the in-between changes. For example, if you change the alpha of the instance in the last frame of the motion tween to 0%, Flash will gradually change the symbol to disappear by the end of the tween.

Once you have created a motion tween, you can always add more keyframes within it to create additional instances of the symbol. The Properties window is accessible for each keyframe and instance to give you more options for changes.

Finally, you can "ease" a motion tween in or out through the Properties window. You can access the Ease option by clicking in either the beginning or ending keyframe of the tween. In the Properties window, manually type in a number between −100 and 100 or use the sliding bar. −100 will slow down the motion for a few frames and 100 will speed up the motion for a few frames. This adds a subtlety that can make the animation seem more natural.

You can also change the timing of an animation by adding or deleting frames between the keyframes. Keep in mind that adding frames will slow down the animation. Deleting frames will speed up the animation.

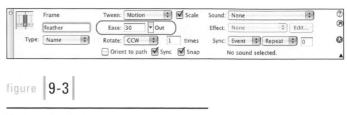

figure 9-3

Easing option in the Properties window

MOTION GUIDES

You can add guide paths to your symbol's movement in a motion tween. The Add Motion Guide Layer button is at the bottom of the timeline.

Flash adds the motion guide layer directly above the layer you select and gives it a default name of *Guide:* followed by the name of the layer you selected. The motion guide icon then appears next to the layer name. Flash also indents the layer linked to the motion guide layer. You can add as many layers as you want to a motion guide.

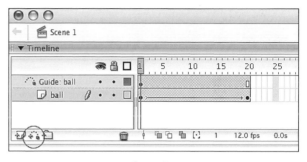

figure 9-4

Add Motion Guide button in timeline

The motion guide layer is the layer that contains the path that will be the guide. To create this path, with the motion guide layer highlighted, use the Pencil tool to draw it on the stage. This path can be curvy and move in any direction. However, too many sharp turns in the path will diminish its effectiveness. This is something to remember. If your graphic doesn't seem to be following your path, no matter how many times you snap, try redrawing your path more smoothly.

In the first key frame of the motion tween, drag the symbol to reposition the registration mark directly over the beginning of this path. (The registration mark is the small circle in the symbol. It is usually in the center of the symbol; its location can be defined in the Create or Convert to Symbol dialog box.)

For Flash to move a symbol along a motion path, the center of the item must snap to both the beginning and the end of the path. In the Properties panel, check the Snap checkbox to have Flash assist you in centering keyframe graphics over the beginning of the guideline. (See Figure 9-3.) This is critical for the animation to work. In the final frame, drag the symbol to reposition its registration mark directly over the end of the motion path. Flash redraws the

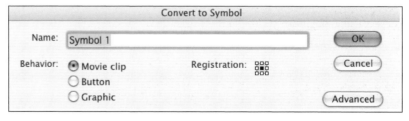

figure 9-5

Convert to Symbol window showing registration mark

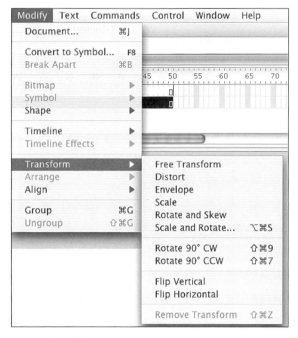

figure | 9-6 |

Modify pull-down menu

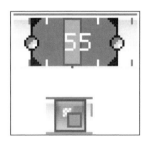

figure | 9-7 |

Onion Skinning icon in the timeline with effects showing on the document stage

in-between frames so that the symbol follows the motion path. In the published document, Flash hides the motion path. You only see the symbol moving.

After you draw the motion path and reposition the registration mark, lock the motion-guide layer to prevent yourself from editing the path accidentally as you snap the graphic to the guideline.

You can orient the movement along the path by choosing Orient to Path in the Properties window. You can also rotate a symbol by selecting Modify>Transform>Rotate and skew from the menu bar.

Choose the Frame in which you would like to reorient your symbol and from the menu bar, select Insert>Timeline>Keyframe. Select the symbol and from the menu bar, select Modify>Transform>Rotate and Skew to reorient the symbol to your liking. Flash will then redraw the in-between frames.

Onion skinning is an option that allows you to see how an item moves along the path. Click on the Onion Skinning icon to engage this setting.

Drag the playhead along the timeline to see the onion skin effect revealing the steps of the Motion Tween.

DRAWING AND EXPORTING IN ILLUSTRATOR

As we have discussed a number of times, Adobe Illustrator is vector-based. Remember that vector-based means that objects are based on formulas for dots and lines rather than pixels. This simplifies and speeds up the process for defining a shape on the screen. Since Illustrator and Flash are both vector-based, files are completely compatible and the drawing capabilities of Illustrator can be used to full advantage in Flash.

In Illustrator, you can export a graphic or series of graphics to .SWF format either as a single .SWF document, Illustrator layers to Flash frames, or Illustrator layers to Flash files. This provides a distinct advantage for Flash users since the drawing tools of Illustrator are so much more sophisticated. See Color Plate 16 for an example of how Illustrator files can be used in Flash.

figure | 9-8 |

"Site" by the Author. Poem by Starr Goode. Adobe Illustrator tools were used to draw these graphics before exporting them as SWF files. The SWF files were then imported into Flash.

When you draw images intended for Flash in Illustrator, you can use any of the tools, including brushes and symbols. Illustrator's symbols do not translate precisely to symbols in Flash. However, they can easily be converted to graphic symbols once in Flash. If you do use a symbol or brush in Illustrator to create graphics, you can expand them from the menu bar of the Object. This converts the graphic to individual shapes. This means that once a symbol or brush has been expanded, instead of a formula-based object sitting on your Artboard, you now have a graphic that can have colors or shapes that can then be altered. This step is important. It allows you to make sure that colors in the Illustrator Symbol or Brush object can now be converted to Web-safe colors.

If you plan to export the entire graphic to one Flash file, then how you use layers to create the graphic is irrelevant. Otherwise, as you determine the use of layers, think about the animation you want to create.

If you would like an Illustrator graphic to appear as an animation in Flash, each layer in Illustrator can be exported to a frame in Flash. If you want to use this option, create the layers to make sequential sense in the animation. In Illustrator, in the Layers palette, you can Release to Layers or Reverse Layers in the Options window. Or you can drag layers around the Layers window simply by clicking and dragging. Consequently, you can build your graphic on one layer and then Release to Layers, or from the very beginning you can build your graphic thinking about how the layers will be translated into animation—perhaps a frame-by-frame animation in Flash. You can always make adjustments to the timeline once the frames have been imported.

Finally, if you want the layers to be exported as separate Flash files, you will again need to be aware of structure. You can import the separate SWF files into one Flash document or each

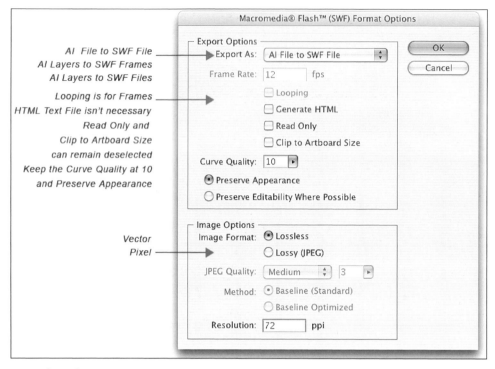

figure | 9-9 |

Annotated AI file to SWF Export dialog box

SWF file can be the beginning of a new Flash document. (We'll revisit this option in Chaper 15.) Or you may want to import separate SWF files onto different layers in one Flash document. The possibilities are quite endless.

You are given several options in the Illustrator dialog box for exporting:

- The Frame Rate option is only available when exporting an AI file to SWF frames. 12 fps (frames per second) is the default in Flash.

- The Looping option is also only available when exporting an AI file to SWF frames. This option isn't necessary, as you can always loop or repeat frames once you are in Flash.

- The Generate HTML option also is not necessary, as Flash will generate its own HTML.

- The Read Only option needs to be deselected, as you will want to convert the graphic to a symbol once you are in Flash.

- The Clip to Artboard Size option really isn't necessary either.

- Curve Quality refers to the resolution of lines and segments. Select the highest choice.

- The Preserve Appearance option should be selected.

- The Preserve Editability where possible should be deselected, as Flash really isn't capable of editing AI files.

- Image Options: Choose Lossless for AI to SWF to maintain vector quality. If you want to convert your object to a JPEG, then export as a JPEG instead of a SWF. There are times

figure | 9-10 |

"Remember" by the Author. Poem by Rose Marcario. This background was created in Adobe Illustrator with a gradient mesh applied. It was then exported as a JPEG.

when you will want to export an AI file as a JPEG. If you have used a Gradient Mesh or rasterized an image, then exporting as a JPEG is a better choice and will maintain the quality of the object.

• Resolution should be 72 ppi for screen resolution.

See Color Plates 19 and 20 for additional images drawn in Illustrator and exported as SWFs for use in Flash Web sites.

SUMMARY

In this Chapter, you have learned a second method of how to create an animation in Flash. You also examined the export options of Illustrator. Furthermore, you've learned how to create a motion tween and a motion guide, and you've learned how to orient an object to a path, change its course, and alter its timing.

in review

1. Where do you locate Create Motion Tween?

2. What is a motion tween?

3. What happens to an object when you apply a motion tween to it?

4. What is a motion guide?

5. How do you make an object follow a given path?

6. How do you transfer an object from Illustrator to Flash?

exercise 9

1. Open a new document in Flash.

2. On the stage, in Frame 1, use the Oval tool to create a circle like you did in Exercise 8. Give it a fill of deep red.

3. Open the `Library` from the menu bar selecting Window>Library (or press Command-L on a Mac, Control-L on a PC). The Library will probably be empty.

figure | 9-Ex1 |

Library window

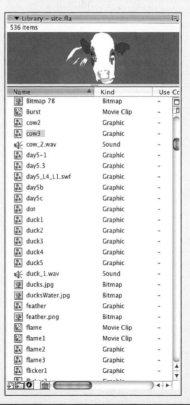

4. Marquis the circle with the Selection tool, making certain to select all of it. From the menu bar, select Modify>Convert to Symbol (or press F8).

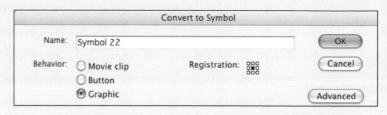

figure | 9-Ex2 |

Convert to Symbol dialog box

5. Name the symbol *ball* and choose Behavior: Graphic. Click OK. Make certain you see the circle in the Library window and then delete it from the stage.

6. In the timeline, double-click the layer name and rename it *ball*. Click and drag your new circle symbol from the Library window to the stage. Place it in the upper left corner.

7. In the timeline, select Frame 20 and choose Insert>Timeline>Frame (or press F5).

8. In the timeline, select Frame 1. From the menu bar, select Insert>Timeline>Create Motion Tween. Flash will define Frames 1 through 20 as a motion tween but with a broken line, indicating that the tween is not yet complete.

9. In the timeline, position the playhead in Frame 20 and choose Insert>Timeline> Keyframe. Flash will now complete the motion tween but you still need to alter the symbol to have it do something. Click in Frame 20 and on the stage, drag the circle to a new position in the far lower-right corner. Flash will redraw the in-between Frames of 2–19 to reflect this reposition.

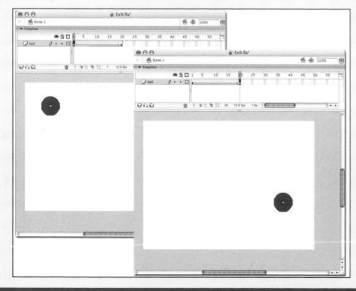

10. Notice that the broken line in the timeline is now a solid line with an arrow at the end. This indicates that the motion tween is complete. It is important to *always* complete your motion tweens.

figure | 9-Ex3 |

Timeline with completed motion tween showing symbol in a new position

11. Move the playhead to Frame 20 and click on the symbol. In the Properties window, choose Color>Tint. Change the tint to R:100, G:0, B:150.

12. Return to Frame 1 and in the Properties window, set the Easing to –100.

figure | **9-Ex4**

Properties window showing easing from frame 1 and tint formula

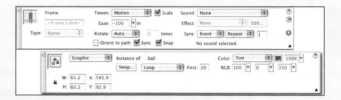

13. From the menu bar, select Control>Test Movie and watch your circle move in a straight path as it changes color. Notice the slower action at the beginning of the movement. This is because of the easing.

    Return to the stage.

14. Now you'll add a motion guide to govern the movement of the circle. Make sure that the playhead is in Frame 1. At the bottom of the timeline, click the Add Motion Guide icon.

figure | **9-Ex5**

Timeline with Motion Guide icon

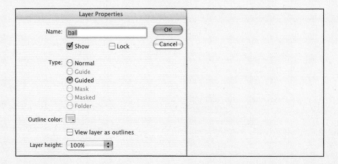

Flash will add the motion guide layer directly above the layer you selected and give it the default name *Guide:* followed by the name of the layer you selected. The Motion Guide icon will appear next to the layer name. Flash will also indent the layer linked to the Motion Guide layer. These linked layers are defined as guided layers in the Layer Properties dialog box. Access this box from the menu bar by selecting Modify>Timeline>Layer Properties.

figure | **9-Ex6**

Layer Properties dialog box

15. With the motion guide layer highlighted, use the Pencil tool to draw a line on the stage showing the path you want the symbol to take. Note that under Options in the

toolbox you can choose straighten, smooth, or ink to affect the flow of your pencil. You can smooth the path even further by selecting it and clicking the Smooth icon as many times as you want.

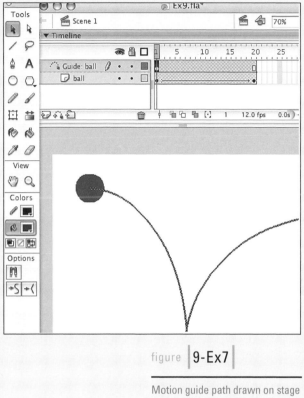

figure | 9-Ex7 |

Motion guide path drawn on stage with Pencil tool and Smooth icon

After you draw the motion path, lock the motion guide layer to prevent yourself from editing the path accidentally as you snap the symbol to the guideline. Make certain that Snap to Objects is checked under the View pull-down menu.

16. Highlight the ball layer and in Frame 1, drag the circle to reposition its registration mark directly over the beginning of the motion path. For Flash to move an item along a motion path, the registration mark of the item must snap to the path. You should be able to feel the snap.

17. In the timeline, on the ball layer, click on Frame 20 and drag the circle to reposition its registration mark directly over the end of the motion path.

18. Test your movie (Control>Test Movie).

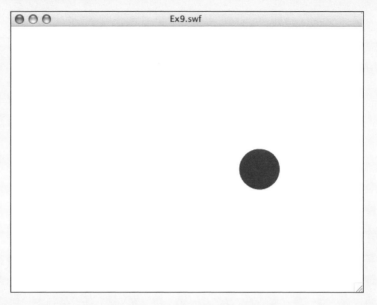

figure | 9-Ex8 |

Exercise 9 in test movie window

If your ball does not follow the path, go back and make certain that the registration mark snapped to the ends of the path in Frames 1 and 20.

19. Save the file as exer9.

20. Open Illustrator. Load the Web-safe color palette from the menu bar by selecting Window>Swatch libraries>Web. Draw a dragonfly, bee, or other bug with a definite head using Web-safe colors. You can draw the entire bug on the same layer if you want, since you will be exporting the bug as an AI file to a SWF file. Be playful and have fun.

21. Save your file, then choose File>Export. Export as bug.SWF with AI File to SWF File chosen in the Format Options dialog box.

figure | 9-Ex9 |

Drawing of bug on Illustrator Artboard

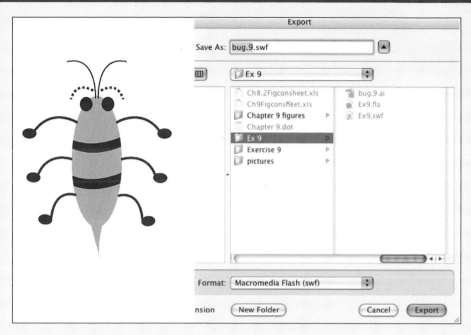

figure 9-Ex10

Illustrator drawing with Export window

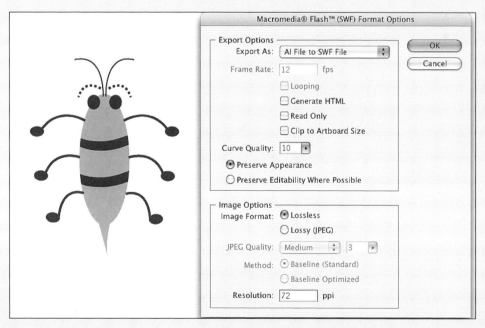

figure 9-Ex11

Illustrator drawing with AI File to
SWF File chosen in the Format
Options dialog box

22. Return to your Flash movie. Add a new layer to the guide by highlighting the Ball layer. Click the Insert Layer button. Flash will add a new indented (guided) layer above the selected layer. You now have two layers that will respond to the same motion guide. Name this layer *bug*.

Timeline showing motion guide layer and Ball and Bug indented layers

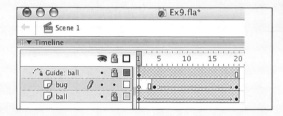

23. Under View>Snapping, deselect Snap to Objects.

24. Select File>Import to stage. Locate bug.SWF and import it to the stage.

25. Once the imported bug is placed on the stage, marquis it with the Selection tool and choose Modify>Convert to Symbol. Name the symbol *bug* and choose Behavior: Graphic. Make certain that the registration mark is set at centered. (See Figure 9–Ex2)

26. Check to see that the bug now shows up in the Library window as a graphic symbol. Then delete the bug object from the stage.

27. Turn on Snap to Objects (View>Snapping>Snap to Objects) again. In Frame 1, drag your new bug symbol from the Library window to the top left corner of the stage, making certain to snap it to the guide path. Rotate the bug to face the direction of the path. From the menu bar, select Modify>Transform>Rotate and skew. Alternately, with the bug selected, click the Transform tool in the toolbox. Transform handles will be applied to the bug. Grab the corner handles of your bug and rotate.

28. On the bug layer, in Frame 1, choose Insert>Timeline>Create Motion Tween. With your cursor still in Frame 1, set the easing to –100 in the Properties window.

29. Click in Frame 20 on the bug layer. From the menu bar, select Insert>Timeline>Keyframe. Drag the bug to the end of the motion path, ensuring that its registration mark snaps to the end point. Rotate appropriately.

30. Finally, orient this graphic along the path by returning to Frame 1 and checking the Orient to Path box in the Properties

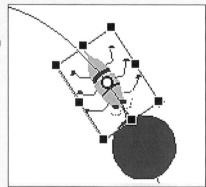

Bug on stage with transform handles

window. Flash redraws the tween. In the in-between Frames, Flash rotates the tweened item to align it with the path more naturally. (The Orient to Path option does not always create the most natural positions for your graphic.)

31. Step through the tween one Frame at a time. You can move forward and backward in the timeline with the comma and period keys on your keyboard.

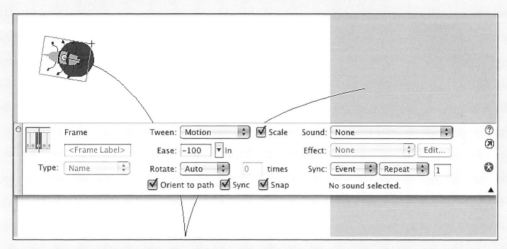

When you get to a frame where Flash has positioned the graphic poorly, you can fix it. In the timeline, select the in-between frame where you want to rotate the Symbol. From the menu bar select Insert>Timeline>Keyframe. In the new keyframe Flash creates, select the graphic and rotate it manually with the Transform tool (or Modify>Transform>Rotate and Skew) to align it with the motion guide. Flash will then redraw the in-between frames.

figure | **9-Ex14**

Bug on stage with Properties window

32. Turn on onion skinning to see how the item moves along the path. Drag the playhead from Frame 1 to Frame 20 to watch the onion skin effect. Then deselect onion skinning.

33. Test your movie.

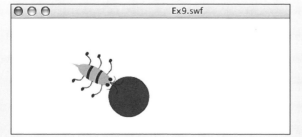

figure | **9-Ex15**

Movie window showing bug and ball

Your movie should look like the bug is on top of the circle moving at the same rate.

34. Now you'll make the bug look like it is chasing the ball. Return to the document. In the timeline, select Frame 1 of the bug layer. Grab the keyframe from Frame 1 and drag it to Frame 4.

figure | 9-Ex16 |

Moving a frame along the timeline

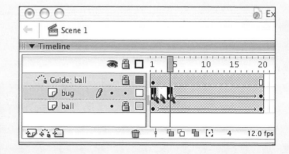

35. Test your movie again. The bug should now appear to be chasing the circle. Move the keyframe further along the timeline if necessary to improve the appearance of a chase.

36. Make changes as desired. Be creative. When all looks correct, save and show your friends!

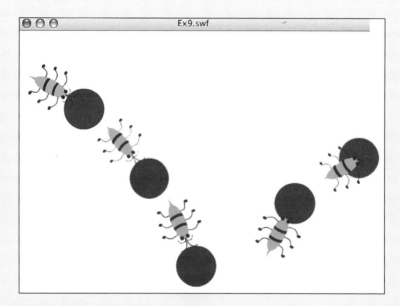

figure | 9-Ex17 |

Complete Exercise 9 in player window

on your own

Create a bird in Illustrator. Export the bird as an AI file to SWF file. Import the bird into the Flash Library. Add a new layer and name it bird. Add a keyframe at Frame 10 and drag the bird from the Library window onto the stage. In Frame 10, create a motion tween, adding a keyframe in the last frame of the document. Then add a motion guide layer to the bird layer and draw a path that crisscrosses the bug path several times. Snap the bird to the path on either end of the motion tween. Have the bird chase the bug, adjusting your document as needed to always have the bird arrive at the crossroads of the bug path just a little too late.

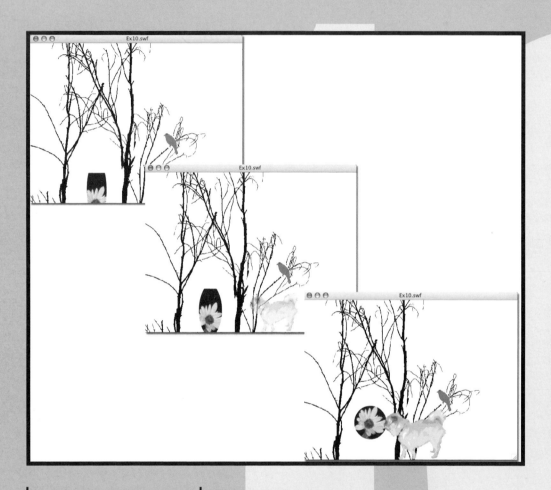

masks and raster images

Objectives

Explore masking.

Learn how to apply animation to both masked images and the mask.

Examine working with raster images in Flash.

Delve into the interactivity between Photoshop and Flash.

Discover the Bitmap Break Apart function.

Introduce the Trace Bitmap function.

Introduction

In this chapter, we'll delve into working with masks and raster images from Photoshop in Flash. A mask can add complexity to your Web site, spark interest, and engage your viewer. Masks create window effects for any number of images that cross the stage. Both the mask (the window) and the masked images can be animated.

Pixel images offer yet another creative venue. We can import images into Flash maintaining transparent areas. We can "break apart" bitmaps, and alter them in a variety of ways. We can also "trace" a pixel image, consequently translating the image into a vector image with the possibility of additional manipulation. We'll explore several of these options.

MASKS AND RASTER IMAGES

MASKS

A Flash mask is like a window envelope. There may be several sheets of papers covered with information inside that envelope, but the outside presents a blank white front with just a little window that lets you see the portion of the letter showing the name and address. The mask is the window of the envelope and the linked, or masked, layers are the papers inside. You can move the window around to see the various bits of information, or you can move the papers beneath the window around, or you can do both. You can also animate the window.

Any filled shape(s) on a defined mask layer becomes a window in the final movie. That window reveals whatever lies on the linked (or masked) layer(s) below. Beneath the mask you can have several layers that act just like any other Flash layers. Any areas of the mask that are left blank hide the corresponding areas of all the masked layers. However, any unlinked layers outside and below the mask will show through both the blank areas and the mask shapes.

figure | 10-1 |

Diagonal mask revealing the page beneath
(by student Orly Osman)

Masks offer you the ability to slowly reveal an image or parts of an image, and can add interest to a page design. For example, if your Web page is rather static, sitting on a horizontal/vertical grid, consider adding a diagonal mask to slowly reveal the entire page or parts of a page.

Creating a Mask

Flash uses only fills to create masks and ignores any lines on a mask layer. A mask may consist of several shapes, but they must all be on the same layer. You can use several editable shapes, or you can create one group or symbol that contains all the shapes. If you combine editable shapes and a group or symbol, Flash uses just the editable shapes to create the mask. If you have two or more groups or symbols, Flash uses just the bottom-most group or symbol. No matter what kind of fill (gradient, transparent, opaque) you use to draw your mask, Flash creates a completely open window out of it.

To create a mask and masked layers, begin by naming the layers. When building a mask, you should create the layer directly above the layer containing the content that you want to mask, although you can always create the mask separately and link the masked layers to it later.

Begin by highlighting the layer you want to turn into a mask. From the Modify pull-down menu, choose Timeline>Layer Properties to display the Layer Properties dialog box. In the Type section, select Mask and rename the layer to identify it as a mask. Click OK. Flash turns the selected layer into a mask and changes the layer icon.

Next, on the stage, draw the shape you want as the window. You can use a shape tool or the pen tool with a fill. And you can apply a motion tween to the shape. For example, you may want the mask to start small, then grow to reveal the image(s) underneath. Conversely, you may want to begin with a full page and diminish the window to conceal the linked image. This would automatically reveal the unlinked images below. You can also have the mask move around to show only bits of information.

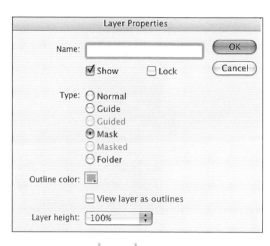

figure 10-2

Layer Properties dialog box

Now you need to add the images for which the mask will serve as a window. Create a new layer and add the image(s) you want to link to the mask. Have this layer sit just below the mask. To link layers to the mask, highlight this layer, then from the menu bar, select Modify> Timeline>Layer Properties to display the Layer Properties dialog box. Alternately, you can double-click on the layer icon to bring up this dialog box.

In the Type section, select Masked, name the layer, and then click OK. Flash links the selected layer to the mask directly above it, changes the layer icon, then indents the icon and layer name to indicate that this is a masked layer and that the mask above it is in control.

You can repeat these steps to create more linked layers. One mask can affect many linked layers. To link existing layers to a mask quickly, simply drag them along the Timeline so that they sit directly below the mask itself or one of its linked layers.

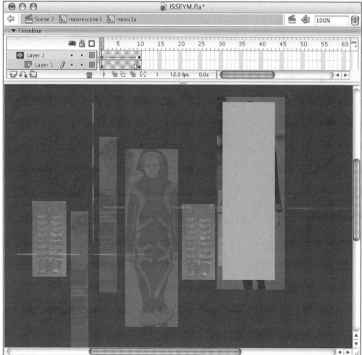

figure 10-3

Mask revealing image (by Student Orly Osman)

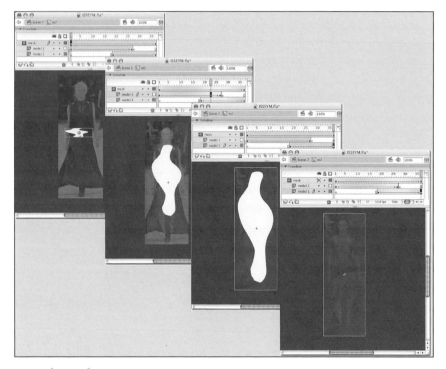

figure | 10-4 |

Timeline showing one mask and several masked layers
(by student Orly Osman)

As mentioned earlier, you can apply motion tweens to masked layers just as you would any layer. The masked layers may move into or out of a mask window or alternate with other Masked layers. You can even use a movie clip in a masked layer so that the animation moves through the window with its own timeline. We'll learn more about movie clips in Chapter 11.

RASTER IMAGES

The word *bitmap* may seem a bit confusing. Macromedia refers to *bitmap* as any raster image. But Adobe Photoshop uses the word differently.

Let's review. When we talk about raster images, we are referring to images defined by pixels or small squares. The term *raster* refers to a grid of pixels and, in fact, this grid can be defined in specific configurations. These configurations are made up of resolution definitions, including image resolution, pixel depth, monitor resolution, screen frequency, and output resolution.

We've talked about resolution versus download time, and we've discussed an image resolution of 72 pixels per inch (ppi) for the purposes of Web design. *Bit resolution* refers to the pixel depth and is the measurement of the number of bits of stored information per pixel. Without getting too technical here, let's just say that this value comes into play when we talk about bitmap images as defined by a Photoshop Mode. With a Photoshop bitmap image, there is only one bit per pixel: black or white. With grayscale and indexed color images, there are eight bits per pixel, and with RGB and CMYK there can be 24 bits per pixel, which translates to millions of colors.

Flash offers tools to play around with bitmapped images. But first you need to make certain that an image is truly defined as a bitmap in Photoshop. To convert an image to a bitmap in Photoshop, you must first convert it to grayscale, thus discarding the color information. From the menu bar select Image>Mode>Grayscale. Once you have converted to grayscale, you can return to the same pull-down menu. Bitmap will now be a choice available to you.

When we convert an image to a bitmap in Photoshop, we are reducing the bits per pixel to one. Again, we have choices here. We can give this conversion a 50% threshold, a pattern dither, a diffusion dither, a custom pattern, or a halftone screen. A 50% threshold is going to give you the most contrast. The different dithers will do just what it sounds like: apply different dithering patterns. Experiment with these settings so that you can see the difference for yourself.

Remember to create your images using the sound design principals we have discussed all along. Think about the concepts of metaphor, less is more, and emotional content. Even simple icons can reference a viewer's sense of play, the bizarre, or intelligence. No image needs to be benign, nor should it be boring.

figure | 10-5 |

Image pull-down menu

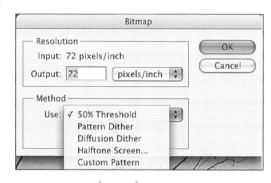

figure | 10-6 |

Bitmap conversion dialog box

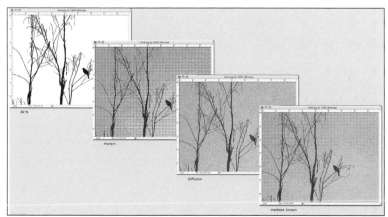

figure | 10-7 |

Four images showing bitmap conversion differences

To be able to transform the bitmap image into an editable image in Flash and edit separate areas, you need to create that separation in Photoshop. If you know you are going to want to paint a certain part of the bitmap in Flash, make sure that part is separated out in Photoshop. In other words, if the image is black in Photoshop, make sure that it has a white border around it. Then you will be able to isolate it for coloring in Flash.

Once you have converted the image to a bitmap, save it for the Web following the steps we discussed in Chapter 3. You can save this image as a 32-bit GIF with no dither.

USING TRANSPARENCY

Flash can import images with transparency and preserve the transparency, as long as the file was saved as a PNG in Photoshop. When Flash imports PNGs, it correctly reads the transparency values of the alpha channel.

To save a file as a PNG with a transparent background in Photoshop, you may need to delete the first default layer, named *Background*. Before deleting this layer, copy and paste what you want to preserve onto a new layer. You can use the Magic Wand tool to select and delete what you don't want.

figure | 10-8 |

Selecting areas with the Magic Wand tool

Alternately, you can duplicate the default layer and then clear the areas that you don't want.

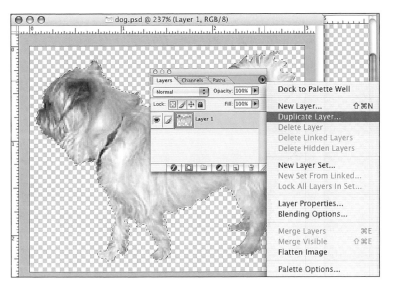

figure | **10-9** |

Photoshop Layers palette showing duplicate layer option

Either way, confirm the transparency. After making certain that everything you want to export is on the new layer, delete the Background layer. Do not flatten the file.

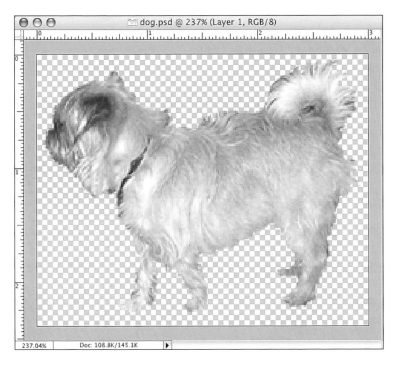

figure | **10-10** |

Photoshop image with transparent background

Save for the Web as a PNG-24 or PNG-128. When you save, make certain that the Transparency option is selected.

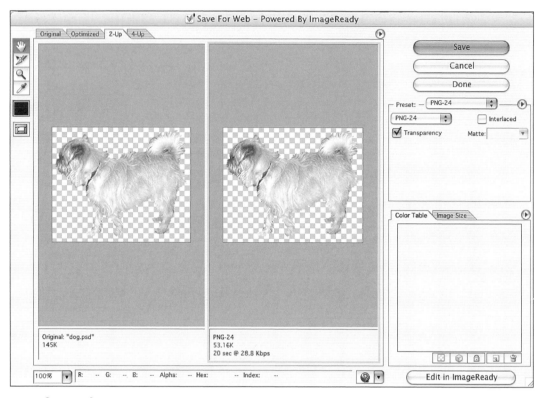

figure | 10-11 |

Save for Web as PNG-24 with Transparency option selected

Now you will be able to import the image into Flash and preserve the transparency.

CREATING AN EDITABLE BITMAP

One reason to convert an image to a bitmap for use in Flash is the increased opportunity for creativity. Once you have imported a bitmap image, you can select it, and from the Modify pull-down menu, choose Break Apart.

figure | 10-12 |

Imported image on stage

Breaking apart means to separate out each pixel into an individual object that is then editable.

After you have broken an image apart, you can use the lasso tool to select areas and repaint them or make other changes. You may need to play around with the Magic Wand settings to achieve the accuracy you need for selecting pixels. Select pixels you want to change by holding down the `Shift` key and clicking on the appropriate pixels. Then choose the Paint Bucket in the toolbox. Select a new fill color from the color palette. You can edit the selection as needed, choosing different colors as you go.

figure | 10-13 |

Modify pull-down menu

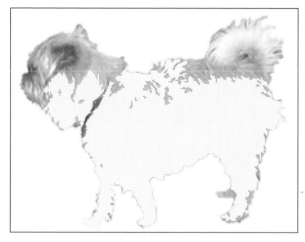

figure | 10-14 |

PNG broken apart and colored

TRACING AN IMAGE

In Flash, you can "trace" a pixel-based image. This results in a translation of the pixel image into a vector image of individual objects.

To begin the tracing process, import a JPG image into Flash. Select it and from the menu bar, select Modify>Bitmap>Trace. A new dialog box will open with setting options. All of these options refer to how detailed the translation will be from pixels to vector objects.

- *Color threshold* refers to how many colors will be chosen to translate to one color. This is a choice of 1 to 500, with 1 representing the most detail. More detail will likely result in a larger file.

- *Minimum area* refers to how many neighboring pixels should be included in calculating the color. Again, the smaller the number, the more detail and the larger a file.

- *Curve fit* refers to the outlines drawn in the creation of the vector shapes.

- *Corner threshold* refers to the sharpness or roundness of the vector shapes.

figure | 10-15 |

Traced image

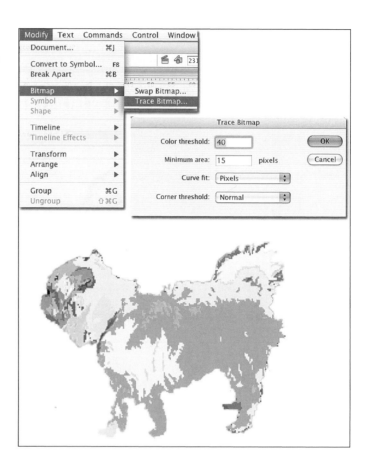

Generally speaking, when you are tracing a pixel-based image, you want to again consider quality versus download time. The more detailed the trace, the larger the resulting vector image. If one pixel equals one vector shape, the file size is going to be huge.

Once converted, the vector shapes can be chosen and altered in any number of ways.

Some designers use tracing to create and export vector image for use in Illustrator. When you are finished altering the vector image in Illustrator, using the software's sophisticated tools, you can export as a SWF file. You then have a new and improved vector image to reimport into Flash.

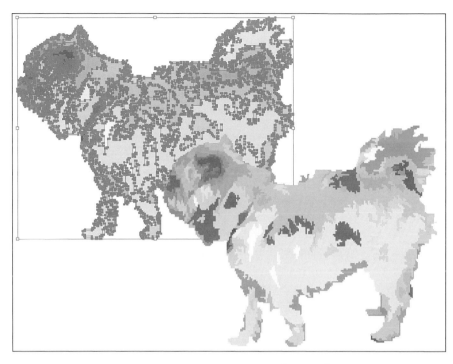

figure | **10-16** |

Image traced in Flash and altered in Illustrator

SUMMARY

In this chapter, you've learned about masks and working with raster images in Flash. Revealing images and transforming bitmaps are easily grasped design tools that can add a great deal of interest to your Web site. But animation is not a substitute for good Web design. The basic design principles that we have discussed throughout the book and will continue to discuss remain essential. Dynamic page layout, great color schemes, and clear, efficient navigation are still the most important issues when creating a compelling user experience—but animation can add interest. After all, we are a multitasking, multiengaging culture. Let your animation reflect this metaphorically and dynamically.

in review

1. What is a mask?

2. How do you define a masked layer?

3. Can you animate a mask?

4. What is a bitmap image?

5. What does it mean to "trace" an image?

6. How can you preserve transparency in an image for import into Flash?

exercise 10

1. From the Exercise 10 folder on the back of book CD, open bird.jpg in Photoshop. From the menu bar, select Mode>Grayscale. When the dialog box opens to ask you if you want to discard the color information, click OK.

2. Return to the Mode pull-down menu, this time choosing Bitmap. Choose Output 72 pixels/inch and 50% threshold.

figure | 10-Ex1 |

Bitmap dialog box

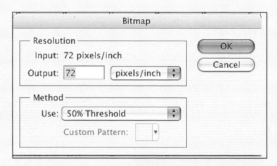

3. Zoom in around the bird image and with the Eraser tool create a white border all around the bird.

figure | 10-Ex2 |

White pixels surrounding bird image

4. Save for the Web as bird.gif, 32-bit, no dither settings.

5. Open a new Flash document. In the timeline, on layer 1 change the name to *bitmap*. Click in frame 100. Add a frame. From the menu bar select Insert>Timeline>Frame.

6. Return to Frame 1, from the menu bar select File>Import>Import to Stage. Import bird.gif.

figure | **10-Ex3** |

7. Select the image and choose Modify>Break Apart. Deselect the entire image.

Bird.gif on stage

8. In the toolbox, select the Lasso tool. At the bottom of the toolbox, under Options, select the Magic Wand properties modifier. When the Magic Wand Settings dialog box appears, set the Threshold to 40 and Smoothing to Pixels. Click OK.

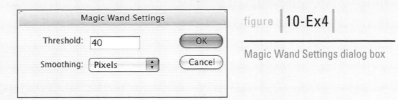

figure | **10-Ex4** |

Magic Wand Settings dialog box

9. Select the Magic Wand tool in the Options section and on the stage, position the pointer over the editable bitmap.

10. Click on the bird. You may need to play around with the Magic Wand settings to achieve a good visual solution. You can add to your selection by first holding down the Shift key and clicking on a nearby unselected pixel. You may need to zoom in a great deal to see what you are selecting.

11. Once your selection feels right, choose the Paint Bucket tool in the toolbox. Select a new fill color. You can edit the selection as needed and choose different colors.

figure | 10-Ex5 |

Paint Bucket swatch color window

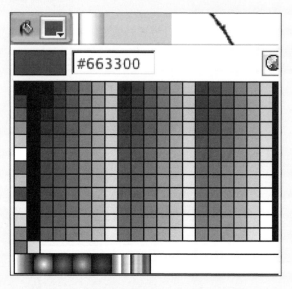

12. Choose the Ellipse tool. With this tool, draw a small circle where an eye would be appropriate to the bird. You can hold down the Option key on a Mac, Alt on a PC to draw from the center out. You can hold down the Shift key to constrain the ellipse tool to a perfect circle. Change the Paint Bucket to black and fill the new selection. Lock this layer.

13. Next, add a new layer and name it *flower*. In Frame 1, import flower.jpg from the Exercise 10 folder.

14. In Frame 1 of your new layer, drag the JPG off of the bottom of the stage so that the flower is somewhat in the center of the trees. Stay in Frame 1 and choose Insert>Timeline>Create Motion Tween.

15. Click in Frame 100 and from the menu bar select Insert>Timeline>Keyframe. Back on the stage, hold down the Shift key and drag the JPG up so that the flower ends up in the approximate center of the trees. (Using the Shift key will constrain the movement to a vertical movement.)

figure | 10-Ex6 |

Flower.jpg imported over bird.gif on stage

16. From the menu bar, select Control>Test Movie. The flower image should grow from off of the stage to the center of the trees.

17. Close the Test Movie window and return to the timeline. Highlight the Masked layer and click the Insert Layer button.

18. From the Modify pull-down menu, choose Timeline>Layer Properties to display the Layer Properties dialog box.

19. In the Type section, choose Mask. Rename the layer to identify it as a mask. Click OK.

figure | 10-Ex7 |

Flower moved to between trees

figure | 10-Ex8 |

Layer Properties dialog box

Flash should turn the selected layer into a mask and change the layer icon.

20. To link layers to the mask, in the timeline, select the Masked layer. From the menu bar select Modify>Timeline>Layer Properties to display the Layer Properties dialog box or, alternately, double-click on the layer icon to bring up this window. In the Type section, choose Masked. Click OK.

Notice that Flash links the selected layer to the mask directly above it, changes the layer icon, and indents the icon and layer name to indicate that the mask above this layer controls it.

figure | 10-Ex9 |

Timeline showing Mask and Masked layers

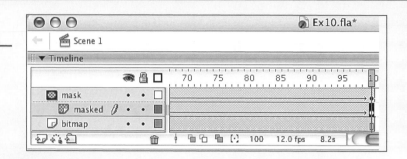

21. Lock the Masked layer. Return to the mask in Frame 1. The layer should be highlighted in the Timeline and the eye and padlock columns should contain bullets.

22. In Frame 1 of the mask, use the oval tool to create a shape between the trees.

23. Back in the timeline, in Frame 1 of the mask, choose Insert>Timeline>Create Motion Tween. This will turn the shape into a symbol.

24. In Frame 100 of this layer, choose Insert>Timeline>Keyframe. Return to Frame 1 and transform the symbol in some way. In Frame 100, transform the symbol to show the entire flower as it moves into position.

figure | 10-Ex10 |

Frames 1 and 100 showing transformation of mask

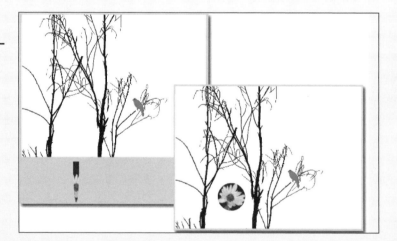

25. Lock the mask and all linked layers.

26. Choose Control>Test Movie.

27. Close the Test Movie window and make any adjustments to your Mask and Masked layers so that the quality of revealing is intriguing.

28. Return to the timeline. With the Mask layer highlighted, insert a new layer and name it *dog*. In Frame 1, import dog.png from the back of book CD. (Feel free to first open this image in Photoshop and make alterations or adjustments.)

29. Note that when you import the dog image, the background is transparent. With the dog image selected, from the menu bar select Modify>Bitmap>Trace Bitmap. When the dialog box opens, choose:

    Color threshold: 40

    Minimum area: 15

    Curve fit: Pixels

    Corner threshold: Normal

    Now you have a vector image instead of a pixel image. You can recolor all or just parts of the dog, choose specific vector shapes to alter, or leave as is.

30. Now create a motion tween for the dog. In Frame 1, choose Insert>Timeline>Create Motion Tween. In Frame 100, choose Insert>Timeline>Keyframe.

31. Return to Frame 1 and with the Transform tool, resize the dog symbol to almost nothing. In the Properties window, under the Color pull-down menu, change the Alpha to 0%. Move the dog to the right of the stage in Frame 1. In Frame 100, move him towards the flower as if he is sniffing it.

figure |10-Ex11|

Stage with dog image transformed
and Properties window

32. Click Control>Test Movie. The dog should gradually appear, moving into the foreground as the bird watches and the flower appears. In the end, the dog should be sniffing a flower that sits in midair, giving the entire image a rather surrealistic quality.

figure | 10-Ex12 |

Final Flash frame in completed
Exercise 10

33. Save your file, embellish as desired, and show your friends.

on your own

Try playing around with PNG images. In Photoshop, create several PNG images with transparent areas and transparent backgrounds. When you save for the Web as a PNG, be sure to choose the Transparency option.

Next, open Flash and create a background layer that will serve as the background for all of the PNG images. Import each PNG image into Flash on its own layer. Trace the images and modify them. Create motion tweens so that the images move in and out of overlapping, creating a sense of one image.

notes

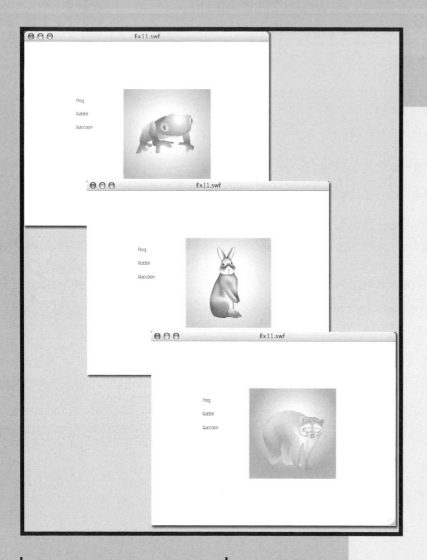

an introduction to ActionScript

Objectives

Learn about ActionScript syntax.

Explore the ActionScript window.

Discover the secrets of ActionScript.

Examine simple navigation systems in Flash.

Revisit navigation aesthetics.

Understand button symbols.

Introduction

Navigation in Flash can be as complex or as simple as you like. You can introduce delightful surprises to your user through Over States of buttons. You can create invisible buttons similar to the hotspots in an image map in Dreamweaver or HTML. Your Web site can look as traditional, static, or flashy as you want. The beauty of Flash navigation is in its versatility. You can create almost anything in any way to move you around a Flash Web site. The key ingredients are button symbols, instances, and ActionScript.

AN INTRODUCTION TO ACTIONSCRIPT

ACTIONSCRIPT

ActionScript can be a truly scary word to the designer who feels little confidence in technical terminology. The word alone can trigger such anxiety that many Web designers shy away from Flash just because of it. The truth is that ActionScript, like everything else in Flash, can be as simple as you need it to be. Flash will help you with ActionScript and if you want to delve more deeply into its capabilities, you can. However, you can produce a beautiful Web site knowing just the basics of ActionScript, so let's start at the beginning.

ActionScript uses punctuation marks much like we use mathematical symbols. It has its own rules (called *syntax*) that organize and control such things as word order, capitalization, spaces, and punctuation. Flash will enter these statements for you and give you hints for filling in the details. The following list briefly describes common ActionScript punctuation marks.

Dot .

The dot (or period) is the primary link symbol in ActionScript. It links objects and properties (characteristics) and methods (behaviors). In the script

Starburst._duplicateMovieClip

the dot links the movie clip named *Starburst* with an action that will copy it.

The dot also indicates the hierarchy of files and folders in path names, similar to a forward slash in HTML.

Semicolon ;

A semicolon indicates the end of a statement. It is not actually required. Flash will usually interpret the end of a line of statements correctly without it, but it is a good practice to use it.

Braces { }

Braces group and separate ActionScript statements. For example, a mouse action connected to the user interaction and the resulting timeline action would be grouped together within a set of braces. Opening and closing braces must pair up evenly. Flash will enter the pairs of braces for you, but you still need to pay attention to where you add scripts within the Actions list and group the actions within the proper braces.

Parentheses ( )

Parentheses group arguments that apply to particular statements. Parentheses also can group operations, such as mathematical calculations, so that they take place in the right order.

One simple ActionScript is a stop action:

```
stop();
```

This action, when assigned to a frame, will stop the movie. The parentheses are automatically added by Flash. When nothing is typed inside of the parentheses, an action has no additional arguments before the end of the statement (signaled by the semicolon). A slightly more complex action is the goto action:

```
on (release) {

gotoAndStop(1);

}
```

Notice that Flash doesn't use spaces in a statement. Spaces would mean something different, so Flash runs the words together using capital letters to begin words. The parentheses in the case of the on action define the conditions for on. In other words *on release* refers to the release of the mouse. The braces then give instructions on what to do with the on release statement. The braces connect the instruction to the statement. In this case, the instruction is *go to and stop*. The next set of parentheses gives the condition of the instruction: (1) tells the statement *go to and stop* to move and then stop at Frame 1. This type of action is applied to an object, such as a button symbol.

ActionScript can be applied to an object or a frame. If an action is applied to an object, it is called an *object-based script*. The object tells the movie what to do next and is usually indicative of a goto action. To apply an action to an object, click on the object itself and assign the action.

If an action is applied to a frame, it is called a *frame-based script*. A frame-based script tells the timeline what to do next, such as stop the movie. To apply an action to a frame, insert a keyframe, click in the keyframe, and assign the action.

It is important to keep actions that are applied to frames on one layer. You can title this layer *actions* or *scripts*. This helps you easily find your actions when you are trying to make changes or find a problematic action. Again, all frame-based actions need to be in keyframes.

All of this may seem foreign and overwhelming, but I think you'll find it easier to understand as we work with ActionScript. It's really quite logical. For the purposes of this book, we'll keep it simple. If you end up feeling a strong affinity toward Flash and want to explore it further, you may want to read *Exploring Flash MX 2004* by James Mohler, published by Thomson/Delmar Learning.

NAVIGATION REVIEW

Before moving on to button states in Flash, let's review a few things about navigation that we discussed in Chapter 6. Remember that we talked about navigation as a potentially dynamic user experience relating human gesture to technology. As the user moves the mouse over a button, this gesture becomes an interaction with technology. We are creating an experience between human cause and technological consequences. What is wonderful about this approach is that, in Flash, we can apply so many different possibilities to this gesture.

Let's reexamine the basics of navigation. A good navigation system must answer the questions "Where am I?" and "Where can I go from here?" Navigation needs to be clear, logical, consistent, efficient, and easy to use. Remember the three basic ingredients?

- Clarity: Navigation should look like navigation. Label everything clearly and use icons logically, making certain that they are easily understood.

- Consistency: Navigation options need to be consistent throughout a site in availability as well as in appearance.

- Efficiency: Keep your user engaged while getting them to the information they seek in an efficient manner.

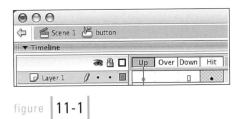

figure **11-1**

Timeline of a button symbol

figure **11-2**

Buttons Library window

BUTTON SYMBOLS

The ruling symbol for navigation in Flash is a button. Buttons are like hotspots in a Dreamweaver image map—they don't have to look like a button and they can be invisible. In Chapter 8, I mentioned that buttons have their own four-frame timeline. These frames are the Up, Over, Down, and Hit States. (These are quite different from the four part navigation of Dreamweaver.)

Flash provides a number of buttons in the common Library window. To access these from the menu bar select Window>Other Panels>Common Libraries>Buttons. When you open this window, notice that there are a number of folders. You can view the contents of the folder through the top right triangle in the window. Click on the triangle and you'll see a number of options. You can highlight a folder and choose Expand Folder in this window, or you can choose Expand All Folders. You can also collapse folders.

Select any one of the symbols listed and notice that it shows up in the upper portion of the Library window. Click on the right-facing triangle (the play button) in the upper-right corner to view the action of the symbol.

To use any one of the button symbols in this window, simply drag it onto your stage. A word of caution about using symbols from the common libraries of Flash: These symbols are very recognizable. As a designer, it is much better to create your own symbols. (You can do this easily in Illustrator.)

You can edit a button symbol on the stage by double-clicking on it. Alternately, you can access button symbols that you are using through the upper-right icon of the timeline, the Symbol icon. Either way, you will be taken to the button symbol's timeline, where you can make changes. You can modify any part of the states Up, Over, or Down. Keep in mind that anytime you change a symbol in its timeline, all occurrences of the symbol will automatically be changed.

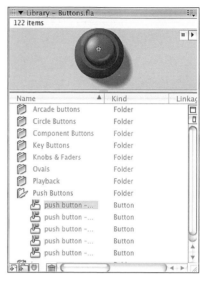

figure | **11-3** |

Buttons Library window with a symbol highlighted

One of the beauties of button symbols in Flash is that you can use the same symbol many times over. Remember that every time you use a symbol, it is an instance. You can change the ActionScript, brightness, tint, alpha, or effect of each instance without adding to the document size.

Additionally, text can be turned into a button symbol. Simply type the text and choose Modify>Convert to Symbol. Choose Button when the Create New Symbol dialog box opens and click OK. Double-click on the symbol to enter the button symbol timeline, where you can add Over and Down States as well as define the Hit State.

To create your own button symbol, draw a shape on the stage and from the menu bar select Modify>Convert to Symbol. Alternately, begin by choosing Insert>New Symbol. In either case the Create New Symbol dialog box will appear.

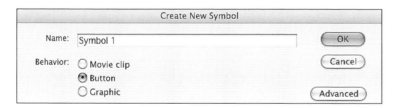

figure | **11-4** |

Create New Symbol dialogue box

Name the button symbol in a manner that will make it easy for you to identify the button. Choose the type of symbol, which in this case is button. If you have used the convert to symbol choice, remember to notice the location of the registration mark. (It's usually best to keep this at center.) If you began with Insert>New Symbol and you click OK, you will be in the four-frame button timeline. If you began with Convert to Symbol, then you will need to double-click in the symbol to enter the button timeline.

If you already drew your shape and chose Modify>Convert to Symbol, it will show up in the first frame of the button timeline. If you did not draw the shape and chose Insert>New Symbol, draw the shape here in the first frame. This is the Up State of the button.

To add different qualities to the different states, you will need to add keyframes to each state. In the Over State, add a keyframe and change something about your shape. (You can even add a movie clip that you already created by dragging the movie clip's symbol from the Library window into this state. We will do this in a later chapter. For now, though, let's keep it simple.) Add a keyframe to the Down State and change something about the shape there—perhaps a visual metaphor of a human gesture? (You can also add text to any of these states. For example, in the Over State, you can add text describing what the viewer is about to see if they click on the button.) Finally, add a keyframe to the Hit State and draw a rectangle large enough to cover the image in the Up State. This will actually be invisible to the user but it defines the area that he or she can click to access the action.

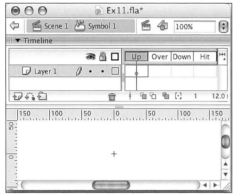

figure | 11-5 |

Button symbol timeline with keyframes showing all four states

A button symbol can be invisible. This option allows you to apply an action anywhere on your stage, mimicking the effect of a hotspot. To make a button symbol invisible, you need to have a keyframe in the Hit State. Draw a rectangle or basic shape in this state and make certain that the other states are empty. When you return to the timeline, notice that the button symbol is now a translucent blue on the stage and in the Library window. This tells you that the button is invisible or works the same as a hotspot. You can drag this invisible button anywhere on the stage.

Buttons don't necessarily need to have an action applied to them. Buttons can be used merely for the purpose of entertaining a user during a rollover. For this type of button, you will need two keyframes. One keyframe needs to be in the Over State and one needs to be in the Hit State. The Hit State frame should contain the shape which will define the rollover area. The Over State frame needs to

figure | 11-6 |

Button symbol timeline for invisible button showing all four states

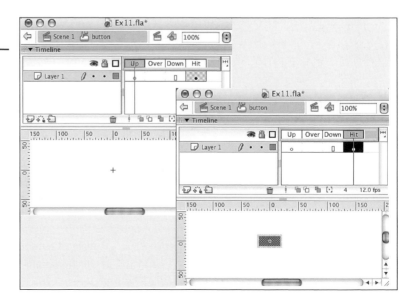

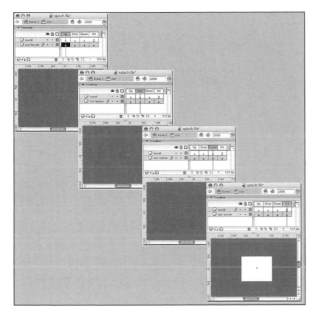

figure | 11-7 |

Button symbol timeline showing all four states

contain the graphic, image, or Movie Clip. For example, see Color Plate 21. Here there are numerous invisible buttons that respond to a mouse moving over them with a burst of stars. This is accomplished using a movie clip of several layers containing motion tweens of stars following a motion guide path. The movie clip sits in the Over State of the invisible button.

APPLYING ACTIONSCRIPT TO A BUTTON SYMBOL

If a button symbol is to be a navigation button, then you need to use ActionScript on the button that tells the movie what to do when the user clicks the button.

One common error that is made with ActionScript is where it is applied. Frequently a gotoAndPlay action is assigned but the button doesn't work. Upon further investigation, if everything is okay with the ActionScript, the problem turns out to be that the frame was selected, rather than the button, when an action was assigned. So make sure you have selected the button symbol before proceeding.

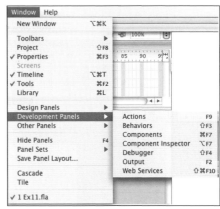

To apply an action to a button, open the Actions panel. From the menu bar select Window>Development Panels>Actions.

figure | 11-8 |

Window pull-down menu

The Actions panel will open. Let's take a good look at this and go over the different elements.

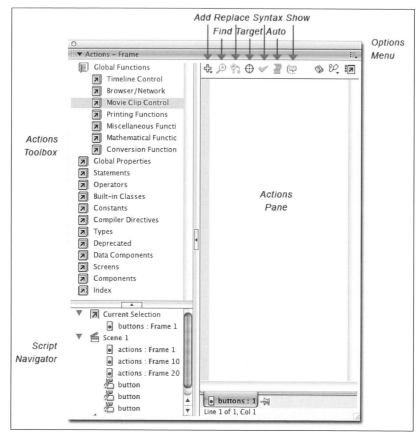

figure | 11-9 |

Annotated Actions panel

The small triangle in the upper left corner opens and closes the window. The Actions panel is divided into sections. On the left is the Actions toolbox, with folders that group actions, properties, and arguments. Inside these folders are the actions of the ActionScript language. Below the Actions toolbox is the Script Navigator, which helps you to locate your scripts. On the right is the Actions pane, where the actions sit. You can bring an action into the Actions pane in one of three ways. You can double-click the action in the toolbox. This will cause the action to appear in the Actions pane. You can also click the action and drag it into the Action pane. Finally, you can use the plus sign in the path tools above the Actions pane to access a pulldown menu of the folders in the Actions toolbox and scroll over to the action.

Above the Actions pane are the path tools. These icons assist you in adding, searching for, and replacing actions; entering a target path for an action; checking the syntax of an action; auto formatting or displaying code hints to help you correctly write the ActionScript.

Finally, above the path tools is a small triangle that will take you to an Options menu, which gives you various options, including the ability to import and export scripts.

SUMMARY

In this chapter you were introduced to ActionScript and learned the basic ActionScript that can guide your user through your Web site. You can actually create an entire Web site with just this much ActionScript. True, there is so much more that can be done—far more than we can cover in this book. But these are the basics: Stop Actions in frames combined with goto actions applied to buttons. Knowing these few things can get you anywhere you need to go.

in review

1. What is ActionScript?

2. What is syntax?

3. How is ActionScript applied differently to a frame than it is to an object?

4. How is the button symbol timeline different from the main document timeline?

5. What are the key ingredients of a button symbol timeline?

6. What are the basic codes used to assign an action to a button symbol?

exercise 11

1. Copy the Exercise 11 folder from the back of book CD onto your desktop. Create a new document in Flash.

2. From the menu bar select View>Rulers. Set a vertical guide at 220 pixels and a horizontal guide at 100 pixels. Set the guide by clicking in the ruler and dragging to the location.

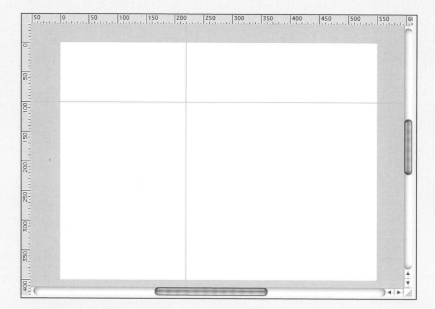

figure | 11-Ex1 |

Guides on stage

3. Return to the Timeline. Click on the layer and rename it *images*. Click in Frame 1.

4. Choose File>Import>Import to Stage. Browse in the Exercise 11 folder and choose frog.jpg, then choose open. The frog image should be imported into Keyframe 1.

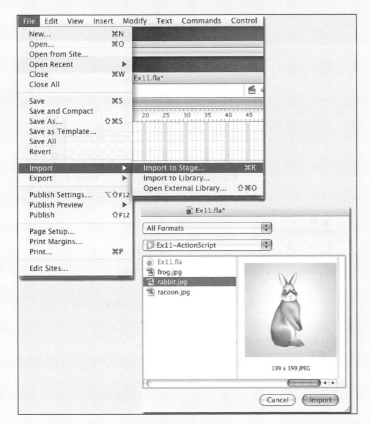

figure | 11-Ex2 |

Import dialog box

Align the top-left corner of the image to the guides.

5. Back in the timeline, click in Frame 10. From the menu bar select Insert>Timeline>Blank KeyFrame. Flash should create a new blank keyframe, eliminating the frog image from the frame 10 onward.

6. On the Images layer, click in Keyframe 10, choose File>Import>Import to Stage, and choose rabbit.jpg. Align the top-left corner of the image to the guides.

7. Back in the timeline, click on Frame 20 and again select Insert>Timeline>Blank KeyFrame.

8. In Keyframe 20, choose File>Import>Import to Stage. Choose raccoon.jpg. Again, align the top-left corner of the image to the guides.

9. Add a frame, not a keyframe, in Frame 25.

The three image files have now been imported into keyframes in Flash. The timeline should look like this:

figure | 11-Ex3 |

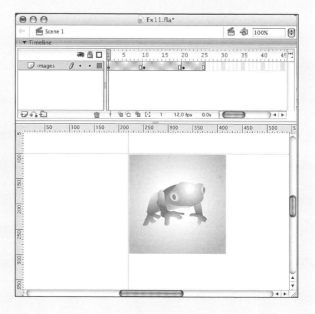

Timeline of Exercise 11 showing 25 frames with keyframes set at 1, 10, and 20

10. Click on the black circle under the Lock icon to lock this layer. Locking the layer prevents everything on the layer from being inadvertently changed.

11. From the menu bar select Control>Test Movie. You should see the three images appearing in sequence over and over. Close the Test Movie window to return to your Flash document.

figure | 11-Ex4 |

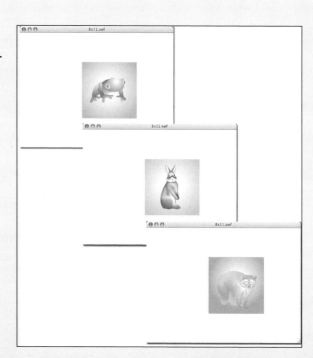

Three images in Sequence in Test Movie window

12. Now add the ActionScript that will stop the playback of the movie. You need to add the stop ActionScript to control the timeline.

13. To set the stop ActionScript, begin by creating a new layer. Highlight the Images layer and click on the Layer icon in the timeline. Alternately, you can add a layer from the menu bar by selecting Insert>Timeline. In either case, name the layer *actions*.

14. In the actions layer, click in Frame 1. From the menu bar select Window>Development Panels>Actions to display the ActionScript window.

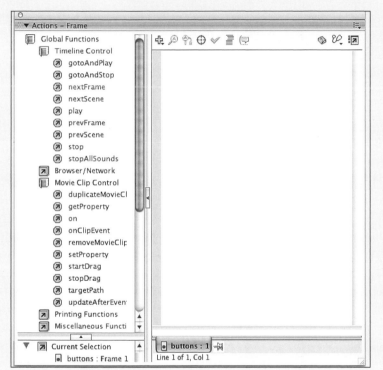

figure | 11-Ex5 |

Actions window

15. From the ActionScript toolbox, choose Global Functions>Timeline Control. Click and drag the Stop icon into the Actions pane.

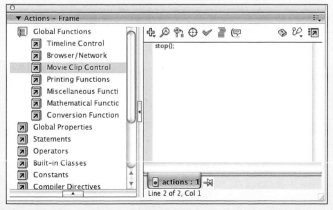

figure | 11-Ex6 |

Actions window with stop action added

16. Back in the main timeline, in the actions layer, click in Frame 10. From the menu bar select Insert>Timeline>Blank KeyFrame. In the Actions pane, again add a stop action.

17. Repeat these steps for Frame 20. Your timeline should now look like this:

figure | 11-Ex7 |

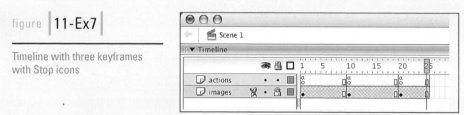

Timeline with three keyframes with Stop icons

18. Test the movie. This time the movie should immediately stop at the frog image with no ability to go any further.

    Close the Test Movie window to return to your Flash document.

19. Next, add the ActionScript that will allow the viewer to move beyond the frog. Start by adding text that will sit under invisible buttons. Create a new layer below the actions layer. Name it *text*.

20. In the left part of the stage, create the visual aspect of your navigation system. Using the Text tool, type the word *Frog*.

figure | 11-Ex8 |

Stage with *Frog* and frog image

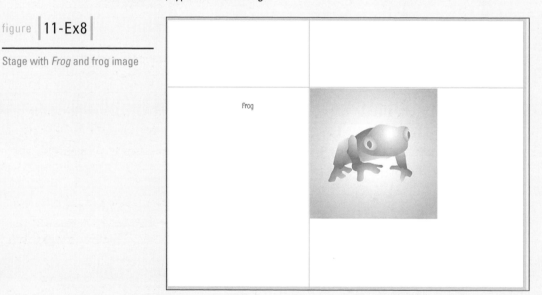

21. Click on the Selection tool in the toolbox. Holding down the Option on a Mac, Alt on a PC and Shift keys, drag the word *Frog* directly below to duplicate it and keep a consistent left margin.

22. With the text tool, change this new word to *Rabbit*. Repeat Step 21, changing the third word to *Raccoon*.

23. Select all three words with the Selection tool, holding down the Shift key to select multiple objects, and choose Modify>Align>Distribute Heights. This will create equal spacing between the words.

    Your stage should now look something like this:

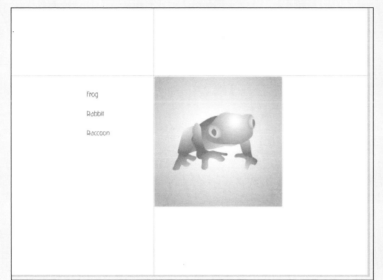

figure | 11-Ex9 |

Stage with *Frog, Rabbit,* and *Raccoon* and frog image

24. Now it's time to add the buttons. Lock the layers and create a new layer just above the text layer. Name it *buttons*.

25. Choose the Rectangle tool. In Frame 1 of the buttons layer, click and drag with the rectangle tool to create a shape on the screen. The shape should be a little larger than the word *Raccoon*. In this case, the color doesn't matter, as we will be converting the shape to an invisible button.

26. Choose the Selection tool in the toolbox. Drag to create a marquee that completely surrounds the rectangle. From the menu bar select Modify>Convert to Symbol. For the name, type *Button*. Choose the Button option and make sure that the registration mark is centered. Click OK.

27. Drag the button to position it over the word *Frog*. You'll make this button invisible next and then adjust the positioning.

28. From the menu bar select Window>Library. Make certain that you see your button with the name *Button* in the Library palette. Notice the different icons there and the information they give you.

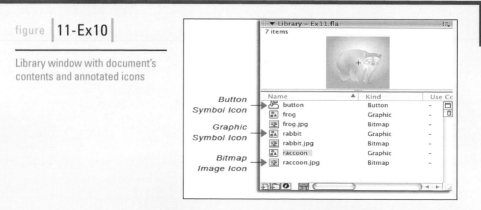

figure | 11-Ex10 |

Library window with document's
contents and annotated icons

29. Now make the button invisible.

Double-click the button that you created. This will bring you to the button symbol editing dialog box. You'll see the four states: Up, Over, Down, and Hit.

figure | 11-Ex11 |

Button timeline

In the next steps, you'll work with the Up and Hit States. The Up State refers to the way the button looks in its normal unclicked state. The Hit State refers to the "hot" area of the button—the shape that responds to the mouse click. Deleting the Up State and leaving a shape in the Hit State of the button will make it invisible but still functional.

30. Click in the frame under the Hit State. Choose Insert>Timeline>KeyFrame. Flash adds a shape for the Hit State that is the same as the current Up State.

31. Click in the frame under the Up State. Using the Selection tool, create a marquee completely around the shape and then delete it. The Up State is now deleted. The button is invisible but can still be triggered because it contains a shape under the Hit State keyframe.

32. Click on the Scene 1 link at the top left of the stage.

This link should return you to the document's main timeline. The button now appears as a transparent light blue, indicating that it is invisible. When you make a change to any symbol in its own timeline, such as this button symbol, all other instances of the symbol are also changed in the same way. This means that you can make changes at any time. Keep in mind that this is not the same as making alterations to *Instances* of a symbol.

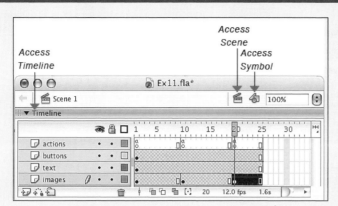

figure | **11-Ex12** |

Annotated top of timeline

33. With the Selection tool, drag the button from the Library window to cover each of the words on the stage. It's okay if the buttons are a little larger than the text, but don't let them overlap. Also, make sure that each button is at least as large as its text. You don't want your user to have to poke around to find the hit area. You can change the size of any instance of a symbol by using the Free Transform tool. In order to change the symbol itself, you must be in its own timeline.

figure | **11-Ex13** |

Free Transform tool applied to invisible button

34. Even though you are reusing the same button, each instance of this button can have a different ActionScript. Using the Selection tool, click on the button you positioned over the word *Frog*. Open the Actions window.

35. In the ActionScript toolbox, open the Global Functions folder. Open the folder for the movie clip control. Drag the on action into the Actions pane. A submenu will appear with options for the on qualifier. Choose release by double-clicking it. Flash should add the argument within the parentheses correctly.

36. Now you need to assign the action statement that is connected to the on (release). With the cursor inside of the braces in the Actions pane, from the Global Functions>Timeline Control folder, drag the gotoAndStop ActionScript inside of the braces. Flash will prompt you to tell it where to stop. You have two choices here.

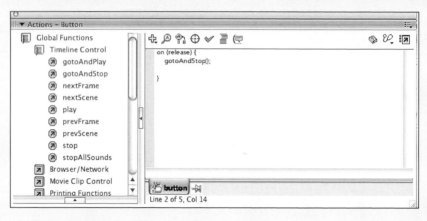

figure | 11-Ex14 |

ActionScript choices for
gotoAndStop arguments

Choice 1 tells the goto action which frame to go to within the same scene. Choice 2 gives you the option to change the scene. To see option 2 of 2, click on one of the triangles next to 1 of 2. Since you are only working in one scene in this exercise, you don't need the second choice. You need only to tell the goto action which frame to go to. Type 1, for the frame for the frog button. Do not press enter or return.

37. Click on the middle button you created over the word *Rabbit*. Follow the same steps as above, only this time type 10 for the frame in the ActionScript.

38. Repeat for the raccoon button, typing 20 for the frame in the ActionScript.

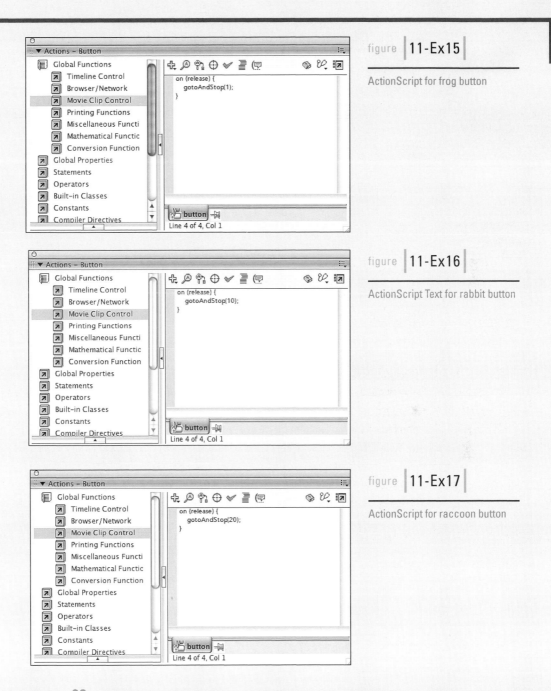

figure 11-Ex15

ActionScript for frog button

figure 11-Ex16

ActionScript Text for rabbit button

figure 11-Ex17

ActionScript for raccoon button

39. Each button should now take the user to its corresponding image. Test the movie.

The buttons should now be functional. Notice that when you test a movie, your Flash document appears slightly larger. This occurs only when you test the movie. On the Web, the movie will appear as the correct size.

figure | 11-Ex18 |

Completed Exercise 11 showing
all three stages of actions

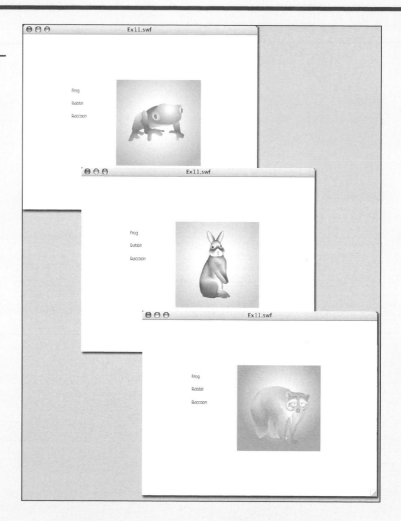

40. Close the Test Movie window to return to your Flash document. When everything
    works correctly and you are happy with the document, save it and show your
    friends.

on your own

Try adding what we've learned from earlier chapters to Exercise 11. Give the images
motion tweens and have them appear from an alpha of 0% to an alpha of 100%. You
will need to add more frames between images so that the appearing act moves a bit
more slowly. If you do this, don't forget to change the frame number in the
ActionScript argument to match.

Additionally, you could add a check mark to the invisible button. To do this, add a
keyframe in the Over State. To the left of the Hit shape, add a check mark graphic.
This will give your user a visual aid to what they are clicking on and add the element
of a user gesture.

notes

_____
_____
_____
_____
_____
_____
_____
_____
_____
_____
_____
_____
_____
_____
_____
_____
_____
_____
_____
_____
_____

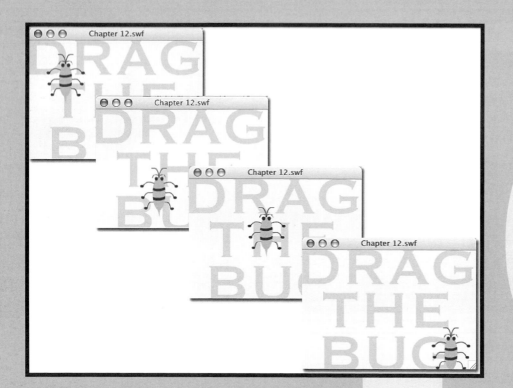

type and movie clips

Objectives

Learn about type in Flash.

Discover the fun of movie clips.

Examine movie clip timelines.

Explore the many ways to use movie clips.

Understand a few ActionScript codes that can control movie clips.

Introduction

Flash offers rather sophisticated tools to work with setting type. When you publish a Flash document, the Publish process converts type into outlines. Consequently, your user is not required to have the same font on their machine, and you can work with the entire array of fonts that are on your machine. Additionally, there is quite a developed capability to format the type. We'll take a look at type in the Flash environment in this chapter.

Movie clips in Flash are another basic organizational element in addition to being a tool for delightful surprises. A movie clip timeline looks the same as a document timeline, but remember that a movie clip sits in one frame of the document Timeline *and* has its own timeline. Confused? In this chapter, we'll explore this and try to gain a clear understanding of the development of movie clips. We'll also look at a few of the ways that movie clips can be used.

TYPE AND MOVIE CLIPS

TYPE

Flash offers a number of ways to work with type, including static text, dynamic text, and device fonts. For the purposes of this book, we'll work with static text, which is editable. Even though the user doesn't need to have your chosen font, while you are still in working mode, you need to carry your fonts with you if you change machines.

Okay, let's take a look at the type environment. Clicking the text tool in the toolbox will access the Properties window for text.

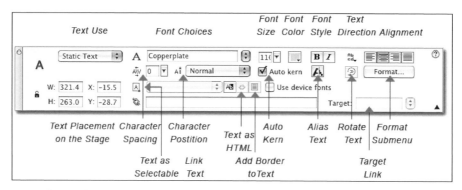

figure 12-1

Annotated Properties window for text

On the left is the submenu for static, dynamic, or input Text. Next is the menu that will display all of the font choices that sit on your machine. Continuing to the right is the font size. You can use the arrows to scroll to a given size or just type in the size. Next is color. Clicking this button will access the Web-safe color palette in which you can choose a color or type in the number of a color.

figure 12-2

Web-safe Color palette for fonts

Next are style buttons for bold and italic. If you are using fonts from your machine, don't use the style buttons. Choose instead the bold or italic options for the font you are using. This will assure a better outline for the user of your site who doesn't have your fonts. The next choice is text direction: horizontal, vertical left to right, or vertical right to left. Finally on this top row are the alignment choices: left, center, right, or justified.

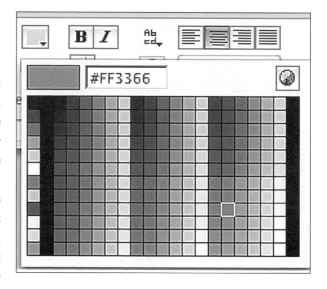

Moving to the next row of the Properties window, the first choice is character spacing. This refers to *tracking*, which is the space between two or more letters and words in a line or paragraph. You can increase or decrease this space. Next is character position. The choices here are normal, superscript, or subscript. The next choice is auto kern. *Kerning* refers to the space between two letters. This is most frequently a formatting tool used to bring sets of letters together, such as *ff* or *tt*.

The next option, alias text, is used to turn off the default that Flash applies to all text by anti-aliasing it. Anti-alias means that Flash slightly blurs the edges of letter forms to smooth them out, for large point sizes, this makes them easier to read. In the case of smaller font sizes, you may want to turn off anti-alias. Use this button to do this. The decision can be a little tricky. You actually need to see the font on different machines to understand when to use the alias and when not to. For now, let Flash do its anti-alias job. You can always go back and change this.

Next up is a handy-dandy tool that allows you to rotate a text selection. This works in conjunction with the Vertical Text tool and resets horizontal text to a vertical rotation. Finally in this row is the Format submenu. Open this to format indents, line spacing, and left and right margins. *Line spacing* refers to the space between the lower margin of one line and the lower margin of the next line. This is particularly useful to tweak when you have large blocks of text. Increase line spacing to make a paragraph more readable. Reduce line spacing when you are trying to fit text into a specified area. If you need to reduce line spacing a lot, try reducing the size of the font to avoid an overcrowded look.

The final two rows begin by showing you the width, height, and xy positions of a text box. Next is a drop-down menu for single line and multiple line, followed by selectable text, text as HTML, and placing a border around text options. The single line drop-down menu is only available for Dynamic and Input text. Link and target boxes are the final options that you can apply.

figure | **12-3**

Format submenu for text

Type a paragraph of text and then poke around the Properties window. Apply different functions to familiarize yourself with these options.

MOVIE CLIPS

Movie clips are symbols. As stated earlier, they sit in one frame of a document's timeline but have their own timeline. A movie clip timeline looks the same as the document's main timeline and can contain as many frames and layers as needed. Any or all of these layers can have motion guides, motion tweens, and frame-by-frame animation. By taking up only one frame of a document's timeline, a movie clip runs independent of it. In other words, as the document's timeline marches on, the movie clip is doing its own thing.

If a movie clip does not have a stop action in the last frame of its timeline, it will continue to run regardless of what the document is doing. If a movie clip *does* have a stop action in its last frame, it will run only once. A movie clip is activated as a result of coding, of reaching the frame in which it sits, or as a result of a user interaction, such as mousing over or clicking a button symbol. Movie clips can be nested inside of button symbols, inside of other movie clips, or simply placed in a document's timeline.

Some designers use movie clips as an organizational tool. In these cases, each "page" of a Web site is in fact a movie clip. The document's timeline simply contains navigation that takes the viewer to each "page" or movie clip. Within a movie clip, secondary navigation can exist, other movie clips can exist, and so on. When there is more than one layer of nesting, Flash controls the navigation through levels in the ActionScript. These levels correspond to the forward slashes that we looked at in HTML and Dreamweaver. Flash uses the root code to reference the main document timeline. We'll look more at this in a minute and again in Chapter 15.

When a movie clip sits inside of the Over State of a button symbol, it is activated simply by the user moving the mouse over the button. Using movie clips in this way is yet another delightful way to surprise and engage your viewer. For example, see Color Plate 21. The Over State of the button symbol has a keyframe with a Movie Clip of a burst of stars. The Hit State responds to the mouseover, but there isn't any ActionScript applied to the button on the stage. The button is simply there to surprise the viewer with a burst of stars and sound as the mouse passes over a seemingly static graphic.

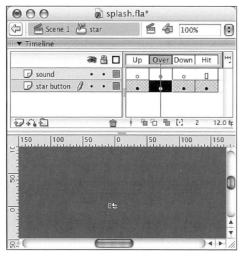

figure | **12-4** |

Over State of a starburst button symbol (at http://www.Moonlightdsn.com)

figure | **12-5** |

Create New Symbol dialog box

To create a movie clip, from the menu bar select Insert>New Symbol. Name your movie clip, select Movie clip in the options, and click OK.

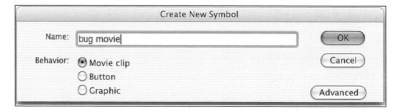

This will take you into the movie clip's timeline. Here you can apply everything you know, creating whatever you want. Once you have created your movie clip, return to the document's timeline or the button symbol timeline. Choose the frame into which you want to insert the movie clip, add a keyframe, and drag the movie clip from the Library onto the stage. Wherever you place the movie clip on the stage is where it will show up when you play the movie. Remember, if your movie clip is placed on the document's timeline and you want it to play only once, add a top-most layer for actions in the movie clip's timeline and place a keyframe in the last frame. Then add a stop action. Otherwise your movie clip will continue to play over and over. However, if you are placing a movie clip in the Over State of a button symbol, then you don't necessarily need a stop action. The movie clip will respond to the mouseover and quit when the mouse is moved away.

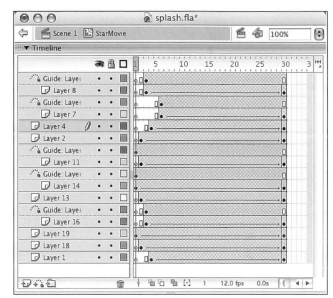

figure | 12-6 |

Timeline for the starburst movie clip

Movie clips, and only movie clips, can be dragged around the stage. Have you ever been to a Web site where you could move something around with your mouse? Did you wonder how they did that? The basic drag action is to click and hold down the mouse button on the movie clip, drag it, release the mouse button, and stop the drag. You might want to use this feature when you want to have your user interact in some way with your site. For example, the drag action could lead your user to an Over State of a button symbol, causing a further action. Or it simply could be an entertainment feature. It could also be a way to guide your user to the next step. In all scenarios, the basic drag action is the same, and there are various steps to guide that drag.

To create a draggable movie clip, you only need a graphic *defined* as a movie clip. The movie clip itself doesn't necessarily need to have any animation or additional layers. The drag is created through ActionScript. Once you have created the movie clip, make certain that it shows

in the Library window. Then drag the movie clip from the Library window onto the stage and open the Actions Window. Use the onClipEvent under Global Functions>Movie Clip Control. A secondary navigation will give you options of load, unload, enterFrame, mouseDown,

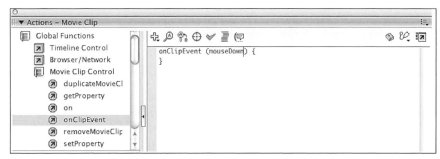

figure | 12-7 |

Actions window

mouseMove, mouseUp, keyDown, and keyUp. Choose any of these options by double-clicking it.

Once you have chosen the action, you will need to give the next set of instructions. In the case of dragging, you would want to add the start drag code:

startDrag(" ");

Make certain that the startDrag(" "); code is before the closing curly bracket. When you test your movie at this point, you will be able to drag your movie clip around the stage. However, you won't be able to stop the drag until you add the stop drag code. This needs to be added to a second onClipEvent with a different secondary function. For example, if your startDrag began with a mouseDown, then you would want your stopDrag to respond to a mouseUp. If you have chosen a keyDown and keyUp set of codes, you will need to tell Flash which key.

Additionally, you can give constraints to the drag. You do this through an if statement together with a property hitTest. First, under Actions>Statements>Conditions/Loops, add the code:

if

When Flash prompts you to name the condition type add:

hitTest(_root._xmouse,_root._ymouse, false)){

_root refers to the main document. This ActionScript then is stating that the xy coordinates are in the main timeline. You now need to add this same code to the stopDrag code. You can copy and paste:

if hitTest(_root._xmouse,_root._ymouse, false)){

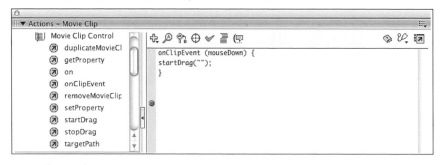

figure | 12-8 |

Actions window with code for dragging

You may want to add even further controlled dimensions to the drag. You can constrain the drag to the stage by including the dimensions in the above code. For example, if your document dimensions are 640 x 480 pixels, then give your conditions the same dimension. The left and top dimensions are 0, the right dimension (width) is 640 pixels, and the bottom dimension (height) is 480 pixels.

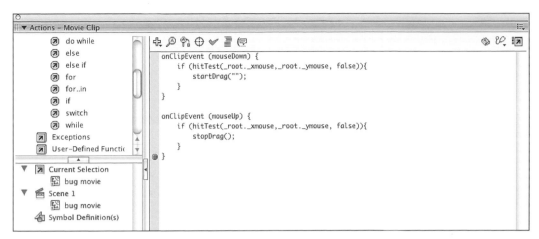

```
onClipEvent (mouseDown) {
    if (hitTest(_root._xmouse,_root._ymouse, false)){
        startDrag("");
    }
}

onClipEvent (mouseUp) {
    if (hitTest(_root._xmouse,_root._ymouse, false)){
        stopDrag();
    }
}
```

You can change these dimensions and have the drag sit inside of the document stage or have it be a vertical or horizontal drag. Simply know that the first dimension is the left boundary of the stage, the second dimension refers to the top boundary, the third is the right boundary, and the fourth is the bottom boundary.

figure | 12-9 |

Actions window with code for constraining drag to the size of the stage

In addition to constraining the movie clip to parameters you enter, you can also use the parameters of the clip itself to constrain. For instance, you could use this to create sliders and scroll bars. Replace the startDrag line from the previous step with the following code:

startDrag (true,0,_y,300,_y);

This uses the _y property of the movie clip to set the constrain for the top and bottom parameters, preventing an up-and-down movement. Additionally, you can snap the drag to the registration mark of the movie clip symbol.

SUMMARY

In this chapter, you have learned about using type in Flash and you have explored movie clips and a few ways that you can use them. I know that learning ActionScript can be a lot like learning a foreign language. However, there are plenty of third-party ActionScripts available on sites such as Flashkit.com. Also, don't be afraid to experiment on your own until you understand the code better. Experimenting with the code presented here will help to give you an understanding of roots and coordinates.

in review

1. What is a movie clip?

2. How many layers can a movie clip contain?

3. Where can a designer use a movie clip?

4. Does a movie clip have to contain animation?

5. Where are ActionScripts that control movie clips?

6. What does the script _root reference?

exercise 12

1. In Illustrator, draw a bug or other character or use your bug from Exercise 9. You can use any of Illustrator's tools, including the Pen tool or shape tools. Be sure to use Web-safe colors. Or, in Illustrator CS, try finding a bug in the Symbol palette. There are several. You can also use the Window pull-down menu to access the symbol libraries. There you will find additional lists that might include a bug you like. The Nature symbol library has several bugs.

When you find an image you like, click the bug in the palette. With the Symbol Spray tool, click once on the document artboard. This will place one instance of the bug on the artboard.

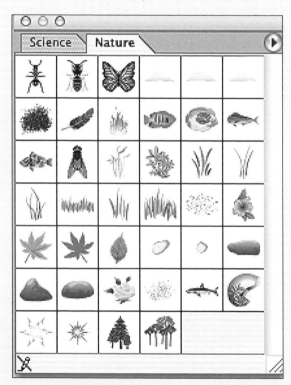

figure | 12-Ex1 |

Nature symbol library in Illustrator

2. You will next need to change the symbol from a formula to an object. Select the bug Symbol. Choose Object>Expand. The Expand dialog box should appear, giving options to Expand Object or Fill. Choose both and click OK. This is only necessary, however, if you want to change something about the bug. For instance, you may want to change the colors and/or make certain that all of the colors used are Web-safe colors. When you think you have a great bug, save the file.

3. Now your bug is ready to export. Export as bug.swf, choosing AI File to SWF File.

4. Open Flash and create a new document sized at 300 pixels by 200 pixels. (Modify>Document)

figure | 12-Ex2 |

Toolbox Highlighting Symbol Sprayer and One Bug on the stage

Macromedia® Flash™ (SWF) Format Options

Export Options

Export As: | AI File to SWF File ▲▼

Frame Rate: | 12 | fps

☐ Looping
☐ Generate HTML
☐ Read Only
☐ Clip to Artboard Size

Curve Quality: | 10 | ▶

◉ Preserve Appearance
○ Preserve Editability Where Possible

(OK)
(Cancel)

Image Options

Image Format: ◉ Lossless
○ Lossy (JPEG)

JPEG Quality: | Medium ▲▼ | 3 | ▶

Method: ◉ Baseline (Standard)
○ Baseline Optimized

Resolution: | 72 | ppi

figure | 2-Ex3 |

Settings for export to SWF

5. Import bug.swf and place it on the stage.

figure | 12-Ex4 |

Bug image on stage

6. Marquis the entire graphic and from the menu bar select Modify>Convert to Symbol.

7. Choose Movie Clip, make certain that the registration mark is centered, and name the clip *bug movie*. Click OK. Open the Library window (F11) to see your movie clip.

8. Next, create a new layer and name it *text*. Choose the Type tool and in the top center of the stage, type *Drag the bug*.

This will open the text Properties window. Poke around to familiarize yourself with the options that Flash provides. Use a font that is somewhat playful and large enough to be easily read. Try tracking the sentence and choose a font color that matches the bug. Cover the entire stage as if the text were wallpaper.

figure | 12-Ex5 |

Stage showing text as wallpaper

9. Return to the movie clip. Select it and open the Actions panel from the menu bar Windows>Development Panels>Actions (F9).

Add the following piece of code from the left pane of the Actions window, under Global Functions>Movie Clip Control:

onClipEvent

Options to control the onClipEvent will show in a second menu. Double-click mouseDown.

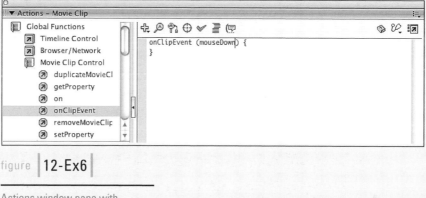

figure **12-Ex6**

Actions window pane with
onClipEvent (mouseDown){}

10. With your cursor placed between the curly brackets, from Global Functions>Movie Clip Control, add the code:

startDrag("");

Make certain that the startDrag(""); code is before the closing curly bracket.

Your pane should now look like this:

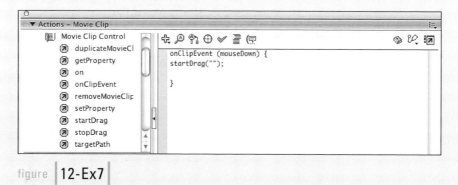

figure **12-Ex7**

Actions pane showing startDrag
code

11. Test your movie. Drag the bug around the stage.

While testing, notice that if you release the mouse button, the bug still moves around as you move your mouse. You need to now stop the drag when the mouse button is released. Return to the stage and make certain that your bug symbol is still selected.

12. In the Actions pane, after the startDrag code, add this code from GlobalFunctions>Movie Clip Control:

OnClipEvent (mouseUp) {stopDrag()

};

Your pane should now look like this:

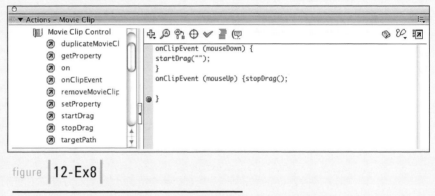

```
onClipEvent (mouseDown) {
startDrag("");
}
onClipEvent (mouseUp) {stopDrag();
}
```

figure | 12-Ex8 |

Actions pane showing onClipEvent stopDrag code

13. Once again, test the movie. You should now be able to drag your bug around the stage and stop the drag when you release your mouse. However, even if you don't place your mouse directly on the bug, notice that you can still drag it around.

Return to the main timeline.

14. Back in the Actions pane, place your cursor before the startDrag(); code. You need to now add an if statement together with the movie clip property hitTest.

First, from Statements>Conditions/Loops, add the code:

if

For the condition type, exactly:

If hitTest(_root._xmouse,_root._ymouse, false))

}

Your pane should now look like this:

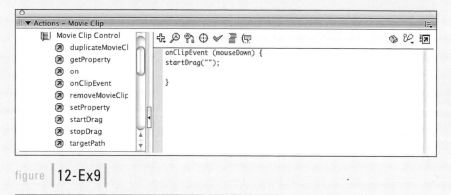

Actions pane showing onClipEvent with conditions added

15. You now need to add this same code to the stopDrag code. You can copy and paste:

If (hitTest(_root._xmouse,_root._ymouse, false))}

into the stopDrag code. Pay close attention to the placement of opening and closing curly brackets. The startDrag and stopDrag commands must fall between the curly brackets of the if statement, and the entire if statement must fall between the curly brackets of the onClip Event.

Your script should now look like this:

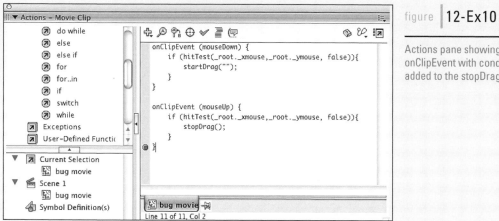

figure | **12-Ex10**

Actions pane showing onClipEvent with condition added to the stopDrag code

16. Test the movie. You should now be able to drag the movie clip around only if you click on the bug.

17. Still, you may want to constrain the drag to the size of the stage window. This will prevent the user from dragging the bug entirely off of the stage.

Return to the main timeline.

18. In the Actions pane, place your cursor inside of the () after the startDrag code. Add the coordinates for the constrain to rectangle. Add the word *true* to lock the mouse to the center registration mark of the bug. Add the coordinates 0, 0, 300, 200. Remember that these indicate the size of your document. Be sure to separate true and each coordinate value with commas.

Your pane should now look like this:

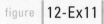

figure **12-Ex11**

Actions window showing coordinates added to code

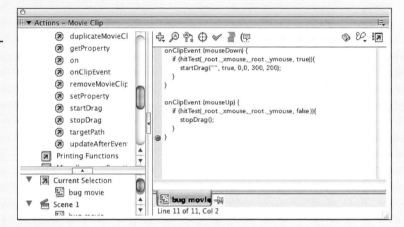

19. Test the movie again. Then, back on the stage, try changing the coordinates to see how this affects your drag and test your movie yet again.

20. In addition to constraining the movie clip to parameters you enter, you can also use the parameters of the clip itself to constrain. To do this, replace the startDrag line from the previous step with the following code:

startDrag ("",true,0,_y,300,_y);

Your pane should look like this:

figure **12-Ex12**

Activities pane showing code constraining the drag to the coordinates of the movie clip symbol

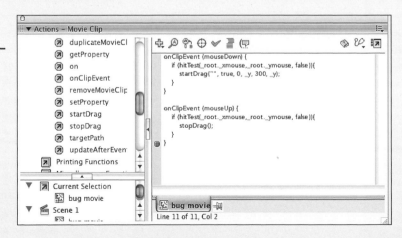

This uses the _y property of the movie clip to set the constrain for the top and bottom parameters, preventing an up-and-down movement.

21. Test the movie one more time. You should be able to drag the clip left and right but not up and down.

22. Save and publish your exercise. Show your friends and let them drag your bug around the Flash player window.

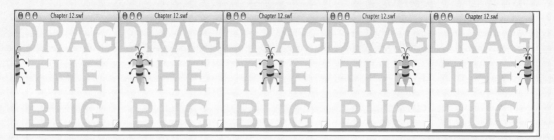

figure | 12-Ex13 |

Completed Exercise 12 showing several locations as a result of dragging

on your own

Try creating a movie clip with several layers of motion tweens that respond to motion guides, so that several objects fly around the registration center of the movie clip. Then create a button symbol. In the button symbol timeline, add a keyframe in the Over State. Leave the Up and Down States empty but add the hit area. Make the hit area quite large so that it will easily activate the Over State. Drag the button symbol onto the stage in a new document timeline. Test the movie and run your mouse across a seemingly blank page. Notice the surprise effect.

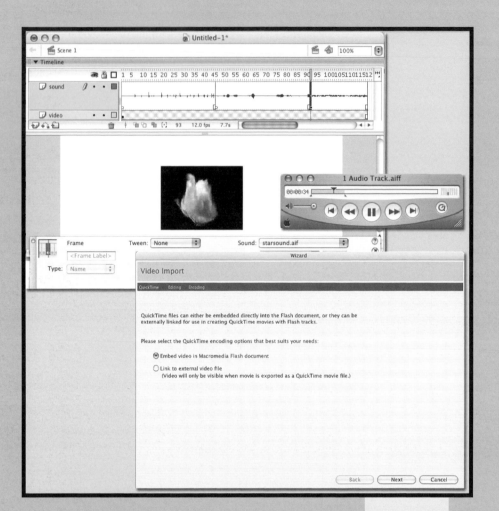

importing audio and video

Objectives

Introduction

One of the most delightful features of Flash is the capability to use sound. You can incorporate sound from anything as simple as a bang to importing music to building your own soundtrack. In this chapter, we'll explore how to find simple sounds, crop more complex music in third-party software, and briefly build your own soundtrack in Flash. We will learn how to manage and edit sounds as well as make the best choices for syncing, compressing, and playing back.

New with Flash MX is the Sorenson Spark video import. You can now embed video clips into your Flash file. The Sorenson Spark codec handles the compression of video needed for import into Flash and the decompression of video data during the playback of a published movie. Consequently, you can include short video clips in your Flash files and still have reasonable file sizes. With Flash Player 6 or 7, any user can view your embedded video without QuickTime or other plug-ins.

IMPORTING AUDIO AND VIDEO

SOUND FILES

We should begin an examination of sound files by discussing ethics. Be conscious of copyrights and permissions. Don't assume that because you are "just" an artist or developing a personal Web site that it is okay to use someone's music without permission. Make sure the sounds you import into your file are royalty free or created by you or someone for you. Otherwise, you must obtain permission to use them which may include paying for their use.

Next, we should take a moment for a word of caution. Sound files can become large and add to your Flash file size very quickly, making download time cumbersome and annoying. It is important that you pay attention to this. You need to balance the quality of the sounds you are using with the file size of your finished movie. In this chapter, we'll learn various ways to manipulate the size of a sound file, to help you with these decisions.

Flash handles sounds with four options: event, start, stop, and stream. Event sounds at a specific frame, but thereafter, event sounds play without relation to specific frames. On one user's computer, a sound may take ten frames to play; on another slower setup, the sound may finish after only five frames have appeared. Unsynchronized sound clips play independently of the frames in a movie and can even continue playing after the movie ends.

You can manipulate sounds through the Edit Envelope, accessible from the Properties window. You can change fades, loops, and edits through the Properties window itself. Choose custom in the Effect drop-down menu or click the Edit button. Either one will open the Edit Envelope window.

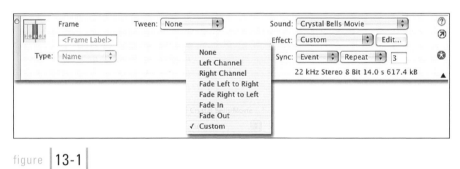

figure | 13-1 |

Properties window showing Edit Effects pull-down menu

In the Edit Envelope, you can shorten your sound in the time bar between the channels. You view sound by seconds or frames. The top envelope is the right channel.

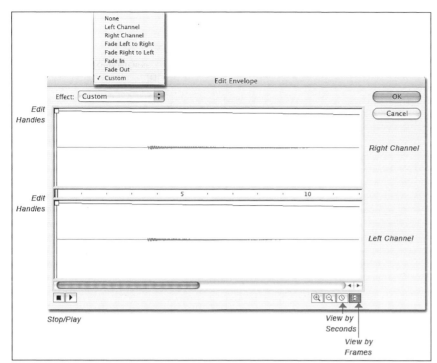

figure |13-2|

Annotated Edit Envelope for sound

There are six predefined volume edits:

1. Left Channel

2. Right Channel

3. Fade Left to Right

4. Fade Right to Left

5. Fade In

6. Fade Out

You can create your own edits by clicking on the sound wave. Click where you want to begin the edit. Click again where you want to end the edit. Drag the wave up or down. You can edit each channel independently.

Because Flash starts a new instance of an event sound, even if that sound is already playing, you have the choice of adding a second instance to the same layer as the first or adding it to a different layer. Choose the layer and frame and from the menu bar, select Insert>Timeline>Keyframe when you want to start a sound again. In the Properties window, from the Sound drop-down menu, choose the sound. (Any sounds you have imported will be listed.) From the Sync drop-down menu, choose Event. The sound is again assigned to this new keyframe. All of the information required to play an event sound lives in the keyframe to which you assigned that sound. When you play the movie, Flash pauses at that keyframe until all the information has downloaded.

It's best to reserve event syncing for short sound clips. In movies that loop, the playback of event sounds can become confusing, since they can stack up on each loop. To avoid playing multiple instances of a sound, set the sound's sync to Start. If the sound is still playing when Flash starts the movie again, Flash lets it play, adding nothing new. If the sound has finished playing, Flash plays the sound again when the playhead enters a keyframe containing the sound. To stop a sound in a specific frame, from the menu bar select Insert>Timeline>Blank Keyframe. In the Property Inspector window, in the Sync drop-down menu, choose Stop.

When you choose Stream as the sync setting for a sound, Flash divides that sound clip into smaller subclips and embeds them in individual frames. A movie's frame rate determines the subclips' size. For streaming sounds, Flash forces the animation to keep up with the sounds. On slower set-ups, Flash draws fewer frames so that important actions and sounds stay together. Flash synchronizes the start of each subclip with a specific frame of the movie. If the sound plays back faster than the computer can draw frames, Flash sacrifices some visuals so that sound and images match up as closely as possible. If the discrepancy between sound-play-back speed and frame-drawing speed becomes too pronounced, however, those dropped frames make the movie look jerky, just as it would if you set a low frame rate to begin with. Streaming sound ensures, for example, that you hear the door slam when you see it swing shut—not a few seconds before.

Flash works with kHz, bits, and mono or stereo. You can assign different options to compress, control playback, and adjust the file size. One way to access a sound's settings is to double-click it in the Library window. This will bring up the Sound Properties dialog box.

figure | **13-3**

Sound Properties dialog box

One final menu can control compression and sample rates for all movie sounds. This is in the Flash Publish settings. From the menu bar select File>Publish Settings>Flash. Here you have choices to affect all audio streaming and all audio events. Click the Set button next to either section to generate a Sound Settings dialog box. Set compression parameters from the Compression drop-down menu. Compression options set for individual sounds via the Sound Properties dialog box will stay the same. All sounds that have not had compression options set individually will be affected by the publish settings. If you've used individual compression methods for some sounds in your movie, you can force Flash to ignore them and publish all sounds with the sound options you've chosen in the Publish Settings dialog box. To do this, on the Flash tab of the Publish Settings dialog box, choose Override sound settings.

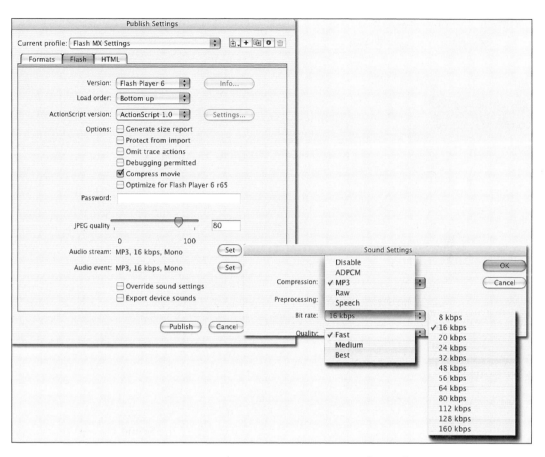

To set compression for movies containing mostly short event sounds, such as handclaps or button clicks, choose ADPCM in the Sound Settings dialog box. Once this is chosen, an ADPCM Bits menu appears. Choose 2-Bit for the greatest degree of compression or lowest quality sound, or choose 5-Bit for the least compression or highest quality sound.

To set compression for movies containing mostly longer streaming sounds, choose MP3. The MP3 options appear and you can choose from 12 different bit rates.

To omit sound compression, choose Raw. This setting still allows you to control the file size by choosing a sample rate and converting stereo sound to mono.

To set compression for sounds consisting of spoken words, choose Speech. Select a sample rate from the menu of options that appears.

Sample rates are measured in kHz or frequency. Recording for music CDs uses 44 kHz. For multimedia CD-ROMs, 22 kHz is the standard rate. For music clips in Flash movies played on

figure | 13-4 |

Flash tab of the Publish Settings dialog box

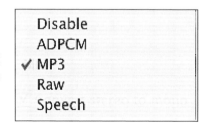

figure | 13-5 |

Compression settings in the Sound Settings dialog box

the Web, 11 kHz is often sufficient. For shorter sounds, including spoken words, you may be able to get away with even lower sampling rates.

It is a good habit to develop to create specific layers for sound. Sounds are easier to update and edit if they are on separate reserved layers. Flash can handle multiple sound layers.

You can adjust the height of a sound layer to better view the waveform. From the menu bar select Modify>Timeline>Layer Properties>Layer Height. Choose 200% or 300% to make the layer taller, then click OK. Back on the timeline, the waveform is shown larger and in more detail.

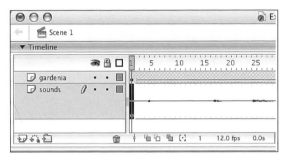

figure | 13-6 |

Timeline with waveform in layer at 300%

Once you have imported sounds and placed them in the timeline, you can see the effect that they have on the play back. When you are in Test Movie mode, choose View>Bandwidth profiler. Notice the surge at the introduction of sound. You want most of your movie to be at the 400 B line with limited surges. Pay attention to how much longer Flash takes to test a movie even with a short sound sampler. The sound continues to replay on top of itself as the movie replays.

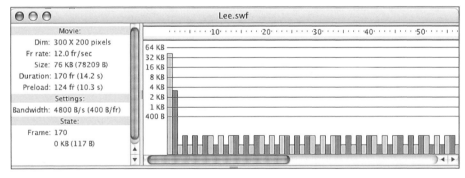

figure | 13-7 |

Bandwidth profiler in Test Movie mode

Notice where the music stops and starts up again and if the edit is what you want. Try changing the loop number to see how this affects your sound.

IMPORTING SOUNDS

There are several sites from which you can download free sound bytes created just for Flash. Try using a search engine—search for *sounds* or *sound bytes* or *sound clips*. Here are a few sites from which you can download sounds either free or for a pretty reasonable price:

- http://www.flashkit.com/soundfx
- http://www.sounddogs.com
- http://www.soundrangers.com

- http://www.webplaces.com/html/sounds.htm
- http://www.freeaudioclips.com/
- http://video.fws.gov/sound.htm

You'll find lots of sound bytes that are clicks, drops, shouts, quacks, etc. These sound bytes are usually royalty free and available to anyone. Pay attention to whether they are .WAV or .AIFF.

Once you have downloaded sounds onto your hard drive, import them into your Flash library through the Import menu. When the sounds exist in your library, you can access them, along with the settings of your choice, through the Properties window. You can sync a sound clip to an action in the document's timeline by adding a keyframe. Add the keyframe to the sound layer in sync with where the action is to take place. In the keyframe, access the sound through the Properties window and set the event to start. You probably won't need a stop event if it is a short sound.

DEVELOPING SOUNDTRACKS

There are several programs out there with which you can build your own soundtracks, including Apple's Garage Band. Garage Band comes with iLife and is free. Another great program for building soundtracks is DoRe Media. It's somewhat expensive but will step you through building a complex soundtrack and provide you with the various necessary components. Regardless of the software program you use, there are some basic components to building a soundtrack in Flash that we can discuss here.

To build a soundtrack in Flash, gather together all of the sounds you plan to use and import them into your library. You will probably need fill sounds, drum sounds, melodies, accent sounds (such as symbol crashes), and solos. Keep your sounds short. This will help to keep your file size down. When building the soundtrack, reuse and loop sounds to develop a full sound, rather than importing large pieces.

Next, create a symbol and identify it as a movie clip symbol. Name it *soundtrack*. You can create the entire soundtrack in a movie clip, using specific layers in the timeline to develop each sound. At the very least, you'll need layers for drums, fills, melodies, solos, and of course, actions.

You can repeat sections of music by sending the playback head back to the frame where the music was cued with an ActionScript of gotoAndPlay (current scene, Frame #).

Also, you can add contrast to repetition by layering other sounds over any section. If you like, you can also add cymbal crashes to keyframes. You may need to mute the last bars of one sound so that the entering musical phrase can be heard clearly. Insert a keyframe to match the frame where the new sound is cued on its layer. Click Edit in the Properties window to open the Edit Envelope. Click the frames button and scroll ahead to where you want to mute the sound. Select Custom from the drop-down menu and create an envelope so that the volume of this track drops out completely at the appropriate frame. When you are finished, click OK.

Let sounds fade in and out, matching up frames and using events to start up new sounds. Play around. Because this is a movie clip, you can have the sound be continuous throughout the main movie. If you only want it to play once, be sure to add a stop action in the last frame of the movie clip.

IMPORTING VIDEO

You can find free video clips on the Internet. Use a search engine, type in *video clips*, and see what you come up with. Once you have downloaded a few, try clipping them in Quicktime Pro. Move the bottom triangles in the timeline to determine the beginning and ending crops. Under Edit, choose Trim. Under File, choose Export. Select Movie to QuickTime Movie and save. This will create a video clip that you can import into Flash.

In Flash, when you import a video, a new wizard will open. Use this to embed the video or link it.

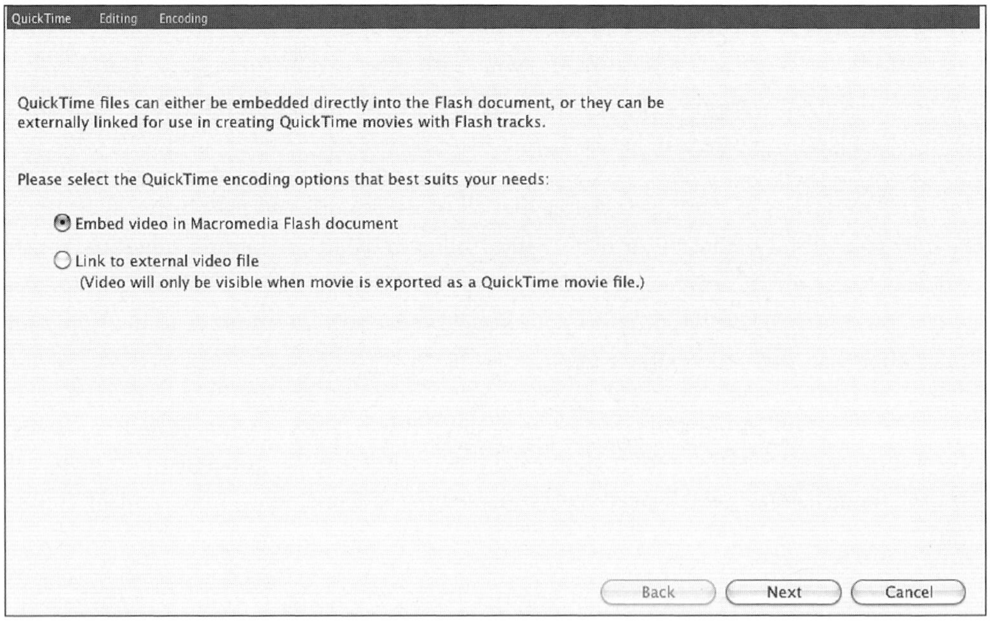

figure | 13-8 |

Video Import Wizard window

You will first have the choice to import or edit. The ability to edit first is new with Flash MX 2004 and a great new feature.

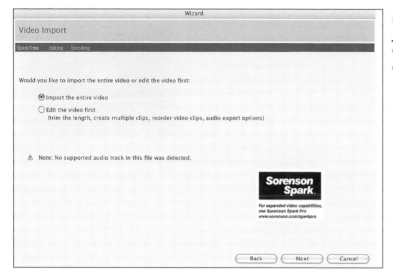

figure | 13-9 |

Video Import Wizard window with import or edit first options

If you choose to edit first, you will be brought to a new window with an editing mode. Move the triangles around to edit, preview, and create clips. The clips that you create will show up in the Clip pane. You can choose to combine the clips into a single library video.

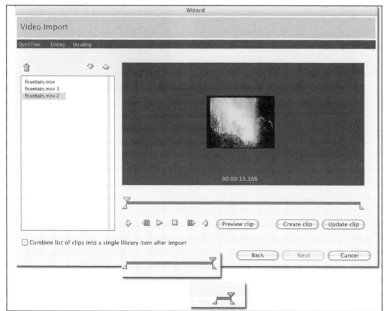

figure | 13-10 |

Video Import Wizard window with several saved clips

The next step in the wizard is to edit the compression settings and synchronize to the document's frame rate. If you synchronize the video to the Flash document frame rate, you will have a frame-by-frame equivalent of your QuickTime movie embedded into the Flash file.

figure |13-11|

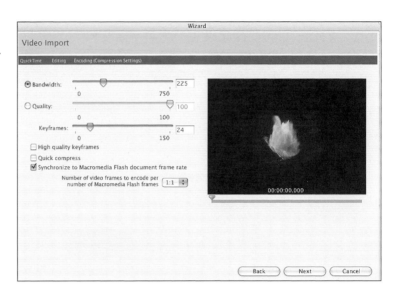

Video Import Wizard compression settings window

At this point, you can go on to the Advanced Settings window and create a new profile. Here you can change color, dimensions, and soundtrack options. You can import sound into the timeline, into a movie clip, or into a graphic symbol. And you can separate or integrate it.

figure |13-12|

Video Import Wizard window with advanced settings for compression

The final window of the wizard will show the compression settings and give you the option to finish or return to a previous menu for changes. At this point, if your Flash document does not have enough frames to play the video, Flash will generate a dialog box telling you how many frames it will take to import the video frame by frame. It will ask you if you want to insert the number needed to synchronize.

figure | 13-13 |

Final window of Video Import Wizard

After you finish with the wizard, you can add a mask to the video, use any of the animation and interactivity capabilities, or use multiple videos or multiple instances that play in and out of each other. One excellent idea for video is to use a short clip with several instances so that it seems to be a longer clip.

SUMMARY

In this chapter, you've explored a variety of sound capabilities and limitations. You've learned about sample rates, compression, looping, and editing. You have examined how sounds can affect file size, playback spikes, and how to view these spikes. You've also looked at copyright issues, downloading sounds, and building your own soundtracks. You've learned how to work with video in Quicktime and edit video with the Flash Video Import Wizard. There are unlimited possibilities with both audio and video in Flash.

in review

1. How can you sync a sound to an action?

2. Where do you go to edit a sound?

3. What tool do you use to view the effects of sound on a movie's profile?

4. What are four ways to compress sound?

5. What is the Video Import Wizard?

6. How can you edit video in Flash?

exercise 13

1. Copy the Exercise 13 folder from the CD onto your hard drive. This folder contains several sounds and video clips that you can use to experiment.

2. Test some of the video clips in Quicktime (or any video player) and choose one.

3. Open a new Flash document. Rename Layer 1 *Video*. Click File>Import>Import to Stage to import the video clip.

4. After the Video Import Wizard Window launches, choose Embed. Click Next and choose the Edit the video first option. Again click Next. You should now be in the editing mode window. Take some time here to experiment. Preview and create your clips. Change the order in the Saved Clip pane. Try out different combinations and check out the Update Clip feature.

figure | 13-Ex1 |

Play/stop and editing tools

5. Choose Combine list of clips into a single library item after import option. After you have created your new video, click Next.

6. In the Encoding window, click Edit. Here you can alter the quality or the bandwidth. If you choose Quality and try out different percentages, you can view the result in the Video pane. This pane also gives you the option to synchronize the video to the document frame rate. Choose this option.

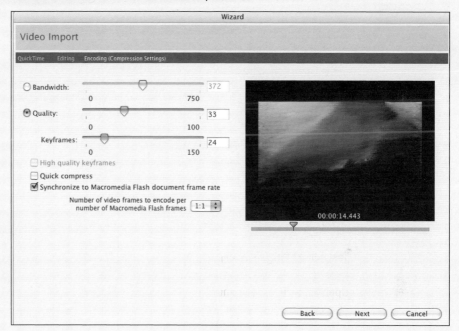

figure | 13-Ex2 |

Video Import Wizard Encoding window with Quality altered to 33

7. Click next. When you are given the option to name this set of choices, click Next and then Finish. If there are not enough frames in the document's timeline, when the dialog box gives you the option to add them choose OK. Synchronizing the video to the document's frame rate and adding enough frames will give you a frame-by-frame equivalent of your video once it is embedded into the Flash file.

8. Test your Movie to view the video.

   Back in the timeline, move the playhead around. Notice that you can watch the video frame by frame. This means that you can sync your own sound to the video. So now add your own sound.

9. Create a new layer and name it *sound*. From the menu bar select Modify>Timeline>Layer Properties. Change the layer height to 300%.

10. If you do not have Quicktime Pro, skip to Step 15. If you do have Quicktime Pro and if you want to use a sound from a CD, insert the disc into your computer and open Quicktime Pro.

Quicktime Pro treats both audio and video tracks as movies. From the menu bar select File>Open Movie in New Player and find the CD. All of the tracks should show in the Open dialog box. Highlight a track and click Open.

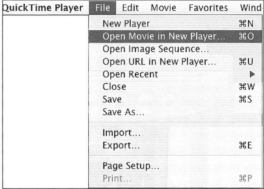

figure | **13-Ex3**

Quicktime Pro File menu

11. Quicktime Pro should open the CD track in a new audio window. You now have options to edit the track. You can move the small triangles around to create a beginning and ending of a new clip. Choose between 15 and 60 seconds.

Next, choose Edit>Trim.

figure | **13-Ex4**

Quicktime Pro window showing editing options

figure | **13-Ex5**

Quicktime Pro Edit menu

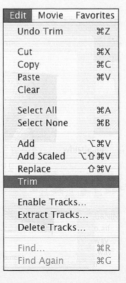

12. From the menu bar select File>Export, then click the Options box. In the Save Exported File As dialog box, you can set compression, rate, size, and use options. Remember: the higher the kHz, the larger the file. 16-bit and stereo will also increase file size, but if you kept your trim to 30 seconds or less, then you can export with higher settings.

13. Click OK when you have made your choices and save. Quicktime Pro should export your trimmed version of the audio track. You can open your new cut in Quicktime to test it. When you are satisfied with all of your sound files, return to Flash and the Exercise 13 document.

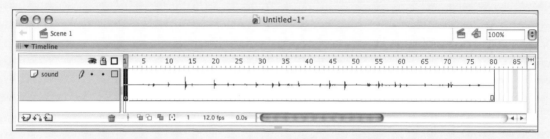

figure | **13-Ex6** |

Flash file with sound layer set at 300%

14. From the menu bar select File>Import>Import to library. Locate the sound(s) that you created or choose from the back of book CD.

15. Open the Library window. Notice the new icon for video clips. Also note that if you had sound in your video file and separated it out, it is still there in the Library window as its own file and available to you. Click on the sound(s) and test by clicking the play button in the upper-right corner.

16. Back in the timeline, click in Frame 1. In the Properties window, open a sound through the Sound drop-down menu. Notice that all of the sounds that you imported to the Library are listed here. After opening a sound, from the Sync drop-down menu, choose Event.

figure | **13-Ex7** |

Testing a sound in the Library window

figure | 13-Ex8 |

Properties window with sound and event chosen

17. Next, click Edit in the window. Envelope Edit should open. At the end of the sound click to start the edit then click again and drag the envelope handles downward to end the edit.

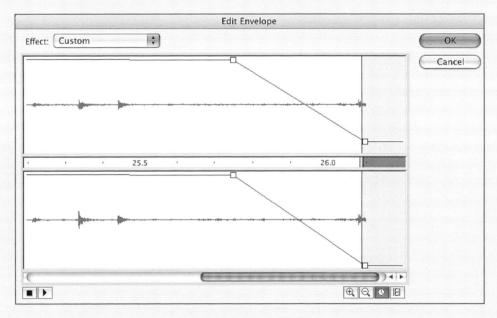

figure | 13-Ex9 |

Envelope Edit window with handles down

18. Click the Play button to hear your edits.

19. Press OK to return to the Properties window. Choose Effect>Fade In. Open the Envelope Edit and notice how Flash has altered the envelope handles.

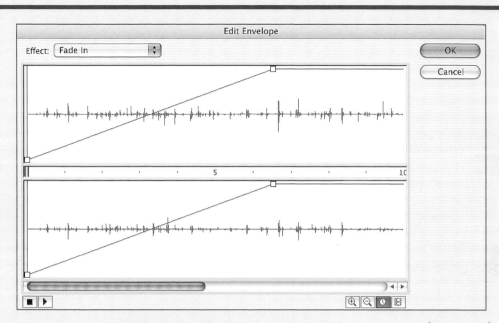

figure | 13-Ex10 |

Envelope Edit window with
handles faded in

20. You can shorten your sound in the time bar
between the channels. Check out View by
Seconds or View by Frames. See how they are
different. Play around with the left and right
channels, changing as desired. (The top envelope
is the right channel.) You can make your sound shorter than the video at this point by
choosing View by Frame.

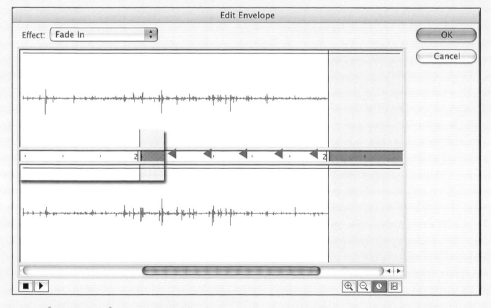

figure | 13-Ex11 |

Shortening sound in the time bar

21. When you are satisfied with your edits, click OK to close the Envelope Edit window. Back in the Properties window, set Repeat to 0.

figure | 13-Ex12 |

Properties window showing repeat setting of 0

22. From the menu bar select Control>Test Movie. Notice how much longer Flash takes to test a movie even with a short sound sampler. Also notice how the sound continues to replay on top of itself as the movie replays.

23. While in Test Movie mode, from the menu bar select View>Bandwidth Profiler. Notice the surge at the introduction of sound. You want most of your movie to be at the 400 B line with limited surges.

figure | 13-Ex13 |

Bandwidth Profiler in Test Movie mode with surge at the first frame

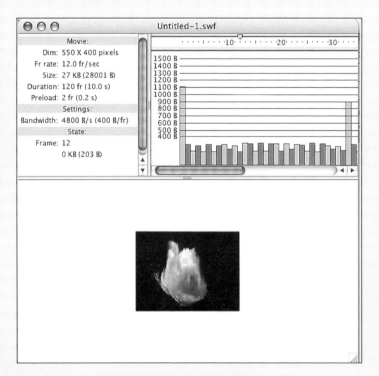

24. Return to the Sound layer. In the Properties window, change the sync to Stream.

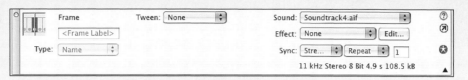

Choose Control>Test Movie again. Notice the difference in how the Bandwidth profiler reads the sound. Pay attention to where the music stops and starts up again and if the edit is what you want. Try changing the loop number to see how this affects your sound. You can change the fades and loops and edit further in the Properties window.

figure | **13-Ex14**

Properties window with sync set to stream

25. Because Flash starts a new instance of an event sound, even if that sound is already playing, you have the choice of adding a second instance to the same layer as the first or adding it to a different layer. Change the sound sync back to Event.

26. When you want to start a new sound or the same sound again, choose the layer and frame and from the menu bar select Insert>Timeline>Keyframe. In the Properties window, from the Sound drop-down menu, choose a sound. From the Sync drop-down menu, choose Event. The new sound (instance) is assigned to the new keyframe.

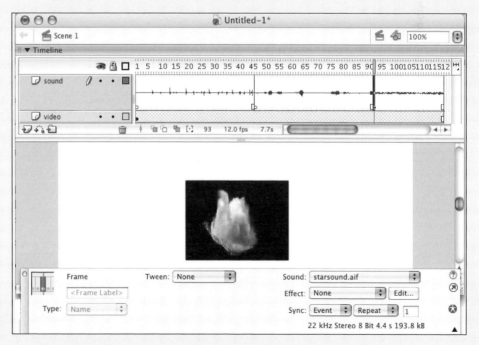

figure | **13-Ex15**

Timeline with sounds attached to additional keyframes

27. Choose Control>Test Movie. Notice how the sounds build upon one another. Play around with this until you have something that sounds pretty good. Try the stop and start options in the sync drop-down menu in the Properties window. You will need to add keyframes to stop or start a sound. Experiment with different settings for the different sounds and instances.

When you are satisfied with what you hear, save your file and play it for your friends.

on your own

Try downloading a few sounds and build your own soundtrack to a video. (There are additional sounds in the Exercise 13 folder on the back of book CD that you can use.) Create the soundtrack in a movie clip. Import a sync sound, drums, accent sounds, and a melody. Use a quack like a symbol crash, creating keyframes in rhythm with the drumbeat. Use bird sounds like a melody. Experiment. Enjoy. See what you can create that syncs up with a video.

notes

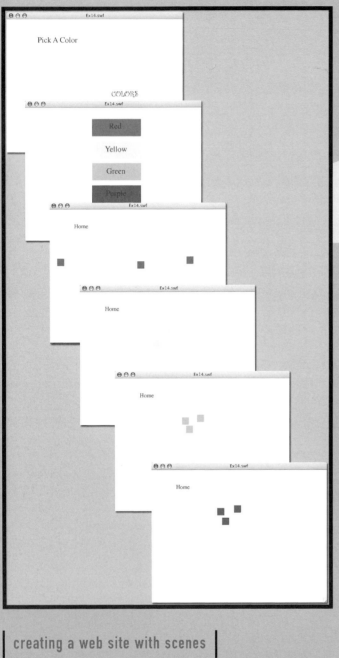

creating a web site with scenes

14

Objectives

Explore one specific way to organize and produce a Web site in Flash.

Discover Copy Frames and Paste Frames.

Understand instances.

Examine BreakApart and Distribute to Layers.

Uncover more ActionScript.

Introduction

Let's take a look at what we've learned so far and put it together to produce a simple Web site. We've touched briefly upon the concept of instances, scenes, and actions, but let's look at how all of these can be organized to structure a Web site that utilizes scenes and symbols repeatedly with different actions and properties assigned to each instance. This chapter will show you one way to consider organizing a Web site in Flash.

CREATING A WEB SITE WITH SCENES

ORGANIZING A WEB SITE IN FLASH WITH SCENES

One approach to organizing a Web site in Flash is through the use of scenes. Each scene can represent a "page" on a Web site, or a section. This can be as simple or as complex as you want; scenes utilize the notion of pages in the same way that we discussed in Chapter 3 regarding hierarchy. Remember when we talked about organizing information effectively? Dreamweaver requires that we create the organization up front with a site directory. Well, in Flash, we don't have to create a site directory. Still, we need to organize our thoughts to match the needs of the Web site. Draw sketches of the organization of the site, including the scenes you will need and what the content and images will be in each scene. Each scene will have its own timeline and layers. All of your Library items can be used and reused in any or all of the scenes.

Organizing with scenes has some disadvantages. If you are working with an image-heavy Web site, and you have embedded the images, it can very quickly become a site that is heavy on the bytes and slow on the download. We'll tackle that in the next chapter. But there are many advantages to using scenes. One advantage is that this is not a complex process in Flash and organization can easily be changed and rearranged. Therefore, when a site is still growing and changing, you can easily add scenes, coding, and additional features. For a text-heavy, image-light site, I choose scenes for navigation and organization.

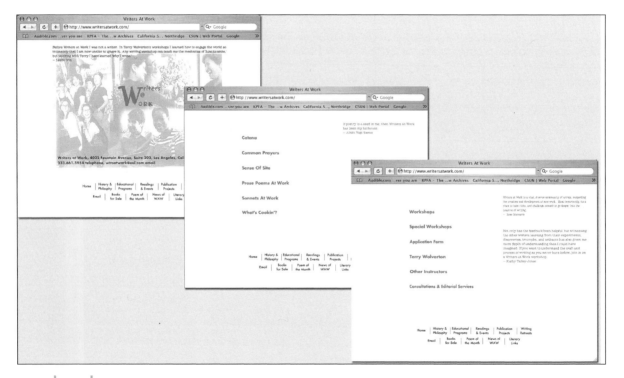

figure | 14-1 |

Example of a site organized by scenes

Okay, let's take a look at how this can be done. Let's say you developed a sketch of a Web site that includes a home page, three first-level pages, and five sublevel pages. This represents nine "pages," or nine scenes. Flash treats the scenes equally. It is you, the designer, who will understand the hierarchy and name the scenes so that they are easily understood later. ActionScript will do the rest.

When you open a new document is Flash, you are automatically in scene one. Use the Insert pull-down menu to create new scenes. Alternately, add scenes through the Scene panel by using the plus sign in the lower right of the window. The Scene panel normally opens with the Flash environment, but if it is not open, from the menu bar select Window>Design Panels>Scenes. Either way, in the Scene panel, double-click a scene to change the name. Name your scenes in a logical, consistent manner. This is where you need to be "clear, consistent, and efficient" for yourself. Look at the sketch you've created for the Web site and name the scenes accordingly. Later, when you apply ActionScript, you will appreciate this early organizational approach. You will use the names of these scenes for your ActionScript.

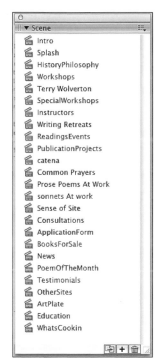

figure **14-2**

Scene window

figure **14-3**

Scene panel showing plus sign to add scenes

COPY FRAMES AND PASTE FRAMES

In a site organized by scenes, the navigation needs to be placed in each scene. As already discussed, you want your navigation to stay in the same place, consistent, efficient, and clear. With scenes as an organizing structure, you can maintain this consistency without a lot of tedious work.

Create the navigation in any Scene and assign ActionScript to each button. Make certain that your navigation placement is going to visually work in each scene. You can check your sketches for this. Once you've created the navigation, you can then highlight the frames and layers that control the navigation. From the menu bar select Edit>Timeline>Copy Frames.

figure | 14-4 |

Edit pull-down menu

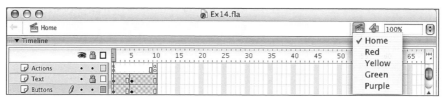

Move to the next scene where you want to add the navigation. You can move between scenes simply by clicking on the name of the scene in the Scene window. Alternately, you can choose a scene through the top-right triangle of the timeline.

In the new scene, use just one layer with a single frame. Click Edit> Timeline>Paste Frames. Flash will paste the frames, layers, layer names, and ActionScript in exactly the same place each time.

figure | 14-5 |

Scene access menu in timeline

figure | 14-6 |

Navigation layers and frames in timeline and on stage

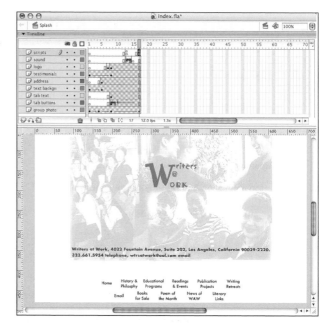

BREAK APART AND DISTRIBUTE TO LAYERS

In Chapter 10, we worked with the Break Apart command with an imported pixel image. Break Apart can also be used with text, objects, and symbols. With text, Break Apart converts a single object of text into individual letters, regardless of the number of words or sentences, so that each letter is an object and can be modified independently of the other letters. When we combine Break Apart with text and another command, Distribute to Layers, we end up with each letter not only as an object with its own bounding box, but also existing on its own layer. This means that we can now apply animation individually to each letter. If we add a keyframe in the anticipated last frame of our animation before we move any letters around, they will end up back together to form the original word, sentence, or paragraph. This is kind of fun and relatively easy.

So how does this work specifically? Let's start with a word, any word. Select it and from the menu bar select Modify>Break Apart. Next, make sure that all of the bounding boxes are highlighted and choose Modify>Timeline>Distribute to Layers. Each letter is now assigned to its own layer and Flash automatically names the layers with the letter.

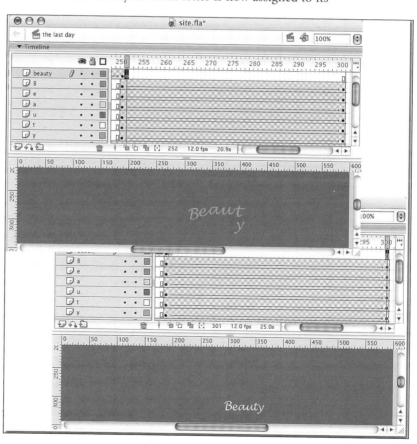

You can now add motion tweens or frame-by-Frame animation to each letter. Move letters off of the stage, change their alphas to 0%, or scale them to be larger or smaller. Just keep the word together in the last frame. Whatever you choose to do, your letters will appear to come flying out of nowhere to settle into a readable word.

As early as it may seem to be, let's move on to Exercise 14, since it is rather long and involved. This exercise puts together several things that you have worked with over the last few chapters to create a complete Web site. Once you have finished the exercise, you'll understand not only how to organize a Web site through scenes but also some new fun and creative ways to animate.

figure **14-7**

Example of Break Apart and Distribute to Layers on timeline and stage

SUMMARY

In this chapter, you've explored how to create an entire Web site using scenes as an organizational scheme. You can apply this method to any image-light site that you are going to design. (In Chapter 15, we'll look at organizing a Web site in a different way.) You can also organize a Web site using movie clips in the same way that you use scenes. Now, when you are designing, you will be able to make choices between these options.

Additionally, you have learned some more fun tools in Flash that allow you to create surprises for the user. You've learned about Break Apart and Distribute to Layers. You've also discovered a few practical tips, such as how to use Copy Frames and Paste Frames, as well as how to work with instances.

in review

1. What is an instance?

2. What does it mean to distribute to layers?

3. How can you add frames to more than one layer at a time?

4. How can you copy frames and layers from one scene to another?

5. What panel do you use to change the name of a scene?

6. How can Scenes be effective in organizing a Web site?

7. When would you want to use Scenes to organize a Web site?

exercise 14

1. Open a new Flash document. You're going to create a Web site about color, so begin by building the elements that will go into it. You'll then use these elements repeatedly as different instances.

   Start by creating two different buttons. One should be the Home button that will be placed on all four pages of the colors. This button will then be used four different times, using the same code with no changes to the properties. You'll use the Copy Frames and Paste Frames functions to achieve this. The other button will be used on the home page to take the user to the inside pages. This button will be used several times with different properties and ActionScript applied to each instance.

   Begin with the Home button. From the menu bar select Insert>New Symbol. Call this one *home* and designate it as a button. When you click OK, you will be taken to the button four-frame timeline. This time you are going to use text to function as a button. In the first frame, in the center of the stage, type the word *Home*, choosing your font size and color in the Properties window. (You may want to keep this a neutral color, since the rest of your site is going to be very colorful.) With the Selection tool, make certain that the text is exactly centered on the registration mark. Click in the Hit frame and add a keyframe. In the keyframe, draw a rectangle slightly larger than the text. Remember that this rectangle will not show up on the Web site. It only functions to tell Flash the location of the clickable area.

figure | **14-Ex1** |

Home button on timeline and stage

2. Change the Over or Down state if you like. Simply move the playhead to the Over State and add a keyframe. You can then change the text in some way. You can additionally alter the Down state. Be careful, though, with how much activity you create in the Home button. Think about where your design focus is. Do you want the Home button to draw a lot of attention or do you want the user to focus on the rest of the site? This is a question that only you can answer—weigh it carefully and balance your ideas. Whatever you decide to do, since you will be using the same button on each "inside" page, the activity of the Over and Down States will be the same.

3. Next, create the button that will be used to take the user to the "inside" pages (actually scenes). This button will only be used on the home page.

| NOTE |

Symbol Registration

It's important to center your symbol drawings to the registration marks of the symbol timeline. This will keep the target point centered in a symbol when you use it in the scene's timeline. Also, centering your symbols this way will help you understand where each symbol sits and what it is adding to the design.

Back in Scene 1, again from the menu bar select Insert>New Symbol. Call this button *colorButton* and designate it as a button symbol. Again, once you click OK, you are taken to the button timeline. In the first frame, in the center of the button stage, draw a rectangle about 50 pixels high by 150 pixels wide.

The color of this rectangle can be a neutral color. You'll be assigning different colors to it through the Properties window in each instance of use, so the color that you use now really doesn't matter.

Remember that you can turn on your rulers through View>Rulers. When you are drawing on the stage with the rulers on, Flash will show you where your drawing is occurring. Use these rulers to measure your rectangle.

4. Click in the Hit frame and add a keyframe. Again draw a rectangle that will tell Flash what the clickable area is (don't worry about the color). Make this rectangle slightly larger than the one in the Up State so that the user can still access it even if there is a slight unintended movement of the mouse. Don't make it too much larger though—you don't want the button's clickable area to interfere with other clickable areas on the stage. Just a few pixels in each direction will do.

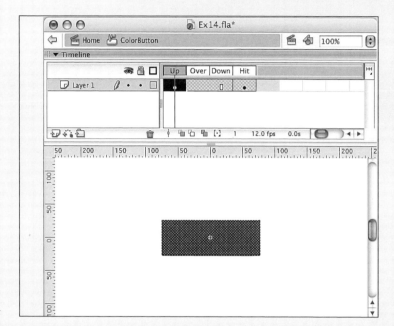

figure | 14-Ex2 |

ColorButton timeline and stage

You can add changes to the Over and Down States if you want, but once again, think about the overall design concept. You could add some surprises here, but you could also do it later, after you've created more of the elements. For example, once you've created a symbol, you can always go back and make changes to that symbol—the changes will show up in each instance that you have used it, along with any changes to the instance.

5. Now add an opening title sequence. Do this by using another movie clip and the Break Apart and Distribute to Layers tools.

Back in Scene 1, click in Frame 1. In the center of the stage, type the word *Colors*. The font choice can be rather playful, as this is going to be purely for entertainment. Make the font size rather large (24 pts or so) as this is your opening title sequence.

6. With the word selected, from the menu bar select Modify>Convert to Symbol. Choose Movie Clip and name the symbol *colorBreak*. Assign the registration mark to the center square. Click OK.

7. Double-click the ColorBreak movie clip symbol to enter its timeline. In the timeline, highlight the word *Colors* and from the menu bar select Modify>Break Apart. Notice now that each letter has its own bounding box.

figure | 14-Ex3 |

Bounding box of each letter on the ColorBreak movie clip stage

8. Make sure that all six letters are highlighted and from the menu bar select Modify>Timeline>Distribute to Layers. Notice that each letter now has its own layer and the layer is renamed with the letter.

figure | 14-Ex4 |

Letters distributed to layers on the ColorBreak movie clip timeline

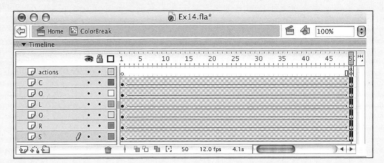

9. In the C layer, click in Frame 50. Hold down the `Shift` key and click in Frame 50 of the S layer. This should highlight Frame 50 in all of the layers. From the menu bar select Insert>Timeline>Frame. This will extend all of the layers to 50 frames.

10. In Frame 1 of each layer, select all of the layers and choose Insert>Timeline>Create Motion Tween.

11. In Frame 50 of each layer, add a keyframe. This will complete the motion tween for each layer. You want to keep Frame 50 as is to bring the word together at the end of the movie clip.

12. Return to Frame 1 of the S layer and move the S somewhere else on the stage. With the S still selected, change the tint in the Properties window. This changes the color of this instance only. At the end of the motion tween, the color will return to its original state.

    Repeat this with each letter. You can scale any of the letters in the first frame to add to the motion tween. You can also add easing in or out.

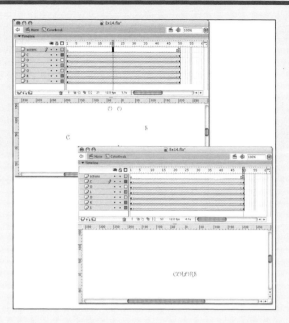

figure | 14-Ex5

ColorBreak timeline and stage showing completed motion tweens

13. Highlight Layer 1. Change the name to *actions*. Click in Frame 50. Add a keyframe. Open the Actions window. With your cursor in the keyframe, drag the stop action from Global Functions>Timeline Control Actions in the toolbox into the Action pane. This will add the stop action to the frame and stop the movie. Make sure that the little *a* appears in the keyframe.

Your movie clip symbol timeline should look something like this:

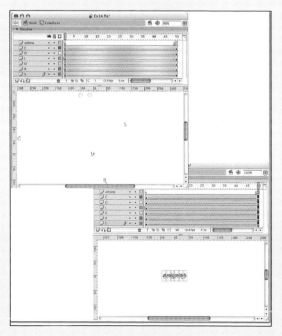

figure | 14-Ex6

Completed ColorBreak movie clip symbol

14. Return to the stage and click anywhere to move your cursor out of the Actions window. Hit the return key and watch your movie clip. You should see the letters move from a scattered, multipositioned configuration to a single word, all the same color in the center of the stage.

15. Return to the Scene 1 timeline. Delete the ColorBreak movie clip from the stage.

16. Now you're going to create a movie clip for use on each of the four "inside" pages (scenes). This movie clip will have different colors applied to it in the Properties window for each instance. Therefore it really doesn't matter what color you use right now. You'll build on your previous experience of using motion guides and motion tweens to create this movie clip.

   From the menu bar select Insert>New symbol. Name this symbol *ColorBurst* and designate it as a movie clip. Click OK, to enter the movie clip timeline.

17. With this movie clip, you are aiming for a bursting-of-color effect. The movie should consist of many little squares of color bursting from the center to fill the stage with color. Focus on the delightful here.

   In the center of the movie clip stage, draw a small square, using a neutral color. This shape could be as small as ten pixels square. In the timeline, click Frame 100 and from the menu bar select Insert>Timeline>Frame. Rename the layer as *square 1* and highlight it. Add a motion guide layer.

figure | 14-Ex7 |

ColorBurst timeline and stage

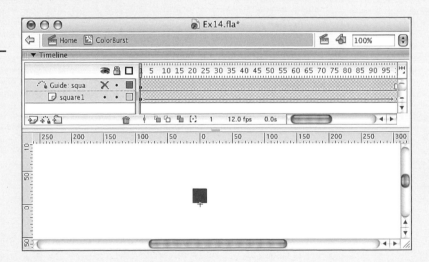

18. In Frame 1 of the motion guide layer, using the Pencil tool with your options set to Smooth, draw a path that begins in the center and spirals outward. You will to add scaling and easing to your motion tweens so you don't want your paths to be too complicated. If you draw a path with many curves and twists and you can't get your

object to follow the path, it may just be too complicated. If that happens, just delete the path and redraw a simpler version. That should eliminate the problem.

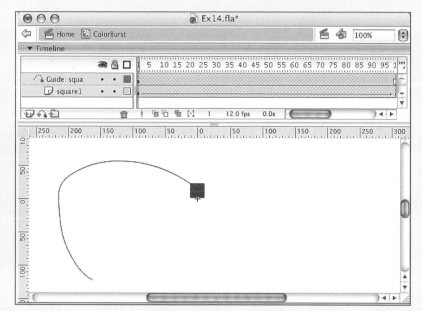

figure | **14-Ex8** |

ColorBurst path for first square

19. Lock the motion guide layer. In Frame 1 of the *Square 1* layer, insert a motion tween. Add a keyframe in Frame 100 and move the square to the end of the path, making sure that you see it snap. Press return to watch the square move along the path through 100 frames. Now you can scale the square in Frame 1 or 100. You can click in either frame and set an easing in or easing out. You can also add keyframes to the in-between frames and ease or modify in some way. Your object will continue to follow the path and react to the changes.

20. Repeat this procedure adding a layer and motion guide for each square until you have four or five different little squares following different paths around the stage of the movie clip. Start them all from the center. This will give that bursting effect. You can stagger the beginnings of the layers by several frames to add interest to the "burst." Press return as you develop each layer to see how your movie is proceeding.

Make this movie clip delightful, energetic, and charming. After all, color is a delightful way to approach life. Since this is a Web site about color, and since the Web is a wonderful venue for color, let this movie clip speak to the delight of the user's soul. Let it sparkle and charm.

figure | 14-Ex9 |

Completed timeline and stage for ColorBurst movie clip

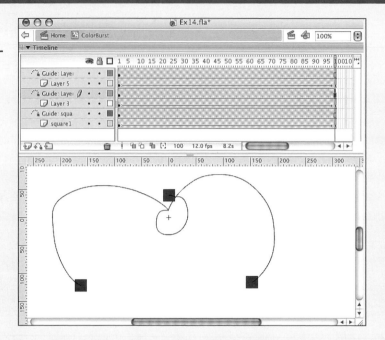

21. Return to the main timeline. It's now time to organize the Web site into scenes.

If the scene panel is not visible from the menu bar select Window>Design Panels> Scene. Click Insert>Scene four times. You should see five Scenes. Double-click each scene and rename it. Name the scenes *Home, Red, Yellow, Green*, and *Purple*.

22. Return to the Home scene by either clicking it in the Scene panel or using the Scene pull-down menu from the top right of the timeline. Create five layers. Name them *ColorMovie, Home, Buttons, Text,* and *Actions*.

figure | 14-Ex10 |

Home scene timeline with Scene panel

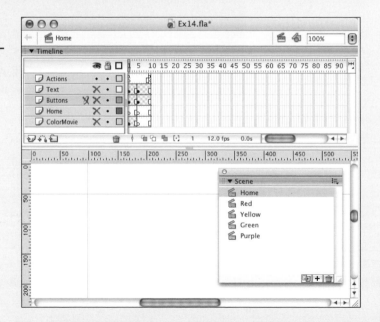

23. Click in Frame 10. Select all five layers and choose Insert>Timeline>Frame.

24. In Frame 5 of the Home, Buttons, ColorMovie, and Text layers, add a keyframe.

25. In the Actions layer, add a keyframe in Frame 10. Add a stop action in both Frames 1 and 10. Your timeline should look something like this:

figure | **14-Ex11** |

Home scene timeline

26. Open the Library window. You should see two movie clips, two buttons, and a few motion tweens.

    In the main timeline, highlight the ColorMovie layer. Click in Frame 1. From the Library window, drag the ColorBreak movie clip to the center of the stage.

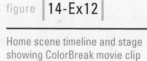

figure | **14-Ex12** |

Home scene timeline and stage showing ColorBreak movie clip

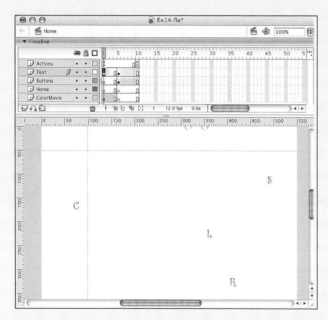

27. Highlight the Button layer and click in Frame 5. From the Library window, drag four instances of the color button and align them vertically in the center of the stage. You can use the Modify>Align>Horizontal Center tool to do this. Additionally, you can distribute heights vertically.

28. Click the first of these four buttons. In the Properties window, change the tint and the instance name to Red. You might want to write down the number of the red tint that you choose to match it with the color burst later.

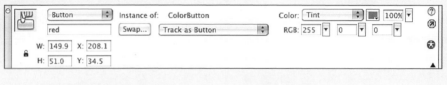

figure | 14-Ex13 |

Properties window for the red color button

29. From the Actions toolbox, choose Global Functions>Movie Clip Control. Drag the action into the Actions pane, choosing Release from the submenu.

30. Next click between the braces in the Action pane. From Global Functions>Timeline Control in the toolbox, add the gotoAndStop action. Make sure you choose the Go to and Stop action rather than the Go to and Play action. Choose 2 of 2 for the arguments. Type in "Red," 1 in the parenthesis area. The spelling here must absolutely match the name of the scene in the Scene panel. Your Action pane should look like this:

on (release) {

gotoAndStop("Red", 1);

31. Click on the second button. Change the tint and ionstance name to *Yellow* (again writing down the number of the color). In the Actions pane, apply the same actions but type "Yellow" for the scene.

32. Repeat this procedure for the Green and Purple scenes.

33. Highlight the text layer. In Frame 5, over the red button, type *red*. Over the yellow button, type *yellow*. Over the green button, type *green*, and over the purple button, type *purple*. Choose a font that is clear and readable, since this is your navigation. You could use the same font as your Home button. Choose a size and color that will show up easily on all four buttons.

figure | 14-Ex14 |

Action panes for all four buttons

34. Return to Frame 1. Draw a horizontal guide at 50 pixels and a vertical guide at 100 pixels. Highlight the text layer and click in Frame 1. On the stage, at the cross point of the guides, type *Pick A Color*. Use the same font as you used for the Home button.

35. Lock the text layer. In the Buttons layer, in Frame 1, drag a color button from the library window to fit over the text of *Pick a Color*. Change the alpha to 0% to make it disappear. (The button will still function even though it is not visible.)

36. Open the Actions window. From Global Functions>Movie Clip Control in the toolbox, drag the on icon into the Action pane. Choose Release from the submenu. With your cursor between the braces, from Global Functions>Timeline Control in the toolbox, add the gotoAndStop. Type *5* for the argument. You don't need to type the scene, as this action will stay in the same scene.

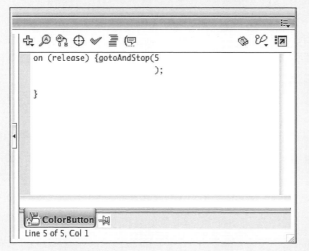

figure | **14-Ex15** |

ActionScript for Pick a Color button

37. From the Scene panel, double-click the Red scene to open it. Or from the upper-right corner of the timeline, under the Scene icon, from the drop-down scene menu, choose Red. Create two more layers. Name the layers *Movie, Home,* and *Actions*. Add a frame at Frame 10 on all three layers.

38. Add vertical guides at 100 and 250 pixels. Add horizontal guides at 50 and 150 pixels. As you work with the different scenes, add these same guides. This will maintain consistency throughout the scenes.

39. In Frame 1 of the Actions layer, add a stop action.

40. In Frame 1 of the Movie layer, from the Library window, drag the ColorBurst movie clip onto the center of the stage. Align the symbol's target to the guides of 250 pixels by 150 pixels. Select it, and in the Properties window, change the tint to the same red as the red of the button in the Home scene. Change the instance name to *Red Burst*.

41. Click in Frame 1 of the Home layer. From the Library window, drag the Home button onto the stage, aligning the symbol's target with the cross point of the 50-pixel and 100-pixel guides. Click the Home button on the stage and in the Actions window drag the on icon from the Global Functions>Movie Clip Control folder. When the arguments submenu shows, choose Release.

42. Next, within the braces of the Actions pane, add the gotoAndStop action from the Global Functions>Timeline Control folder. After the gotoAndStop action, type in "*Home*", *1*. This directs the action to go to the Home scene, Frame 1. It should look like this:

on (release) {

gotoAndStop("Home", 1);

Your stage for the Red scene should look something like this:

figure 14-Ex16

Completed timeline and stage for the Red scene

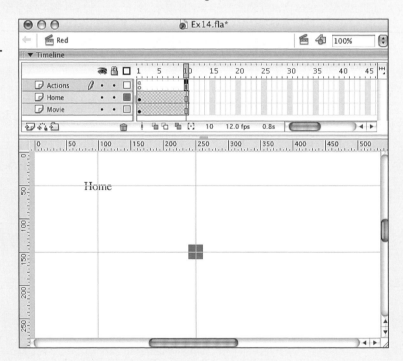

43. Highlight all ten frames of all three layers of the Red scene and click Edit>Timeline>Copy Frames.

44. Open the Yellow scene and in Frame 1 of the unnamed layer, from the menu bar select Edit>Timeline>Paste Frames. This will add the entire contents of the Red scene to the Yellow scene.

45. In the Yellow scene, click the ColorBurst movie clip symbol. In the Properties window, change the tint and instance name to *Yellow*, using the same yellow as the button in the Home scene.

Check the Home button to make sure the actions copied properly.

46. Repeat this procedure with each of the remaining scenes (Green and Purple), changing the ColorBurst movie tint and instance name to the appropriate color.

47. Return to the Home scene. Test your Web site. It should look something like this:

Check out Color Plate 26 to see how student Richard Hogge completed this exercise.

Is everything working correctly? Do all of the actions take you where they should? If not, you can go back and fix them. Are all of the colors consistent? Is your Web site fun and engaging? When all of these answers are yes, save your file and show your friends.

See Color Plates 22 and 23 for a look at http://www.mariaclaudia cortes.com, a Web site thesis project devoted to color communication and symbolism.

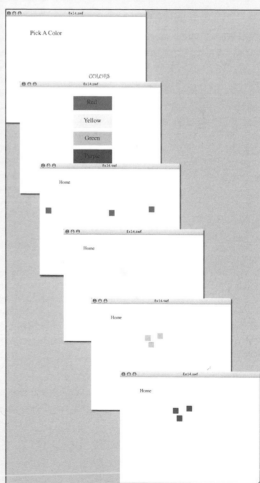

figure | **14-Ex17**

Completed five scenes of Exercise 14 in the Test Movie window

on your own

Add some sound to the scenes in Exercise 14. In each of the color scenes, add a short, rather dramatic sound (like a symbol crash) that matches with the burst of color. You can find some short sounds in the Chapter 13 Exercise folder.

Also, try organizing a Web site with scenes to show the color wheel. You can refer to Color Plates 4 and 5 for help. Using the same steps as in Exercise 14, create a site with navigation for the primary colors of red, yellow, and blue. In the scenes of the primary colors, add a secondary navigation that takes you to the secondary colors green, orange, and purple. Finally, add a third level of navigation to take you to the complementary colors. Continue to use the same ColorBurst movie clip symbol throughout, changing the tint in each instance to match the color. In the scenes containing the complementary colors, place two instances of the movie clip symbol on the same "page," showing the two different colors.

notes

creating a web site with root ActionScript

Objectives

Introduction

As you have read and seen, there are many approaches to organizing and developing a Web site in Flash. We've already explored the use of scenes. Another excellent organizing feature is the root ActionScript loadMovieNum. If your Web site is text-heavy, then scenes are the better choice for organization. If your Web site is image-heavy, particularly pixel-based images, then loadMovieNum is a better choice. It is also an especially good choice for a portfolio site.

CREATING A WEB SITE WITH ROOT ACTIONSCRIPT

LOADMOVIENUM

LoadMovieNum is a root ActionScript that loads a SWF file on top of another SWF file. It doesn't actually replace the original SWF file. Instead, it treats the background of the top SWF as transparent. In fact, you will need to use a background of some sort in order to have the second SWF file be opaque. This results in everything in the second SWF showing up on top of the background of the original SWF. You can load as many additional SWF files over the original SWF, one at a time, as you want. This offers the advantage of reducing the number of pixel-based images per SWF document, thus keeping your site running smoothly without waiting for either all of your images to load into one file or boring your user with a preloader. Let's face it. Aren't preloaders getting to be a drag?

The Web sites in the following were both created with the loadMovieNum organizational structure.

figure 15-1

http://www.francisco-x.net (by student Francisco Ruiz)

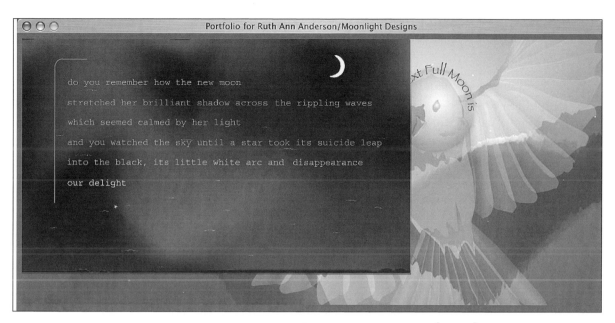

You can view more of these two Web sites in Color Plates 25, 26, and 27.

figure **15-2**

http://www.moonlightdsn.com (by author, poem by Rose Marcario)

Here is the code to use to set up this type of organization:

```
on (release) {

loadMovieNum("home.SWF", 1);

}
```

In the above code, *on* refers to the mouse. *(release)* refers to the action of the mouse. *{loadMovieNum* is the argument that tells the movie what to do when the action is carried out. (*"home.SWF"* is the published Flash file to load. *1* is the frame that loading should start playing from. *);}* closes the action.

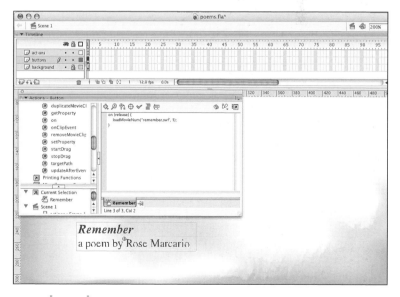

figure **15-3**

ActionScript for Remember button on http://www.moonlightdsn.com

NAVIGATION AS A MOVIE CLIP

You can create navigation inside of a movie clip to use in conjunction with the ActionScript loadMovieNum. Everything goes inside the movie clip, including the buttons and the ActionScript loadMovieNum. This results in a button symbol nested inside of a movie clip symbol, which will sit in one frame of the document's timeline. Remember that you can have another movie clip nested inside of any state of the button symbol, resulting in several levels of nesting.

Each navigation button will load a different .SWF file with this ActionScript, placing it directly on top of index.swf. It will stay in this position until the user clicks on another button.

It's important to be conscious of the navigation placement in the index file when you are creating additional Flash files. You don't want to cover this up. Additional SWFs are centered horizontally and vertically by default, but you may need to experiment with this.

Again, sketching is very important. Sketch out a diagram of your site, only this time plan each "page" as a separate Flash document. Create sketches for the organization of your site, the contents of each "page," and the possible images you will need.

CREATE AN E-MAIL LINK

Adding an e-mail link to a Web site created in Flash is quite easy. You can use the Actions window to add the script just as you would add a script to any button. In this case, the button can be text or a graphic. The Over State can have a nested movie clip. As with any navigation button, make it clear and efficient.

The code to add an e-mail link is:

on (release) {

getURL("Mailto: emailaddress.ext");

}

figure | 15-4 |

Code for Moonlight Designs e-mail button

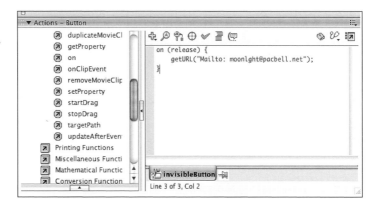

WEB DESIGN BRIEFLY REVIEWED

So now that we're putting this all together, let's step back and review some of the design concerns that we've discussed throughout the book.

Page Layout

Page layout needs to be clear and understandable. You want your user to know what is going on, not get confused, and not be overwhelmed. This means breathing space around images. It means a logical grid of text and images. It means knowing one's whereabouts. It also includes guiding your user's eye around the page, through animation and navigation.

A page format gaining popularity is the widescreen look of a theatrical presentation. This can be a fun approach, offering a level of subconscious emotional response.

figure | 15-5 |

Page layout for http://www.maryperson.com (See Color Plate 28 to view this Web site in color.)

Navigation

As we've discussed repeatedly, navigation should be clear, concise, efficient, and consistent. With loadMovieNum, consistency is not an issue. The navigation is only placed once and therefore cannot move around, functioning much the same as a navigation frame in a frames-based Dreamweaver site. Still, you want to remain conscious of clarity. Remember that you want your user to be able to answer the questions "Where am I?"; "Where can I go from here?" "How can I get there?", and "How can I get back?" You want user movements to be efficient and concise.

figure | 15-6 |

Widescreen format of http://www.francisco-x.net (See Color Plate 25 for color details.)

figure | 15-7 |

Example of clear and efficient navigation at http://www.lorilindland.com

Typography

Type should be easy to read, have plenty of breathing space, and fit the style of the design. On larger Web sites, type can be used to show hierarchy. Titles can be larger and possibly a different font. Navigation can be a specific font. Beyond these two, stick to one font, using italic, roman, and bold where necessary. On a smaller site, use just one font with different sizes or attributes.

Color Scheme

Don't make your Web site confusing by using too many colors. Remember that today's user spends a lot of time on the Internet; a lot of color can be very tiring on the eyes. Be conservative with a simple color scheme and maybe one or two highlight colors.

figure | 15-8 |

Example of good typography (by student Chelsi Jenkins)

figure | 15-9 |

Example of a nice color scheme (by student Natalia Wehba; see Color Plate 29 to view in color)

Images

Remember that images are still the most powerful tool of communication. Images grab you emotionally, subconsciously, and effectively. Make sure you allow plenty of time to create strong images.

Sketching

One final time: Don't forget to sketch out your ideas, your organization, and the most logical way to move around your Web site. Take your time with this process. Sketching offers the opportunity to erase, reconsider, and ultimately create the most effective images and site management possible.

When we are sketching, we receive visual feedback that is easily edited, rethought, and reconsidered. When we try to "sketch" on the computer, we tend to get caught up in the tricks and glamour of the program and monitor. We also tend to become invested in the amount of work we've already completed just in this initial phase. Suddenly it is harder to erase and let go. Sketching promotes a deeper level of understanding, creativity, and feedback *before* we are seduced by the computer. So sketch, sketch, and sketch some more.

figure | 15-10 |

Duck and Bun Kiss the Moon (by Mary Peterson)

SUMMARY

In this chapter, you learned how to create a Flash Web site by using the loadMovieNum ActionScript for the navigation combined with separate SWF files for each "page." This is an excellent way to organize a Web site in Flash. There are several advantages to this method. To add to the navigation, just return to the editing mode of the movie clip. You only need to edit the navigation once. Additionally, loading separate .SWF files spreads out your images throughout your Web site, guaranteeing faster downloads and adding to a more compelling user experience.

in review

1. What is loadMovieNum?

2. How does loadMovieNum work?

3. Do you need HTML documents beyond index.html?

4. Can you place navigation inside of a movie clip?

5. When would you want to use the loadMovieNum method to organize a Web site?

exercise 15

1. On your desktop, create a new folder called *Exercise 15*. Copy the Exercise 15 files from the CD.

2. Begin by sketching out your ideas. You can use the provided artwork and text or create your own. In either case, you will create a background in Photoshop or Illustrator. Your site will include an index page, a home page, a page about raccoons, and a page about frogs. Your index page will contain the navigation that will be visible regardless of which page is loaded. You may want to include shapes for the navigation on the background graphic, or you can create these in Flash. For this exercise, the shapes were created on the background in Photoshop.

3. Create the background in Photoshop or Illustrator. Make this document 640 pixels wide by 300 pixels high.

4. Create a color scheme from the Web-safe palette, limiting your colors to no more than two analogous colors and one complementary color. Your document should have a monochromatic look with one highlight. Write down the Web-safe numbers of your colors so that you can use them in your Flash file.

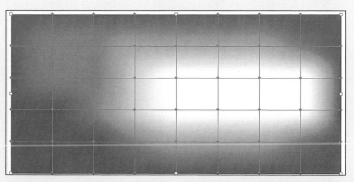

figure | 15-Ex1 |

Background created in Illustrator using a gradient mesh

5. Create the background to include "tabs" where your navigation system will be. You'll need tabs for the raccoon link, the frog link, the home link, and the e-mail link.

6. Add a highlight area where your information/images/etc. will go.

7. If you are creating your background in Illustrator, you can use the gradient mesh to add interest and a highlight area. This is a great tool to create ambience. If you use this filter, you should Save for the web as a JPG. Otherwise, export from Illustrator as AI file to Flash file.

From Photoshop, Save for the web as a JPG.

When you are saving an entire background as a JPG to import into Flash, choose a low or medium resolution in order to keep the file size smaller.

figure | 15-Ex2 |

Completed background in Illustrator with tabs

8. Next, create a new document in Flash. Then from the menu bar select Modify>Document>Dimensions: 640 pixels wide by 300 pixels high. Call out the background color to match the basic color of your Photoshop or Illustrator document. This leaves some room for error between Flash and the JPG.

9. Save the document as index.fla.

10. On the default layer, import the JPG or SWF background that you created in Photoshop or Illustrator to the stage. It should fit exactly to the size of the document. Convert the image to a graphic symbol to reduce the download time. Name the layer *background* and lock it.

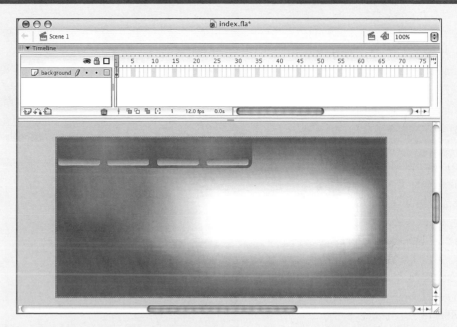

11. Now it's time to create a navigation system. Remember that you want it to be clear, efficient, and consistent. Choose a typeface that matches the style of your image; remember that it will lose a little clarity on the Web, so avoid a funky typeface. Save the funky for exclamations, not navigation. Choose something solid, not too thin, and clearly readable.

    Above the background layer, create a new layer and name it *navigation*. On the stage, over the navigation "tabs" background, create a rectangle.

figure | 15-Ex3 |

Flash document with JPG imported

12. Select the rectangle and from the menu bar select Modify>Convert to Symbol. Name it *navigation*, choose movie clip, make certain that the registration mark is centered, and click OK.

figure | 15-Ex4 |

Stage with rectangle over the navigation background tabs

| NOTE |

By drawing a shape on the main document stage, converting it to a symbol, and then entering Edit mode, Flash can maintain the document stage in a softened background behind the symbol. This allows you to create the symbol's attributes and reference the placement of the symbol at the same time. If you were to choose Insert>New Symbol and go from there, you wouldn't be able to see the document stage at the same time.

13. Double click the rectangle to enter edit mode. In the edit mode of the navigation movie clip, begin by creating three layers. Name them *text*, *buttons*, and *actions*. Delete the rectangle.

14. Type the word *email* on top of the first graphic "tab." Play around with the font, size, tracking, and color until you get something that looks clear, efficient, and great.

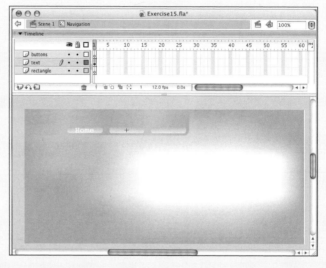

figure | 15-Ex5 |

Movie clip timeline with named layers and *Home*

15. Now you can copy-drag this text to the next three "tabs." Remember that if you hold down the `Shift` key, you can restrain the copy drag to a horizontal drag.

16. Change the second word to *Home*, the third word to *Raccoon*, and the fourth to *Frog*.

figure | 15-Ex6 |

Completed text

17. Next, you need to create an invisible button, and, for entertainment purposes and to add some clarity for the user, we'll add a movie clip in the Over State of the button.

Stay in the navigation movie clip timeline. From the menu bar select Insert>New Symbol and choose Button. Name the symbol *invisible button*.

figure

Button timeline with Hit State graphic

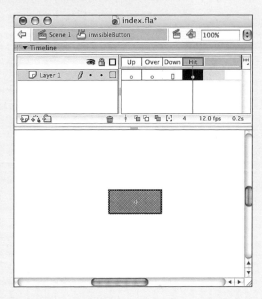

18. In the invisible button symbol, add a keyframe in the Hit State. Draw a rectangle to become the live area of the button.

19. Add a Keyframe in the Over State. Click Insert>New Symbol. Name the new symbol *moving dots*, choose Movie Clip, and click OK.

20. In the movie clip timeline, create some moving dots using motion tweens and layers.

figure

Moving dots movie clip with timeline, layers, and stage

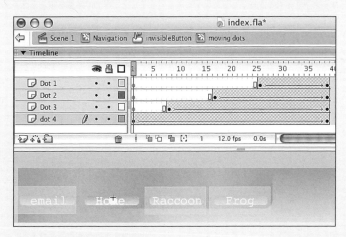

21. Return to the invisible button Over State. You can return to the Invisible Button by double-clicking on the symbol in the Library window or using the drop-down menu from the symbol icon in the upper-right corner of the timeline. Drag the moving dots movie clip from the Library window into this state. At this point, you can add some sound to the Over State. It could be a short, one-second sound or even a longer, five-second sound.

22. Return to the navigation movie clip timeline and drag the invisible button onto the stage four times. You want these buttons to sit exactly on top of the four text areas. This is where you are going to assign the ActionScript loadMovieNum. You can adjust the size of the buttons to fit the text with the Transform tool. Don't allow the button shapes to overlap and size each one to be slightly larger then the text.

figure |

Button with Transform tool applied to scale button size

23. Save your file.

Before we add the ActionScript to the buttons, let's create the three movies that you are going to access with the navigation.

24. Create a new document in Flash and give it the same pixel height and width as the index document. Leave the background color as white.

25. In the timeline, create two layers. Name them *text* and *image*.

26. On the stage, draw horizontal guides at 80 and 130 pixels and vertical guides at 75 and 295 pixels.

27. On the stage, on the image layer, import frog.jpg from the Exercise 15 folder. Place the top-left corner of the frog image at the cross-section of the guides at 80 and 75 pixels. Convert frog.jpg to a symbol. Name it *frog* and choose Graphic. The JPG will be replaced by the symbol on the stage.

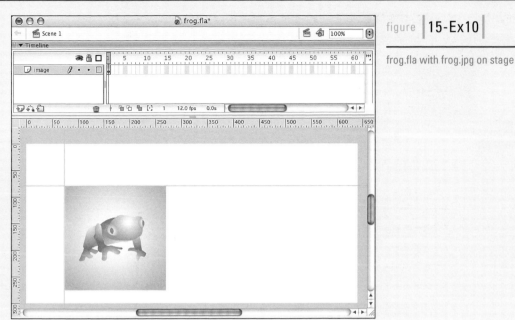

figure | 15-Ex10 |

frog.fla with frog.jpg on stage

28. In the text layer, type the following text from the dictionary:

frog/frawg/n. 1. small amphibian having a tailless smooth skinned body with legs developed for jumping

Because this is a dictionary definition, format the text in a way that visually describes it as such. Use the Format menu in the Properties window to track, lead, and generally enhance the presentation of the text.

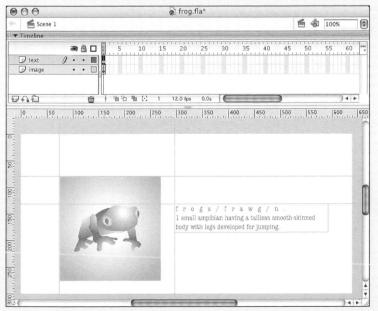

figure | 15-Ex11 |

frog.fla stage with frog image and text on stage

29. Save the file as frog.fla.

You will need to publish all of these files in order for loadMovieNum to work. We will thoroughly examine the Publish tool in Chapter 16 but for now, just choose File>Publish Settings. Make certain that on the Formats tab the default names are called out and that the Flash and HTML options are selected. (See Figure 16-3.) Click Publish. Flash should create the SWF and HTML files for you in the same folder. Click OK to close the Publish Settings window.

30. Save frog.fla as raccoon.fla.

Onto the image layer, import the raccoon.jpg and place it in exactly the same place as the frog. Use the guides to line up the image. Delete the frog symbol. Convert the JPG to a graphic symbol. Name the symbol raccoon.

On the text layer, change the text to:

raccoons/rakoon/n. 1 N. American nocturnal mammal with a brushy, ringed tail and masklike band across the eyes. 2 its fur.

figure | **15-Ex12**

raccoon.fla stage with raccoon image and text

Use the same tracking and leading and line up over the frog definition. Delete the frog definition.

Save the file as raccoon.fla and publish it, making certain that the default names are used in the Format Tab.

Save raccoon.fla as home.fla.

31. Place the frog graphic symbol on the image layer next to the raccoon image. If the frog symbol is not in the home.fla Library window, open frog.fla to access its Library window. You can then drag the frog symbol from the Library of frog.fla onto the stage of home.fla. You may need to reduce the size of both images.

32. In the text box, change the text to:

animals. We hope to bring together literature and nature by presenting you with Webster's dictionary of an animal and showing you an artist's rendering of that same animal.

Use the same font, leading, and tracking as the definitions. Treat the word animals as a title.

figure | 15-Ex13 |

home.fla stage with frog and raccoon images and text

33. Save the file and publish it.

You should now have three versions of three Flash documents published in your Exercise 15 folder. You should have a .fla, .html, and .swf file for the frog document, the raccoon document, and the home (index) document.

34. Return to the index document and the navigation movie clip timeline editing mode.

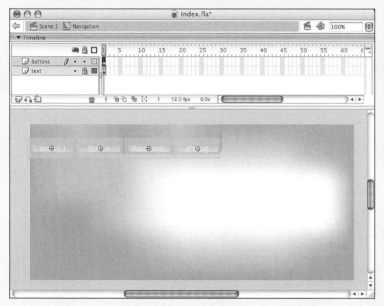

figure | 15-Ex14 |

index.fla navigation movie clip timeline editing mode

Click the invisible button placed on top of the *Home* text. Add the following ActionScript in the Action pane:

```
on (release) {
loadMovieNum("home.swf", 1);
}
```

figure 15-Ex15

loadMovieNum ActionScript for home.swf

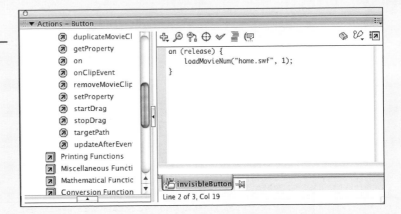

35. Click the invisible button placed on top of the *Raccoon* text. Add the following ActionScript to the Action pane:

```
on (release) {
loadMovieNum("racoon.swf", 1);
}
```

figure 15-Ex16

loadMovieNum ActionScript for raccoon.swf

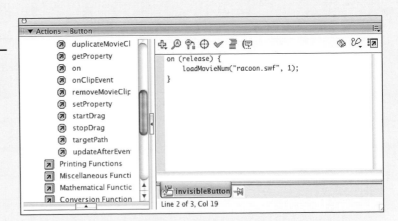

36. Click the invisible button placed on top of the *Frog* text. Add the following ActionScript to the Actions pane:

```
on (release) {
loadMovieNum("frog.swf", 1);
}
```

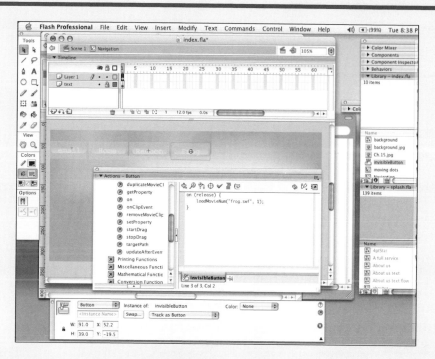

figure | 15-Ex17

loadMovieNum ActionScript for
frog.swf

37. Make sure that each of these conditions are spelled exactly the same as the
published Flash files (including treatment of upper and lower case).

38. Click the invisible button placed on top of the *e-mail* text. Add the following
ActionScript to the Action pane:

```
on (release) {
getURL("Mailto: youremailaddresshere.ext");
}
```

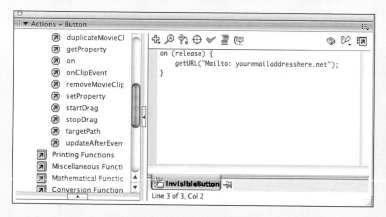

figure | 15-Ex18

e-mail ActionScript

39. Return to Scene 1. The navigation movie symbol should be sitting on top of the tabs, since you started with a rectangle in this location and converted it to a symbol. If it isn't there, drag it from the Library window and place it.

Your document stage and timeline should now look like this:

figure | 15-Ex19 |

index.fla showing layers, timeline, and stage

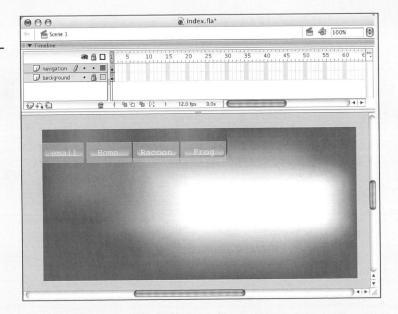

40. Save index.fla and publish it, again making certain that the default names are used on the Format tab of Publish Settings.

Check your exercise folder and make certain that all of the published files are inside of it. You should see SWF and HTML files for index, frog, raccoon, and home.

41. Open a browser window. From the File pull-down menu, open the index.html file. Test your buttons. Your additional .swf files will load directly on top of index.swf, with the edges lined up. This ensures a consistent look with navigation that stays clear and efficient.

Make sure that everything is working right. Make any necessary changes or adjustments, then show your friends.

figure | 15-Ex20 |

Completed Exercise 15 with three
SWFs and e-mail window

See Color Plate 32 for a color version of this exercise.

on your own

Try adding sound to your index document. You could add sound to the Over State of
the invisible button symbol. You could also add sound to the main timeline. Check out
the extra sounds in the Exercise 13 folder.

Additionally, try adding more animals to your Web site. Create each animal in a
separate Flash document and publish it. For home.fla, instead of having each image
of an animal sit on the page, turn them into a movie clip. Create a mask the size of one
image and have it sit in the same location as the frog in frog.fla file. Assign the movie
clip of all of the animals as the masked layer and have it move through the Mask.

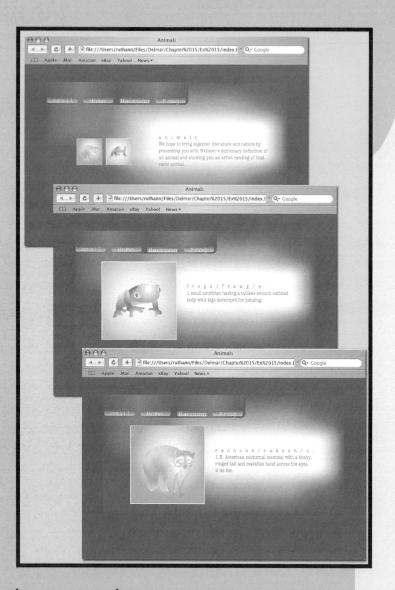

the big finale

16

Objectives

Examine the Bandwidth Profiler.

Revisit the discussion of quality versus quantity.

Discover optimizing in Flash.

Explore publishing in Flash.

Understand how to augment HTML for search engines.

Discuss hosting, connection speeds, and uploading to the Internet through an FTP program.

Introduction

Okay. It's time to test the waters. It's time to put yourself out there and see how you look. This chapter will show you how to read the Bandwidth Profiler in Flash, decipher the publish settings, and optimize and publish your Flash document. We'll examine how to augment a published HTML document in a text edit program. We will also take a look at hosting and modem speeds. Finally, we will upload your entire Web site to the Web. (Check out Color Plates 30 and 31 for additional inspiration for Flash Web sites.)

THE BIG FINALE

BANDWIDTH PROFILER

When you are satisfied with your Web site and you are ready to upload, the first thing you need to do is to look at the Bandwidth Profiler. This is truly a gift from Macromedia. Through the Bandwidth Profiler, you can determine how fast your site is going to download at what rate. As always, choices need to be made regarding quality versus quantity. Higher quality increases file size, thus increasing download time and slowing down your site. Things that increase the size of your file include bitmaps (especially animated bitmaps), sounds, keyframes, frame-by-frame animation, multiple areas of simultaneous animation, embedded fonts, gradients, and separate graphic elements in place of symbols and instances. In the Bandwidth Profiler, you cannot only see *if* but also *where* there might be problems.

To access the Bandwidth Profiler, when you are in Test Movie mode, from the menu bar, select View>Bandwidth Profiler.

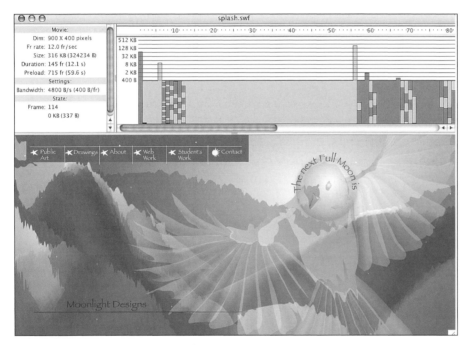

figure | 16-1 |

Bandwidth Profiler

At the top of the Test Movie window, you'll now see the amount of data that is being transmitted against the movie's timeline. The bars represent the number of bytes of data per frame. The bottom line (highlighted in red) at 400 B represents the amount of data that will safely download fast enough to keep up with the movie's frame rate. Any frame that contains a greater amount of data than this will force the movie to pause while the data downloads.

On the left is the Profile window, which presents various bits of information. You can grab the dividing line between the graph and your movie and drag it up or down to view more of the Profiler or more of the movie.

You can view the Bandwidth graph frame by frame or streaming. These choices are available under the View pull-down menu. Viewing frame by frame will present a single bar for each frame in the graph. Select a bar and specifics about that bar will appear in the Profile window.

To display streaming bandwidth from the menu bar select View>Streaming Graph. Now you will see the frames displayed as alternating bars of light and dark gray, sized to reflect the time each one takes to download. For frames that contain very little data, you might see several bars in a single time unit in the graph. Frames that have lots of data will stretch out over several time units. With View>Show Streaming, animation will play in the Profile window highlighting the numbers of the timeline in green to show where you are in the download progress.

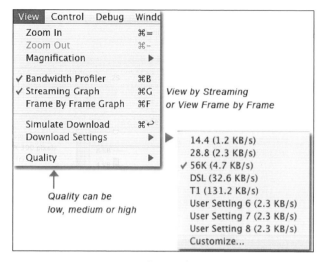

A red line in the timeline of the Profile window indicates the optimal download time. If the top of a bar falls on or below the red line it means that the amount of data is downloading fast enough to keep up with the frame rate of the movie. Occasional spikes (a bar that goes above the red line) are not usually a problem. Long periods of spikes can be. If you have problem frames, this is the time to look back at your movie. Look at the corresponding frames in your document to locate the problems. Are there large bitmaps that could be sized down in Photoshop and then re-imported into Flash? Are there bitmaps that could be converted to symbols? Are there large areas of type that could be converted to symbols? Is there sound that could be reduced to a lower kHz before publishing? Are there numerous spot graphics that could be converted to a symbol and then used in separate instances? Making changes to reduce the spikes and final size of your site is a process referred to as *optimizing* your files in preparation for publishing. It is an important step. Take the time to be thorough.

Once you have optimized as much as possible, your Bandwidth Profiler looks manageable, and the streaming download time seems reasonable, you are ready to publish your site.

PUBLISHING A FLASH FILE FOR THE WEB

The next step is to publish your document. Flash will help you with this process.

First, Flash asks you to look at the settings you will use in publishing. Settings need to be determined for HTML configurations, Flash configurations, and the formats. Access these settings from the menu bar by selecting File>Publish Settings. The first choice in the Publish Settings dialog box is Formats. Here you determine the file names and extensions that will be

figure | 16-3 |

Format tab of the Publish Settings dialog box

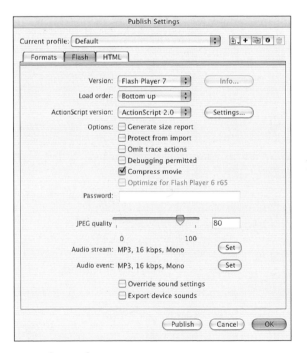

figure | 16-4 |

Flash tab of the Publish Settings dialog box

read by the browser. In Chapter 1, we talked about common protocols and addressing. This is the practical application of that discussion. What the browser reads is the HTML file. The HTML file accesses the SWF, GIF, JPEG, PNG, or MOV. The projector choices on this tab are for different uses and a different book.

For uploading your Flash document, you need only the HTML and the SWF files. In the case of a file that responds to the ActionScript loadMovNum, such as we discussed in Chapter 15, you will only need the SWF document. In all other cases, whether it's the home page on the Web or a getURL page, you will need both the HTML and the SWF files.

In all cases, you want to keep your published files with the same names as your Flash document for organizational purposes. Name your home page file *index* in Flash. Then when you publish it, the browser will recognize it as index.html. After that, you can name the Flash documents as you create them in a logical, organized fashion that matches your ActionScript. Then when you publish each one, the published file will match the ActionScript. The Publish Settings Format menu accomplishes more than the obvious. If document names and published names are different, or if you rename a published file on the desktop, the internal coding will not be changed and problems will occur with the ActionScript.

Next, let's take a look at the Flash tab of the Publish Settings dialog box. The settings here are going to determine who can view your site and what the quality of that viewing experience will be.

The first choice here is the Flash Player that your user needs to have installed. You need to make some important choices here. Some ActionScript and features in the latest version of Flash will not be available in earlier versions of Flash Player. Alternately, you need to consider that using an earlier version of Flash Player may make your Web site more universally available. I suggest that you try a version or two earlier than the latest and see if everything works properly after you have uploaded your files. If so, then your site is going to have a broader audience. If your audience is a highly technical one, then by all means, choose the latest version of Flash Player. The same decision-making process applies to the ActionScript choices on the Flash tab. Just remember that the user can pretty much always download the latest version of Flash Player for free.

Next you have a variety of options:

- Generate size report
- Protect from import
- Omit trace actions
- Debugging permitted
- Compress movie

The Generate size report option is for your use. Flash will generate a text file that will list all amounts of data. This works similarly to the Bandwidth Profiler.

Select the Protect from import option if you wish to prevent users from obtaining the SWF file.

The Omit trace actions option refers to an ActionScript which we did not cover in this book. You can try selecting it. It may reduce your file size if there are any trace actions used in the document.

The Debugging permitted option is only desirable if you want to remotely debug your file. I recommend leaving this option deselected. If you do use it, assign it a password.

The Compress movie option is a great choice for Versions 6 and above of Flash Player. It will compress text both in viewing and in ActionScript.

The final tab of the Publish Settings dialog box is the HTML tab.

The HTML tab controls the published HTML file—the actual file that the browser will read. The first option here is the Template option. For our purposes, based on what we have discussed in this book, Flash Only is the appropriate choice. We really didn't cover any

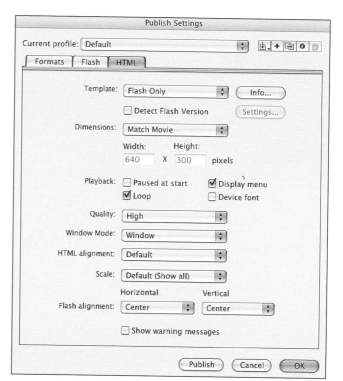

figure | 16-5 |

HTML tab of the Publish Settings dialog box

information that would merit the other Template options. Flash Only places the OBJECT tag (Windows) or EMBED tag (OS) in the HTML document.

The next option is the Detect Flash Version option. If you are trying to reach the broadest audience possible, then select this option and take a look at the settings that guide it. Here you will see the file alternate.html, which will be published. You can go into that HTML file later and revise it. This file gives you the opportunity to type a description of the Flash content for users who cannot view the SWF. This functions similarly to the ALT coding we discussed in Chapter 2.

The next choice on the HTML tab is the dimensions. Match Movie is the option of choice here. Choosing percentage or pixels brings up other choices in which you tell the Flash how to scale your movie to fit in the browser window. It is better to match the movie, as this will fit it into the browser window at 100%. This is the best viewing option for both text and graphics.

Playback options include those for Playback, Quality, and Window Mode. You have four choices for Playback. Paused at start, if selected, will require the user to begin the movie manually. Loop, if selected, will make the movie start over when it reaches the last frame. Display menu will create a contextual menu with playback options that become available to the user. Device font allows a substitute font for Windows only if you enabled device fonts when you were creating the document. Long story short, based on what you have learned thus far about Flash, deselect all four of these options.

Quality controls the antialias and smoothing during playback, based upon the movie's specified frame rate. Let's look at each Quality option:

- Low—Flash keeps the antialias off, creating the fastest download and poorest quality of your movie.

- Auto Low—Flash begins the playback with antialias off, but searches the user's computer for a connection that can handle antialias and keep the movie's frame rate. If Flash finds what it is looking for, it will turn antialias back on.

- Auto High—This is just the opposite of Auto Low. Flash begins with antialias on but turns it off if playback drops below the specified frame rate.

- Medium—This option takes the middle ground. There is some antialias but no bitmap smoothing.

figure | 16-6 |

Version Detection Settings dialog box, accessed from HTML tab

- High—With this option, Flash keeps antialias turned on throughout, but bitmap smoothing is only turned on if there is no animation.

- Best—Flash keeps antialias and smoothing on all of the time.

All of our previous discussions regarding quality resolution versus download time come into play here. You're the designer. You need to make decisions based upon your knowledge of the Web site and the intended audience. Feel free to experiment. You can publish your file as many times as you want. Try out some of these options and view changes in your browser to determine the differences in quality for a particular file.

The next choice on the HTML tab is Window Mode. This references how the Flash file is displayed in the browser. To have the Flash movie in its own window, choose Window. This is the option of choice. To have the Flash movie on top of another Web page and make the transparent areas of the Flash file block the background and other elements of the bottom Web page, choose Opaque Windowless. Finally, to have the Flash movie on top of another Web page and have all elements show through the transparent areas, choose Transparent Windowless. This third option is not fully supported by browsers. You may want to avoid this choice.

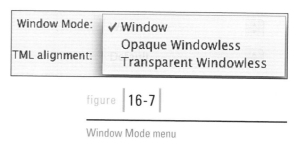

figure | **16-7** |

Window Mode menu

HTML alignment is next. You have choices of Default, Left, Right, Top, or Bottom. This alignment takes place within the Window Mode. We'll come back to this when we discuss adjusting the HTML published file. For now, choose Default.

The next set of options concern scale. *Scale* refers to how the movie's original aspect ratio fits into the movie display window that you defined earlier. There are four options.

- Default—Shows all.

- No border—Scales the movie to match the Window Mode with no border.

- Exact fit—Scales the movie to match the Window Mode exactly.

- No scale—Matches the movie.

You need only to define a scale if you changed the dimensions in the Window Mode. Default is the scale of choice, particularly if you chose Window in the Window Mode.

The last choice on this tab is Flash alignment. This references the alignment of the movie window within the movie display window, not the HTML browser window. This can be somewhat confusing. Again, we'll come back to this setting when we discuss adjusting the HTML published file. For now, choose Center for Vertical and Horizontal.

Finally, click Publish. Flash creates all of the necessary coding for both the HTML and the SWF files that you will need to upload. That's it. The next step is to upload.

Before we upload though, let's look at one in-between step. Flash is rather limited as to what gets published in the HTML file. Since you know a bit about HTML, you can open the published HTML file in TextEdit, Notepad, or Dreamweaver and make some changes. Let's take a look at this.

ADJUSTING THE HTML FILE

In Chapter 1, we discussed the <head> tag. Remember that within the <head> element, all that is required is the <title> element. The <meta> tag, along with keywords and content description, are not. However, we do want to add these elements so that search engines will find our Web site. So let's review the coding:

<head>

   <title>Portfolio for Ruth Ann Anderson and Moonlight Designs</title>

   <meta name="keywords" content="Ruth Ann Anderson Moonlight Designs

Sculpture Professor Illusutrations Drawings Public Art Animated Poetry Web Sites">

   <meta name="description" content=A portfolio site of images and projects by Ruth Ann Anderson>

   </head>

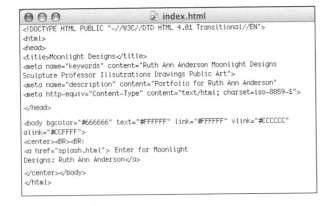

```
<!DOCTYPE HTML PUBLIC "-//W3C//DTD HTML 4.01 Transitional//EN">
<html>
<head>
<title>Moonlight Designs</title>
<meta name="keywords" content="Ruth Ann Anderson Moonlight Designs
Sculpture Professor Illsutrations Drawings Public Art">
<meta name="description" content="Portfolio for Ruth Ann Anderson">
<meta http-equiv="Content-Type" content="text/html; charset=iso-8859-1">

</head>

<body bgcolor="#666666" text="#FFFFFF" link="#FFFFFF" vlink="#CCCCCC"
alink="#CCFFFF">
<center><BR><BR>
<a href="splash.html"> Enter for Moonlight
Designs: Ruth Ann Anderson</a>

</center></body>
</html>
```

figure | 16-8 |

Revised HTML document with META elements and TITLE and CENTER codes

Make sure you put spaces, equal signs, quote marks and <> in all the right places. Then just add the code into your HTML published document in the correct location.

Additionally, you may want to center your SWF document inside of the HTML document. The Flash publishing process does not do this. However, you can easily add <center> in the <body> tag and </center> in the </body> tag. This will center your Web site in a browser window. Also, if you want your SWF document to sit slightly below the top of the HTML document, add a couple of <br> tags prior to the SWF coding.

HOSTING AND UPLOADING

The first thing that you need to know about hosting is that purchasing a domain name does not purchase space on a host server. These are two different things. Choose your domain name first. There are a number of sites that will search, establish, and protect a domain name for you.

Next you find a host. This is not an easy task—there are literally hundreds of sites out there vying to be your host. How do you begin to narrow the search? Don't necessarily choose the cheapest service, regardless of how serious you are about Web design at this point. Cheap can include down server time, limited space, and questionable user accessibility. Also, avoid Web hosting by companies that require you to go through their application program to create a Web site.

Surf the Web to locate quality hosting sources. You can also find sites that will rate hosting services. Try your phone company to see what it has to offer. Talk to your friends. Who has trouble with what service and who is really happy with their service? As we discussed earlier in this book, you want to go for good reputations, 24-hour technical support, and quality service.

Once you sign a contract with an Internet host, your user ID and password will be established. Now all you need is an FTP program. FTP programs are quite inexpensive and easy to come by. Some hosts are very specific about which FTP program they want you to use and will let you know how to obtain it. Fetch is a popular FTP program and is downloadable from the Internet.

In any case, in the New Connection FTP dialog box, type the host, user ID, and password in the appropriate fields. Your own Web site folder will open in a new window.

figure | 16-9 |

Fetch dialog box

figure | 16-10 |

Web site in Fetch window

To upload a file, click Put Files and browse to the documents in your desktop folder that you want to upload. In this case, it will be at least index.html and index.swf. Highlight each dcoument and click `Put Files`.

Type of file to be uploaded

The type of files to upload now becomes important. With MacSMTP, as well as other FTP programs, the type will be determined for you. With Fetch, you can choose the type of file. There are several choices.

When using Fetch, in the Format pull-down menu, use Text for the type for HTML files and Raw Data for the type for SWF files. These choices tend to be the most stable. Once you have uploaded, open your browser and check out your Web site. You can keep the FTP window open while you check things out in the browser.

When you want to make changes, add files, or delete files, follow the same steps. If you have made changes and are replacing a document, delete the current file in the FTP program first through the File pull-down menu. Then Put the replacement document.

figure **16-12**

File pull-down menu in browser

If you do make changes and replace files and the browser doesn't recognize the new uploaded file(s), you may need to refresh the browser or empty the browser cache. Generally, you can empty the cache from the browser's File pull-down menu.

Generally speaking, unless you make changes to the document size, you won't need to replace the HTML document. Just note that when you republish the Flash document, it will replace your HTML document, deleting the META and CENTER elements that you added. Therefore, when you first create these elements, it is wise to save the information in a separate document. Name it something like *head Info*. Then you can always copy and paste this information into a new HTML document if you do need to replace the one that is uploaded.

Finally, when uploading, don't forget to FTP any additional SWF or HTML documents you may have created that link to the index.swf document.

SUMMARY

In this chapter, you learned how to optimize your Web site. You examined the three tabs in the Publish Settings dialog box of Flash. You learned how to publish your Flash file. And you discovered how to augment the published HTML document to make it more available to search engines. You know how to upload your Web site. The final hurrah! Congratulations! Enjoy your new adventure in Web design.

in review

1. What does the Bandwidth Profiler show you?

2. What can you accomplish on the Formats tab of the Publish Settings dialog box?

3. What can you accomplish on the Flash tab of the Publish Settings dialog box?

4. What can you accomplish on the HTML tab of the Publish Settings dialog box?

5. How can you identify information for a search engine?

6. How can you upload a SWF file from your computer to the Internet?

exercise 16

1. Open your completed Exercise 15 Flash index.fla document.

2. From the menu bar select Control>Test Movie, choose View>Bandwidth Profiler.

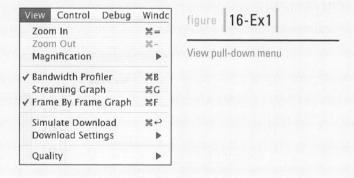

figure | 16-Ex1 |

View pull-down menu

3. From the menu bar select File>Publish. Flash should create an HTML document using the same name as the SWF document, creating all of the necessary links. Check the settings on all three of the tabs in the Publish Settings dialog box.

You want the Formats tab to look something like this:

figure | 16-Ex2 |

Formats tab for index.fla

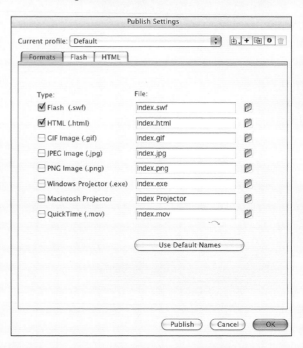

You will most likely only be using the SWF and HTML files. Make sure that you have clicked the Use Default Names button.

4. Next is the Flash tab. Make your choices based on the discussion earlier in this chapter. Basically, you want the tab to look something like this:

figure | 16-Ex3 |

Flash tab for index.fla

5. Last is the HTML tab. It should look something like this:

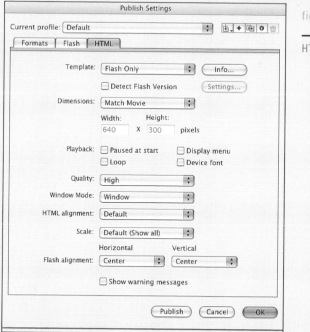

figure | 16-Ex4 |

HTML tab for index.fla

6. Once you have your settings adjusted, click Publish. Flash should inform you that it is publishing and when it is finished.

figure | 16-Ex5 |

Exercise 15 in browser prior to HTML revisions

7. Once the publish process is complete, close the Flash document and open index.html in either Text Edit (selecting Ignore rich text commands) or Dreamweaver with just the code showing.

figure | 16-Ex6

Opening a file in TextEdit with Ignore rich text commands selected

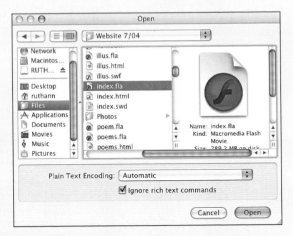

8. Find the <title> and </title> tags. Type the title for your Web site. This is what will show in the browser window, so be concise and clear.

9. Now, just below the <title> tags, but still inside of the <head> tags, add some information for search engines. These will be the meta names or keywords that we discussed in Chapter 1. You don't need any commas or other punctuation between these words. Spaces will do the trick. Add up to about 15 keywords that you can think of to bring viewers to your site via a search engine.

figure | 16-Ex7

META information

```
<!DOCTYPE html PUBLIC "-//W3C//DTD XHTML 1.0 Transitional//EN" "http://www.w3.org/
TR/xhtml1/DTD/xhtml1-transitional.dtd">
<html xmlns="http://www.w3.org/1999/xhtml" xml:lang="en" lang="en">
<head>
<meta http-equiv="Content-Type" content="text/html; charset=iso-8859-1" />
<title>Animals</title>
<meta name="keywords" content="Ruth Ann Anderson Animals Defined Images of Animals
Raccoons Frogs">
<meta name="description" content="A Website About Animals">
</head>
<body bgcolor="#006666"><center><BR><BR>
<!--url's used in the movie-->
<!--text used in the movie-->
<!--
Home

Racoon

Frog

email

-->
<object classid="clsid:d27cdb6e-ae6d-11cf-96b8-444553540000" codebase="http://
download.macromedia.com/pub/shockwave/cabs/flash/swflash.cab#version=7,0,0,0"
width="640" height="300" id="index" align="middle">
<param name="allowScriptAccess" value="sameDomain" />
<param name="movie" value="index.swf" />
<param name="quality" value="high" />
<param name="bgcolor" value="#006666" />
<embed src="index.swf" quality="high" bgcolor="#006666" width="640" height="300"
name="index" align="middle" allowScriptAccess="sameDomain" type="application/x-
shockwave-flash" pluginspage="http://www.macromedia.com/go/getflashplayer" />
</center></object>
</body>
</html>
```

10. Next center the Flash file inside of the browser window.

Find the <body> tag. Follow the <body> tag with a <center> tag. Find the </body> tag. Proceed it with a </center> tag. Finally, add a couple of <br> codes just after the opening body tag.

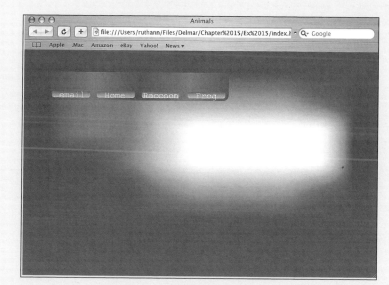

figure | 16-Ex8 |

Exercise 15 in browser after HTML revisions

11. Save your HTML document.

12. Okay, time to upload. By now you have contracted with a host and have all of your server information. Using Fetch (or a similar FTP program) to upload, type your host, user ID, and password in the appropriate fields.

This should take you directly to the folder that your host has provided for your Web Site with your domain name. (Usually, the domain name is either in the host name or the user ID.)

13. From the menu bar select Remote>Put Folders and Files. Browse for your site folder in the Open window and open it.

figure | 16-Ex9 |

Fetch Remote pull-down menu

14. Locate the HTML and SWF documents you want to upload. Select the HTML document and choose Text before uploading.

figure | **16-Ex10** |

Uploading a text file via Fetch

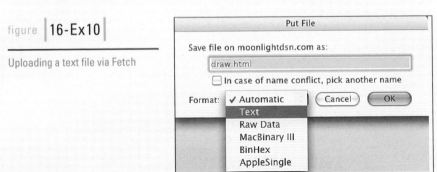

Next, select the SWF document and choose Raw Data before uploading.

figure | **16-Ex11** |

Uploading a SWF file via Fetch

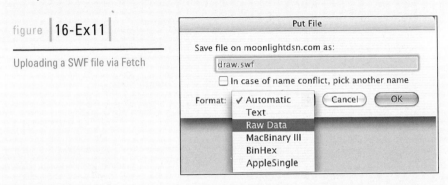

15. The progress of the upload will appear in the status bar of the site window while the files are being sent to the remote server. When you have finished uploading your documents, click Done.

16. Open the browser of your choice. Check out your site. Is it what you expected? You can always go back and make changes. Just remember that if you do go back and make changes, before you upload a new file, delete the old one. Highlight the file in the FTP window and choose Delete Folder/File from the Remote pull-down menu.

Most likely, you will not need to replace an HTML file. However, if you need to make changes to the Flash document size, then you will need to replace it. Be sure to copy and paste the TITLE, META, CENTER, and BR elements first.

Don't forget to check your site in different browsers. If you can, view it on a variety of computers. You may want to make some changes or compromises based on different computer environments. When everything looks great, call your friends. Tell them to visit your site. Enjoy the compliments!

figure | 16-Ex12 |

Final Web site displayed in browser (See Color Plate 32 to view in color.)

on your own

Try revising one of your files other than the index file. Make some sort of change and then republish the document. Open your Web site through your FTP program. Find the SWF that you want to replace and highlight it. Under the Remote pull-down menu, delete the SWF. Then Put the new SWF to upload it.

Return to the browser and refresh the Web site. Notice your new changes. If they do not show up, you may have to empty the cache of the browser.

Imagination by student Cam McCarley

index